SCOTT HUTCHESON, PhD
WITH **MATTHEW D. JONES**

BIOHACKING

LEADERSHIP

LEVERAGING THE
BIOLOGY OF BEHAVIOR
TO **MAXIMIZE YOUR IMPACT**

WILEY

Copyright © 2025 by John Wiley & Sons, Inc. All rights reserved, including rights for text and data mining and training of artificial technologies or similar technologies.

Published by John Wiley & Sons, Inc., Hoboken, New Jersey.
Published simultaneously in Canada.

No part of this publication may be reproduced, stored in a retrieval system, or transmitted in any form or by any means, electronic, mechanical, photocopying, recording, scanning, or otherwise, except as permitted under Section 107 or 108 of the 1976 United States Copyright Act, without either the prior written permission of the Publisher, or authorization through payment of the appropriate per-copy fee to the Copyright Clearance Center, Inc., 222 Rosewood Drive, Danvers, MA 01923, (978) 750-8400, fax (978) 750-4470, or on the web at www.copyright.com. Requests to the Publisher for permission should be addressed to the Permissions Department, John Wiley & Sons, Inc., 111 River Street, Hoboken, NJ 07030, (201) 748-6011, fax (201) 748-6008, or online at http://www.wiley.com/go/permission.

The manufacturer's authorized representative according to the EU General Product Safety Regulation is Wiley-VCH GmbH, Boschstr. 12, 69469 Weinheim, Germany, e-mail: Product_Safety@wiley.com.

Trademarks: Wiley and the Wiley logo are trademarks or registered trademarks of John Wiley & Sons, Inc. and/or its affiliates in the United States and other countries and may not be used without written permission. All other trademarks are the property of their respective owners. John Wiley & Sons, Inc. is not associated with any product or vendor mentioned in this book.

Limit of Liability/Disclaimer of Warranty: While the publisher and author have used their best efforts in preparing this book, they make no representations or warranties with respect to the accuracy or completeness of the contents of this book and specifically disclaim any implied warranties of merchantability or fitness for a particular purpose. No warranty may be created or extended by sales representatives or written sales materials. The advice and strategies contained herein may not be suitable for your situation. You should consult with a professional where appropriate. Further, readers should be aware that websites listed in this work may have changed or disappeared between when this work was written and when it is read. Neither the publisher nor authors shall be liable for any loss of profit or any other commercial damages, including but not limited to special, incidental, consequential, or other damages.

For general information on our other products and services or for technical support, please contact our Customer Care Department within the United States at (800) 762-2974, outside the United States at (317) 572-3993 or fax (317) 572-4002.

Wiley also publishes its books in a variety of electronic formats. Some content that appears in print may not be available in electronic formats. For more information about Wiley products, visit our web site at www.wiley.com.

Library of Congress Cataloging-in-Publication Data is Available:

ISBN: 9781394351510 (cloth)
ISBN: 9781394351527 (ePub)
ISBN: 9781394351534 (ePDF)

COVER ART & DESIGN: PAUL MCCARTHY

SKY10106183_052725

To three remarkable individuals who have profoundly shaped my understanding of leadership:

Ed Morrison, for his visionary thinking and unwavering belief in the power of collaboration

Peter Robertson, for his groundbreaking insights into complexity and ecosystems

Bob Sadler, whose wisdom, generosity, and guidance remain a touchstone for me

This book is also a tribute to Bob, who passed away as I was writing these pages. His impact on my life and work is immeasurable, and his presence is deeply missed.

Contents

	Foreword	*vii*
	Introduction	*ix*
1	**Keystone Leaders**	**1**
2	**The Biology of Leadership**	**21**
3	**The Biomechanics of Leadership**	**35**
4	**From Executive Presence to Leadership Biodynamics**	**55**
5	**Biohacking Warmth**	**73**
6	**Biohacking Competence**	**97**
7	**Biohacking Gravitas**	**123**
8	**The Neuroscience of Storytelling**	**143**
9	**The Neuroscience of Conversation**	**173**
10	**The Neuroscience of Play**	**199**
	Conclusion	*213*
	Notes	*215*
	Bibliography	*227*
	Acknowledgments	*247*
	About the Author	*249*
	Index	*251*

Foreword

Leadership, much like elite sports, is about optimizing performance—tapping into the full potential of individuals and teams to achieve something extraordinary. As someone who has spent their career in the worlds of government, education, and professional sports, I've seen firsthand that the highest-performing leaders, much like the highest-performing athletes, don't rely on talent alone. They train, they adapt, and most importantly, they understand the science behind their success.

That's what makes *Biohacking Leadership* such a powerful and timely book. Dr. Scott Hutcheson has taken what elite coaches and performance experts have long known about the biology of human behavior and applied it directly to leadership. Just as an athlete learns to control breath, body mechanics, and mental focus, leaders can learn to regulate the physiological signals they send, the trust they build, and the cultures they create.

This book gives leaders a new kind of playbook—one rooted in the biology of behavior, the mechanics of presence, and the neuroscience of influence. It's not about charisma or positional power; it's about understanding and applying the fundamental forces that drive human connection, collaboration, and impact.

Whether you're leading a boardroom, a locker room, or a classroom, the insights in these pages will help you elevate your leadership game. Just like championship teams, great leaders don't leave performance to chance. They train for it.

—Allison Barber, PhD
Former President & COO, Indiana Fever

Introduction

Leadership is behavioral.

Behavior is biological.

Biology can be hacked.

These principles form the foundation of this book.

Rethinking Leadership Through Biohacking

Leadership today demands more than technical expertise or magnetic charisma. In a world characterized by complexity, rapid innovation, and constant change, leaders must do more than manage; they must guide, inspire, and unite. The stakes are high, and traditional leadership models—rooted in static traits or narrowly defined competencies—often fall short of addressing the real dynamics at play.

This book offers a bold new perspective: examining leadership from a *biology of behavior* perspective in which we unearth the evolutionary underpinnings of influence, trust, and collaboration. It introduces the concept of *leadership biodynamics* as a set of three channels that represent the essential dimensions of effective leadership: warmth, competence, and gravitas. These are not abstract ideals but concrete, measurable behaviors that leaders can learn to tune, much like adjusting channels on a mixing board, to meet the demands of any situation.

The premise is simple: If leadership is behavioral, and behavior is biological, then we can hack it. *Biohacking leadership* means that we can understand the science behind what drives human connection and performance—and apply it to unlock full leadership potential.

The Biodynamics Model: Leadership as a Mixing Board

Imagine leadership as a sound engineer's mixing board. Each biodynamic channel—warmth, competence, and gravitas—represents a distinct yet interconnected aspect of how leaders influence and inspire. Mastering leadership biodynamics means learning to dial up or dial down these channels in real time, tailoring your approach to the needs of your team, your goals, and the context in which you operate.

You won't find a set rigid rules to follow in this book or a one-size-fits-all framework. Instead, you'll be challenged to cultivate agility and precision—developing the ability to modulate your leadership presence with the same finesse as a musician shaping the sound of a symphony.

Why Biohacking Leadership Matters Now

The challenges of leadership in the 21st century demand an evolutionary leap. Teams are increasingly interdisciplinary, ecosystems are interconnected, and the problems we face—whether in business, society, or science—are more intricate than ever before. Leaders must not only navigate complexity but also create environments where innovation thrives, trust flourishes, and diverse perspectives align toward shared goals.

Biohacking Leadership meets this moment, leveraging insights from biology, neuroscience, and organizational behavior to bridge the gap between the science of human behavior and the art of leading people. It equips leaders to harness the invisible forces that shape how we connect, collaborate, and perform.

An Evidence-Based, Practice-Proven Approach

This book is built on a dual foundation of rigorous research and real-world application. Each concept and strategy is informed by science, but the insights are presented in an accessible, actionable way. While you'll find references to key studies and thought leaders, the focus remains on practical tools and techniques that you can implement immediately.

For those seeking deeper academic context, a full list of sources and resources is provided at the back of the book, ensuring the balance of credibility and readability.

What You Will Learn

This book is organized around the following three themes.

The Biology of Behavior

Chapters 1–3 explore the biological and ecological principles that underpin effective leadership.

1. **Keystone Leaders: Lessons from Ecosystem Formation:** Learn how insights from nature's keystone species—beavers, wolves, and sea stars—illustrate the impact of creating balance, inclusivity, and shared value.

2. **The Biology of Leadership:** Discover the physiological and emotional drivers of leadership, from heart rate variability to emotional regulation, and their influence on team dynamics and performance.

3. **The Biomechanics of Leadership:** Understand how intentional physicality, including posture, movement, and gestures, shapes your leadership presence and reinforces your influence.

Leadership Biodynamics

Chapters 4–7 focus on the three biodynamic channels that define leadership excellence.

4. **From Executive Presence to Leadership Biodynamics:** Introduces the biodynamic framework, outlining how warmth, competence, and gravitas function as actionable leadership behaviors.

5. **Biohacking Warmth:** Explore the biology of trust and psychological safety and cultivate behaviors that build genuine connections and foster inclusive environments.

6. **Biohacking Competence:** Learn to deliver results with clarity and credibility by mastering complexity, decision-making, and alignment with strategic goals.

7. **Biohacking Gravitas:** Develop calm authority, composure, and resilience to align teams, inspire confidence, and navigate complexity effectively.

The Biohacking Leadership Toolkit

Chapters 8–10 provide actionable tools to amplify your leadership impact.

8. **The Neuroscience of Storytelling:** Harness the power of narrative to inspire action, connect deeply, and drive collaboration across diverse contexts.

9. **The Neuroscience of Conversation:** Master the art of dialogue to foster collaboration, bridge divides, and create shared understanding within teams and organizations.

10. **The Neuroscience of Play:** Discover the critical role of creativity, adaptability, and play in fostering innovation, resilience, and team cohesion.

A New Way to Lead

Biohacking Leadership is a path to transformation. Through this book, you'll gain access to:

- **Practical tools** for identifying and cultivating leadership behaviors

- **Actionable strategies** to adapt your leadership style to any situation
- **Real-world examples** that bring the science to life

Whether you're an emerging leader seeking to amplify your impact or an experienced executive navigating the demands of complexity, this book will provide you with the insights and techniques to lead with greater precision, agility, and purpose.

Are You Ready to Biohack Your Leadership?

The pages ahead will challenge you to think differently about what it means to lead. Together, we'll dismantle outdated paradigms and explore how you can use the biology of behavior to optimize your leadership presence and create lasting impact.

By the end of this journey, you'll have not only a deeper understanding of the science of leadership but also a clear blueprint for putting it into action. It's time to reimagine leadership. Let's get started.

Chapter 1

Keystone Leaders

B*eavers, wolves, and sea stars, oh my!*

No, it's not a rewrite of the *Wizard of Oz*, but just as Dorothy Gale learned important life lessons from a scarecrow, a tinman, and a lion, we can discover valuable leadership lessons from a beaver, a wolf, and a sea star.

Getting Things Done When You Can't Tell Anyone What to Do

One of my early experiences in leadership development work was in an environment in which the person at the top of the organization had virtually no ability for command and control. The people they were leading were highly skilled. They could find work anywhere and be well compensated for that work. This was in the 1980s and it represented a relatively new leadership challenge. Value was being produced differently, as talent was highly mobile and supply chains were becoming globalized. I began looking far and wide for new leadership models.

I would eventually find one hiding in plain sight, all around me—natural ecosystems and the emergent and evolutionary patterns of behaviors that result in sustainability, resiliency, and the shared-value creation. Often there is a specific living creature that helps create and sustain many natural ecosystems.

These remarkable creatures are known as keystone species. Remove them and balance is disrupted, leading to significant changes that can affect countless other species. Understanding the role of keystone species offers profound insights into the dynamics of leadership and the influence one individual can wield. As we navigate the complexities of leadership and life in general, we can draw valuable lessons from these three fascinating keystone species, each demonstrating unique behaviors that inform and enhance our leadership practices.

Evolutionary Drivers

At the heart of nature's ecosystems are forces that have shaped behaviors over millennia—forces that can illuminate how leaders influence their organizations today. Evolutionary biology highlights three critical drivers: individual selection, kinship selection, and reciprocal altruism.

- Individual selection focuses on traits that benefit the individual, ensuring survival and leaving behind a legacy.
- Kinship selection emphasizes collaboration within close-knit groups, ensuring the survival of shared interests.
- Reciprocal altruism fosters cooperation beyond kin, creating relationships built on mutual benefit and trust.

By understanding these principles, leaders can adopt the strategies of keystone species—beavers, wolves, and sea stars—to build resilient systems, strengthen collaboration, and promote diversity.

First, we will consider beavers as ecosystems architects, constructing intricate dams that create wetlands teeming with life. Their proactive approach to building structures parallels the way effective leaders create systems and processes that support their teams. Just as beavers ensure the stability and sustainability of their environment, leaders must establish frameworks that enable their organizations to thrive.

Next, we will turn to wolves as balancers within their ecosystems. As apex predators, they regulate herbivore populations, ensuring that no single species overwhelms the landscape. This balancing act reflects the role of leaders who navigate complex team dynamics, strategically intervening when necessary to foster collaboration

2

Biohacking Leadership

and maintain harmony. Like wolves, effective leaders understand the importance of timing and influence, knowing when to step in and when to allow their teams to flourish independently.

Finally, we will examine the sea star, a species that plays a critical role in promoting diversity. By preying on dominant species, sea stars prevent any single organism from monopolizing resources, thereby fostering a rich tapestry of life. In leadership, this translates to the importance of inclusivity and resilience. Sea star leaders create environments where diverse voices are heard and valued, ensuring that every team member can contribute their unique perspectives.

As we explore the insights offered by these keystone species, we will uncover practical strategies for biohacking leadership— optimizing our impact and effectiveness by integrating principles from the biology of behavior into our leadership practices. By understanding the roles these species play in their ecosystems, we can navigate challenges and seize opportunities with greater skill, creating spaces where innovation flourishes and performance soars.

As we look at these lessons from nature, I invite you to reflect on your own leadership style. Are you more like the beaver, focused on building and maintaining the foundational structures of your team? Do you embody the characteristics of the wolf, balancing dynamics and fostering collaboration? Or perhaps you resonate more with the sea star, promoting diversity and resilience in the face of challenges? The lessons drawn from these keystone species offer a roadmap for enhancing your leadership presence, ensuring that you can guide your teams and organization toward success.

The Beaver: Builders of Foundations

Beavers are known for their extraordinary ability to construct intricate dams that fundamentally alter their environments. These structures do more than create homes; they play a pivotal role in shaping ecosystems, flooding areas that transform into rich wetlands, thereby supporting diverse flora, fauna, and animal life. Understanding the behaviors of beavers through the lens of evolutionary biology and the biology of behavior provides valuable insights into their ecological roles and adaptability—lessons that inform how a leader can take on a similar keystone-like role in their teams and organizations.

The dam-building behavior of beavers exemplifies evolutionary adaptation at its finest. Over millions of years, beavers have developed physiological traits that enable them to thrive in aquatic environments. Their webbed feet facilitate efficient swimming, while their large incisors, which continuously grow, allow them to fell trees and manipulate their surroundings effectively. This anatomical adaptation serves not just as a tool for construction but also as a survival mechanism that has ensured their success as a keystone species. The habitats they create provide protection from predators and easy access to food resources, including aquatic plants and tree bark.

Beavers exhibit an instinctive drive to build dams primarily to create stable aquatic habitats. The benefits of flooding an area far outweigh the energy costs associated with construction, because these altered environments offer both safety and abundant resources. This behavior reflects an evolutionary strategy where beavers optimize their chances of survival by transforming their immediate environment into one that is conducive to their needs.

Insights from ethology underscore the cognitive complexity inherent in beaver behavior. Beavers demonstrate problem-solving abilities when it comes to dam construction. They assess their environment and determine the most advantageous locations for building, often selecting sites that maximize water flow and material availability. This capacity for spatial awareness and environmental understanding highlights a level of cognitive sophistication that extends beyond mere instinct.

Beavers engage in a form of planning before initiating construction. They gather materials from nearby sources and exhibit an understanding of resource availability and suitability. This behavior illustrates not only their adaptability but also a learned component that reflects their ability to navigate complex ecological interactions. Beavers may modify their construction techniques based on past experiences, showcasing behavioral plasticity—a trait that enhances their resilience in changing environments.

4

Biohacking Leadership

Beavers are inherently social creatures, living in family units that contribute to their success as builders. The collaborative nature of their construction efforts enhances efficiency and effectiveness. By working together, beavers can tackle larger trees and build more substantial structures than an individual could manage alone. This social aspect facilitates resource gathering and reinforces bonds within the family unit, enhancing their ability to thrive in shared habitats.

The communal nature of beaver life extends to their ongoing maintenance of dams. Regular inspections and repairs demonstrate a commitment to sustaining their environment. This proactive behavior not only maintains the structural integrity of their dams but also reflects an evolutionary advantage; well-maintained dams provide optimal conditions for survival.

A striking feature of beaver behavior is their plasticity—the ability to adapt their construction techniques based on environmental conditions. In areas with abundant trees, beavers may construct large, complex dams. Conversely, in environments with fewer resources, they may opt for smaller, simpler structures. This adaptability underscores the importance of environmental context in shaping their behavior and highlights their resilience as a species.

Beavers also exhibit flexibility in their social dynamics. When faced with ecological changes, such as habitat loss or competition for resources, they adjust their building habits and social structures accordingly. This plasticity enables beavers to maintain their ecological roles even in the face of adversity, reflecting an intrinsic adaptability that is crucial for long-term survival.

Beavers exemplify a complex interplay of evolutionary adaptations, cognitive abilities, and social dynamics that enable them to thrive as architects of their ecosystems. Their remarkable dam-building behavior is a product of natural selection, rooted in the necessity for survival and community. Understanding these biological insights offers a deeper appreciation for the intricacies of beaver behavior, highlighting the significant ecological roles they play. As keystone species, their presence not only influences their immediate environment but also contributes to the overall health and diversity of the ecosystems they inhabit.

Beavers demonstrate individual selection, the drive to optimize personal survival and success. Their dam-building behavior begins as an act of self-preservation, creating stable environments for safety and sustenance. Yet these structures transform the entire ecosystem, fostering wetlands that support countless other species.

For leaders, this mirrors the act of building systems and frameworks that endure. Leaders who exhibit individual selection focus on establishing processes, structures, and cultures that allow their teams to thrive, long after their direct influence fades. By prioritizing sustainability, they create a legacy of stability and opportunity.

Leadership Lessons from the Beaver

The behaviors of beavers offer several leadership lessons that can be applied within organizational contexts:

- **Strategic Resource Management:** Just as beavers assess their environment to gather materials effectively, leaders should be adept at evaluating the resources available to their teams. This includes recognizing individual strengths and deploying them where they can have the most significant impact.

- **Cognitive Flexibility:** Beavers' ability to modify their building techniques based on past experiences illustrates the importance of adaptability in leadership. Leaders should cultivate a mindset that embraces change and encourages innovation within their teams.

- **Collaboration and Teamwork:** Beavers thrive in social units, working together to achieve common goals. Leaders can learn from this by fostering a collaborative environment where team members are encouraged to contribute and support one another, ultimately enhancing collective performance.

- **Proactive Maintenance:** The regular upkeep of their dams reflects a commitment to sustaining their environment. Leaders should prioritize ongoing assessment and improvement of their organizational structures, ensuring they remain effective and responsive to challenges.

- **Behavioral Adaptability:** Beavers demonstrate a remarkable ability to adapt to changing conditions. Leaders, too, must be willing to adjust their strategies in response to evolving circumstances, leveraging their team's resilience to navigate challenges successfully.

Case Study: Emily's Transformation of Team Dynamics

Let's examine the case of Emily, a manager who transformed a struggling product development team within a tech startup. Take note of some of the similarities between Emily's work with her team and the beaver's effort building and maintaining the dam.

Upon her arrival, Emily quickly assessed the situation and recognized that the team was operating in silos, with little collaboration and communication among members. Morale was low, and deadlines were frequently missed. Drawing inspiration from the beaver's approach, Emily set out to build a strong foundation for her team.

Emily began by articulating a clear framework for the product development process, outlining how collaboration would lead to innovative solutions. She facilitated brainstorming sessions that encouraged team members to share their ideas and insights openly, much like how beavers work together to tackle large trees. This not only fostered a sense of ownership but also helped establish a more cohesive team dynamic.

Understanding the importance of structure, Emily introduced agile methodologies to streamline workflows. She defined clear roles and responsibilities, ensuring everyone understood how they contributed to the team's success. Like a beaver carefully constructing its dam, she built processes that would allow her team to thrive.

However, Emily recognized that building the foundation was just the start. She implemented regular check-ins to gauge team sentiment and gather feedback, mirroring the beavers' commitment to ongoing maintenance. This proactive approach allowed her to identify and address any issues before they escalated. When one team member expressed frustration with the new processes, Emily worked with them to refine the system, demonstrating her commitment to adapting the structures for optimal performance.

As a result of Emily's efforts, the team not only improved its collaboration and communication but also exceeded its product development goals. The transformation was evident, much like a thriving wetland, as team members began to take pride in their work and support one another.

Emily's case illustrates how adopting a beaver leadership style—focused on building and maintaining effective systems—can lead to significant improvements in team dynamics and performance.

In examining the role of beavers as architects of their ecosystems, we uncover profound lessons in strategic resource management, cognitive flexibility, collaboration, proactive maintenance, and behavioral adaptability. These attributes not only define beavers as keystone species but also serve as essential qualities for effective leadership. By building solid foundations, engaging in continuous improvement, and fostering a collaborative environment, leaders can create the conditions necessary for their teams to thrive.

As we shift our focus from the beaver to the wolf, we will explore another vital keystone species that offers distinct yet complementary leadership insights. Wolves play a crucial role in maintaining balance within their ecosystems as apex predators. Their ability to regulate populations, promote healthy dynamics, and act strategically provides rich lessons for leaders navigating the complexities of team dynamics and organizational environments. Join us as we delve into the world of wolves and uncover the leadership lessons that emerge from their behaviors and social structures.

The Wolf: Guardians of Balance

Wolves are apex predators that play a critical role in maintaining the balance of their ecosystems. By regulating herbivore populations and influencing various ecological processes, wolves create conditions that promote biodiversity and ecological health. Understanding the behaviors of wolves through evolutionary biology and the biology of behavior provides valuable insights into their ecological roles and the lessons they offer for effective leadership.

Wolves have evolved specific traits that enable them to thrive in diverse environments. Their social structure, characterized by pack living, is one of their most notable adaptations. This social behavior allows wolves to hunt cooperatively, increasing their efficiency in taking down larger prey, such as elk and deer. The ability to work as a cohesive unit not only enhances their hunting success but also strengthens the pack's survival odds against competitors and predators.

Wolves possess keen senses, including exceptional hearing and smell, which are critical for locating prey and detecting potential threats. These adaptations highlight their evolutionary strategy of living in dynamic ecosystems, where adaptability and cooperation are essential for survival.

The social structure of wolf packs is integral to their success as predators and maintainers of ecological balance. Packs are typically matriarchal, led by an alpha pair, with hierarchical dynamics that help regulate behavior and decision-making within the group. This hierarchy enables effective coordination during hunts and conflict resolution, contributing to the pack's overall stability.

Wolves demonstrate strong loyalty and bonding within their packs, often engaging in social behaviors that reinforce relationships, such as grooming and play. These interactions foster a sense of community and trust, which are vital for the pack's cohesion and effectiveness as a hunting unit.

Wolves exhibit significant behavioral adaptability, allowing them to adjust their hunting strategies and social behaviors in response to environmental changes and prey availability. For example, in regions where prey populations decline, wolves may shift their focus to alternative food sources or modify their hunting techniques to target smaller or more abundant species. This adaptability reflects their resilience as a species and underscores the importance of being responsive to changing conditions.

Additionally, wolves know when to intervene in their social dynamics. They may diffuse tensions within the pack or redirect efforts to ensure collective goals are met. This strategic intervention is a key characteristic of wolf behavior and highlights the importance of timing and influence in maintaining balance within the group.

Wolves embody kinship selection, the principle that prioritizes the success of the group to ensure shared survival. A wolf pack cooperates to hunt, protect their territory, and raise their young, recognizing that collective strength ensures individual well-being.

In leadership, kinship selection translates to fostering team cohesion and loyalty. Leaders invest in mentoring, developing, and protecting their teams, ensuring that success is shared and sustained. The "genes" of a leader—their values, principles, and strategies—are carried forward by those they empower.

Leadership Lessons from the Wolf

The behaviors of wolves provide several leadership lessons that can be applied within team and organizational contexts:

- **Strategic Intervention:** Wolves exemplify the importance of knowing when to step in and influence team dynamics. Effective leaders must be adept at recognizing critical moments when their intervention can foster collaboration and restore balance within their teams.

- **Team Cohesion:** The social structure of wolf packs highlights the value of building strong relationships and trust among team members. Leaders can learn from this by nurturing a collaborative environment that emphasizes teamwork and mutual support.

- **Adaptability in Approach:** Wolves demonstrate remarkable adaptability in their hunting strategies, showcasing the need for leaders to remain flexible and responsive to changing circumstances. Embracing change and encouraging innovation can lead to more effective problem-solving within teams.

- **Social Learning and Development:** The learning dynamics within wolf packs emphasize the significance of mentorship and knowledge sharing. Leaders should prioritize creating opportunities for team members to learn from one another, fostering an environment where continuous improvement is encouraged.

- **Balancing Individual and Collective Goals:** Wolves operate within a hierarchical structure that balances individual roles with the overall goals of the pack. Leaders must recognize the importance of aligning individual aspirations with team objectives to ensure collective success.

Case Study: Mark's Revitalization of Team Performance

To illustrate the principles of wolf leadership in action, let's examine the case of Mark, a team leader in a marketing agency struggling with low morale and high turnover rates.

Mark took the time to assess the team's dynamics and identified that communication breakdowns and lack of collaboration were contributing to the issues. Drawing inspiration from the wolf's approach, he sought to create a cohesive team environment.

Mark initiated regular team-building exercises that encouraged open communication and collaboration. He organized brainstorming sessions where everyone could contribute ideas and voice concerns, much like wolves working together during a hunt. This not only fostered a sense of ownership among team members but also built trust and camaraderie.

Recognizing the importance of adaptability, Mark encouraged team members to explore new marketing strategies and techniques. He created a safe space for experimentation, allowing individuals to learn from both successes and failures. This openness to innovation mirrors the wolves' ability to shift their hunting strategies based on prey availability.

As a result of Mark's efforts, the team began to flourish. Collaboration improved, and members reported feeling more engaged and valued. The revitalization of team dynamics led to a significant increase in productivity and a decrease in turnover rates, illustrating the power of adopting a wolf leadership style.

In exploring the role of wolves as balancers of their ecosystems, we uncover critical leadership lessons centered on strategic intervention, team cohesion, adaptability, social learning, and the importance of aligning individual and collective goals. Wolves exemplify how effective leaders can foster collaboration, maintain balance within their teams, and respond adeptly to changing circumstances. Their social dynamics and cooperative hunting strategies illustrate the power of collective effort in achieving common objectives.

As we shift our focus to the sea star, we will examine one more keystone species that offers unique insights into leadership through its role in promoting diversity and resilience. Sea stars play a vital part in maintaining ecological balance by preventing any single species from dominating their environment. Their behaviors provide valuable lessons for leaders aiming to create inclusive and adaptive organizational cultures. Join us as we delve into the fascinating world of sea stars and uncover the leadership principles that emerge from their ecological contributions.

The Sea Star: Champions of Diversity

Sea stars, also known as starfish, are often overlooked in discussions of keystone species, yet their ecological significance cannot be underestimated. These remarkable organisms play a vital role in their marine ecosystems by regulating populations of other species, particularly mollusks like mussels, which can otherwise dominate the seafloor. Understanding the behaviors of sea stars through the lenses of evolutionary biology and ethology provides essential insights into their ecological contributions and the leadership lessons they offer.

Sea stars possess unique physiological traits that enhance their adaptability and survival in varied marine environments. Their radial symmetry allows them to move easily in any direction, making them efficient predators. Additionally, their tube feet, equipped with suction capabilities, enable them to pry open the shells of bivalves, facilitating access to food sources that might otherwise be inaccessible.

The regenerative abilities of sea stars are one of their most fascinating evolutionary adaptations. If a sea star loses an arm, it can regenerate it over time, which not only allows for recovery from injury but also enables them to survive predation. This capacity for regeneration underscores their resilience, providing an excellent model for adaptability in fluctuating environments.

Sea stars play a critical buffering role in their ecosystems by preventing any one species from monopolizing resources. By preying on dominant organisms like mussels, sea stars maintain a balance that allows for a diverse array of species to coexist in the same habitat. Without the presence of sea stars, mussel populations can explode, leading to overgrazing of kelp forests and a decrease in biodiversity.

This buffering action highlights the importance of biodiversity in maintaining healthy ecosystems. Sea stars ensure that no single species becomes too dominant, allowing various organisms to thrive and contributing to overall ecological stability.

Sea stars exhibit behavioral plasticity that enables them to adapt to changing environmental conditions. For example, they may alter their feeding strategies based on prey availability or environmental pressures. In some instances, they can even switch to a more generalist diet when preferred prey becomes scarce, demonstrating their resilience and adaptability.

Additionally, sea stars are known for their ability to respond to environmental cues, adjusting their behavior based on factors like temperature and salinity. This adaptability allows them to occupy a range of ecological niches, reinforcing their role as key players in maintaining ecosystem balance.

Sea stars illustrate reciprocal altruism, where cooperation extends beyond immediate kin for mutual benefit. By preying on dominant species like mussels, sea stars prevent monopolization of resources and foster an environment where diverse species can thrive.

For leaders, reciprocal altruism can help create inclusive and equitable environments. Leaders who model reciprocity—by lifting others, sharing resources, and building trust—create systems that benefit everyone. In such environments, diverse perspectives contribute to innovation, adaptability, and resilience.

Leadership Lessons from the Sea Star

The behaviors of sea stars provide several leadership lessons that can be applied within organizational contexts:

- **Promoting Diversity:** Sea stars exemplify the importance of fostering diversity within teams. By preventing any single voice or perspective from dominating, leaders can create an environment where all members feel valued and empowered to contribute.

- **Resilience and Recovery:** The regenerative abilities of sea stars underscore the significance of resilience in leadership. Effective leaders should model adaptability and demonstrate how to recover from setbacks, encouraging their teams to embrace challenges as opportunities for growth.

- **Resource Management:** Just as sea stars manage populations of mussels, leaders must be skilled at managing resources within their teams. This includes balancing workloads, recognizing individual strengths, and allocating resources where they are needed most.

- **Strategic Intervention:** Sea stars demonstrate the importance of timing in intervention. Leaders should be aware of when to step in to prevent dominance or conflict within their teams, promoting harmony and collaboration.

- **Adaptability:** The ability of sea stars to adjust their feeding strategies reflects the necessity for leaders to be flexible and responsive to changing circumstances. Embracing innovation and adapting to new information can lead to better decision-making.

Case Study: Maria's Approach to Fostering Inclusivity

To illustrate the principles of sea star leadership in action, let's examine the case of Maria, a director at a nonprofit organization focused on community development.

Upon stepping into her role, Maria recognized that the organization was facing challenges related to inclusivity and representation within decision-making processes. Drawing inspiration from the sea star's buffering role, she set out to create a more inclusive environment.

Maria initiated open forums where team members could voice their opinions and share ideas, ensuring that everyone had an opportunity to contribute to discussions. This practice mirrored the way sea stars maintain balance by allowing diverse species to coexist and flourish. By actively encouraging participation from all members, Maria fostered a sense of belonging and ownership within her team.

Additionally, Maria implemented mentoring programs that paired experienced team members with newer staff, facilitating knowledge sharing and promoting professional growth. This approach not only empowered individuals but also reinforced the importance of collaboration and learning from one another, like the way sea stars promote diverse interactions within their ecosystems.

As a result of Maria's efforts, the organization experienced a cultural shift. Team members reported feeling more valued and engaged, leading to increased collaboration and innovative solutions to community challenges. The transformation demonstrated the impact of adopting a sea star leadership style—focused on inclusivity and resilience.

In exploring the role of sea stars as buffers in their ecosystems, we uncover vital leadership lessons centered on promoting diversity, resilience, strategic resource management, and adaptability. By preventing any single species from dominating their environment, sea stars create conditions that allow for a rich tapestry of life to flourish. Their regenerative abilities and flexible feeding strategies further exemplify the importance of resilience and adaptability in navigating challenges.

As we transition to the next section, we will integrate the lessons learned from beavers, wolves, and sea stars, examining how these insights can be synthesized to enhance our leadership practices. By combining the strengths of each animal—builders, balancers, and buffers—we can develop a more holistic approach to leadership that embraces collaboration, inclusivity, and adaptability.

We will explore practical strategies for integrating these nature-inspired lessons into our leadership frameworks, empowering us to create environments where innovation thrives and teams perform at their best. Join us as we delve into how we can combine these approaches to enhance our effectiveness as leaders.

Integrating Lessons from Nature

The lessons we can learn from beavers, wolves, and sea stars offer a valuable set of insights that can transform our approach to leadership. By synthesizing the unique qualities of these keystone species—builders, balancers, and buffers—we can have a better understanding of leadership framework informed by the biology of behavior, one that emphasizes collaboration, inclusivity, and adaptability. This integration allows leaders to cultivate an environment where innovation flourishes and team dynamics thrive.

Each of the three keystone species we've explored brings distinct yet complementary strengths to the table. By examining their roles through a unified lens, we can develop a multifaceted leadership style that incorporates the best practices from nature.

1. **Building Foundations (Beaver):** Leaders can take inspiration from beavers by focusing on establishing strong systems and structures within their organizations. This involves creating clear processes, defining roles, and fostering a culture of accountability. By laying a solid foundation, leaders ensure that their teams have the stability necessary to thrive.

2. **Balancing Dynamics (Wolf):** Incorporating the wolf's balancing act means recognizing the importance of team dynamics and knowing when to intervene. Leaders must develop the ability to assess situations and strategically step in to promote collaboration and harmony. This includes mediating conflicts, ensuring equitable participation, and fostering a shared sense of purpose among team members.

3. **Promoting Diversity (Sea Star):** Embracing the sea star's role as a buffer involves actively promoting diversity and inclusivity within teams. Leaders should create environments where multiple perspectives are valued and encouraged, allowing for a rich exchange of ideas. This approach not only enhances creativity but also strengthens the resilience of the organization.

By combining these approaches, leaders can cultivate a dynamic and adaptive organizational culture that mirrors the complexity and balance of natural ecosystems. This integrative perspective allows for more effective responses to challenges, promotes innovation, and ultimately leads to greater success. To effectively integrate the lessons learned from nature into our leadership practices, consider the following practical strategies:

- **Create a Collaborative Environment:** Foster a culture that encourages teamwork and open communication. Implement regular team-building activities and brainstorming sessions to strengthen relationships and promote idea-sharing. For example, adopt practices from beaver leadership by establishing clear processes that facilitate collaboration.

- **Assess and Adapt:** Regularly evaluate the effectiveness of your team dynamics. Just as wolves adapt their strategies based on the behavior of prey, leaders should remain vigilant and responsive to changing conditions within their teams. This might involve soliciting feedback from team members and adjusting processes or roles as needed.

- **Encourage Diverse Perspectives:** Actively seek out and embrace diverse viewpoints within your team. Create opportunities for individuals to share their ideas and experiences, fostering an inclusive environment like the sea star's role in maintaining ecological balance. This can be achieved through diverse hiring practices and by encouraging participation from all team members during discussions.

- **Emphasize Continuous Learning:** Promote a culture of learning and growth within your organization. Encourage mentorship and knowledge-sharing initiatives that allow team members to learn from one another. Like wolves that benefit from social learning, your team will be stronger when individuals can draw on each other's experiences and expertise.

- **Develop Resilience:** Instill a sense of resilience within your team by framing challenges as opportunities for growth. Encourage team members to embrace failure as part of the learning process, like how sea stars regenerate and adapt to loss. Create an environment where experimentation is supported, and individuals feel safe to take risks.

- **Align Individual and Team Goals:** Ensure that individual aspirations are aligned with team objectives, much like the hierarchical structure of wolf packs. This can involve regular one-on-one meetings to discuss personal goals and how they contribute to the team's success. Clear communication about how individual efforts impact the broader mission fosters a sense of ownership and accountability.

By integrating these strategies into your leadership approach, you can harness the strengths of beavers, wolves, and sea stars to create a thriving, innovative, and resilient organization.

Reflection

As you consider the insights gained from beavers, wolves, and sea stars, take a moment to reflect on your own leadership style and practices. The following questions are designed to help you identify areas for growth and enhancement:

1. **Building Foundations:**
   - Am I building systems that ensure immediate success and long-term resilience?

- How effectively am I establishing clear processes and structures within my team?
- What specific systems can I put in place to create a more stable and supportive environment for my team members?
- In what ways can I proactively maintain and improve these systems to ensure they meet the evolving needs of my team?
- What legacy will my leadership leave behind?

2. Balancing Dynamics:

- How am I strengthening bonds within my team to ensure resilience?
- Am I mentoring and developing future leaders to carry forward our shared success?
- Am I aware of the dynamics within my team, and do I recognize when intervention is necessary?
- How can I cultivate a sense of trust and collaboration among team members to enhance overall team performance?
- What strategies can I implement to address conflicts or imbalances in participation and ensure that every voice is heard?

3. Promoting Diversity:

- Am I fostering an environment where diverse perspectives thrive?
- How diverse is my team, and what steps can I take to encourage inclusivity in our processes?
- What mechanisms do I have in place to seek out and value different perspectives?
- How can I create an environment where team members feel safe sharing their ideas and experiences?
- How am I modeling reciprocity to build trust and mutual success?

By thoughtfully engaging with these questions, you can deepen your understanding of how to apply the lessons from nature to your leadership style. This reflection can guide you in developing a more adaptive, inclusive, and effective approach to leading your team.

Chapter 2

The Biology of Leadership

As we explored in Chapter 1, nature offers us profound insights into leadership through the lens of keystone species—builders, balancers, and buffers—that shape their ecosystems with precision and impact. The behaviors of beavers, wolves, and sea stars teach us that effective leadership transcends individual actions and is deeply connected to the systems and relationships we foster. Now, as we transition from the natural world to the inner workings of human beings, we turn to the biology that drives us. Just as keystone species adapt and thrive through evolutionary mechanisms, leaders can harness biological principles to influence their environments. This chapter delves into the physiology of leadership, uncovering how our bodies and behaviors interact to shape perceptions, build trust, and drive performance in ways that are as instinctive as they are strategic.

Leadership as a Biological Process

Leadership extends far beyond observable actions and strategic decisions; it is deeply influenced by biology. The next step in our exploration takes us beneath the surface to examine the physiological underpinnings that shape every interaction a leader has. Beyond the research, there lies a biological reality—one that affects how leaders are perceived and how they impact others on a fundamental level. This chapter will delve into how the bodies of those we are leading (or hope to lead) respond instinctively to the signals we send, revealing the often unseen ways that tone, posture, and presence can influence emotions, build trust, or create tension. By recognizing

21

these biological dynamics, leaders can refine their approach not just to connect but to resonate deeply with those they lead.

The truth is that the biological processes at play in leadership are the same ones that shape all human relationships. Whether or not we realize it, the signals we send and receive from others—through our tone, our posture, even our facial expressions—are processed by our bodies before our brains have even fully understood them. These signals help us decide who we want to keep close as friends, who we choose as mates, and who feels trustworthy or dangerous. In the same way that we get a "gut feeling" about someone we're just meeting for the first time, we're constantly picking up on the biological cues sent by those around us, and leaders are no exception.

Think back to a time when you were introduced to someone new, whether a future close friend, a romantic partner, or even a colleague. Often we can't explain why, but we feel an immediate pull toward—or push away from—that person. Or perhaps you've been in a situation where you sensed something was off with someone you once trusted. These reactions occur at a biological level before you've even fully processed the thought. Your body receives signals—whether through body language, eye contact, or tone of voice—and your nervous system responds accordingly. This isn't just perception; it's your biology guiding you, helping you determine who is friend or foe, whom you can trust or who might be a threat.

For leaders, these same biological dynamics are at play. Every time you walk into a room, speak to your team, or even interact casually in the hallway or a Slack channel, you're sending out signals that affect others on a deep physiological level. The way you carry yourself, the tone of your voice, the expressions on your face, and even the emojis you use send messages that others' bodies respond to instinctively. You may calm the room, putting people at ease, or you may heighten their anxiety, leaving them tense and on edge. In the same way that we unconsciously scan for trustworthiness in our personal relationships, our teams and colleagues are constantly reacting to the signals we emit.

Take a moment to consider a time when someone's presence or tone completely changed the mood in a room. Maybe it was a leader who brought a calming influence when tension was high, or perhaps it was the opposite—a tense and uncertain leader who raised everyone's stress levels. These reactions aren't just perceptual; they're biological. We are hardwired to react to these cues in ways that affect us emotionally and physically, whether we're aware of it or not.

The biological basis of leadership is a frequently overlooked but deeply significant part of how we lead and influence others. The signals you send don't just stay at the surface—they penetrate deeper, shaping how others feel and, ultimately, how they perform. Just as a calm voice can ease the nerves of a team under pressure, a harsh or abrupt tone can trigger the body's stress response, flooding the system with cortisol and setting off a cascade of biological reactions that make clear thinking and effective performance harder to achieve.

In this chapter, we'll delve into the biology of leadership by exploring how physiological signals—both the ones we send and the ones we receive—affect how we lead and how we are led. We'll look at the biological processes that underpin everything from building trust to managing stress, and how understanding these dynamics can help leaders more effectively influence their teams. By recognizing these biological realities, leaders can fine-tune their behaviors to create environments where people not only feel safe and motivated but are biologically primed to perform at their best.

This exploration of the biology of leadership is crucial to understanding the next step in this journey: the biomechanics of leadership. Before we dive into how physical movements and body mechanics influence leadership effectiveness, we must first understand how biology—the foundation of all human relationships—affects every interaction a leader has.

The Physiology of Leadership

Much of what we perceive as influence happens before a word is spoken. Our bodies are constantly reacting to the signals we receive from those around us—whether it's a leader's posture, tone of voice, or even the subtle tension in the air. We'll be exploring the often overlooked physiological responses that shape how we lead and are led. We'll begin by examining how our bodies instinctively react to leadership cues, sometimes faster than our brains can process them. From there, we'll dive into the impact of stress, showing how leaders can either amplify or calm team tension. We'll also explore heart rate variability (HRV), a powerful tool for measuring resilience under pressure, and end with practical breathing techniques that leaders can use to regulate both their own and their team's physiological responses in high-stress moments. By understanding these physiological factors, leaders can create environments that foster calm, focus, and high performance.

Leading with Instinct: How Our Bodies Respond Before Our Brains Catch Up

When we think about leadership, we often focus on communication, decision-making, and emotional intelligence. However, what's happening beneath the surface—at the level of our physiology—is just as important. The body reacts to leadership signals before the brain fully processes them. This means that when a leader enters a room, speaks, or even moves, the people around them are experiencing subtle but powerful physiological responses.

One simple way to think about this is through the analogy of a reflexive "flinch." When something unexpected happens, like a loud sound or a sudden movement, we instinctively flinch before we even have time to think. This is the body's natural way of protecting itself, reacting faster than the brain can process what's happening. Similarly, when leaders send signals—whether through body language, tone of voice, or facial expressions—the body reacts before the mind has a chance to catch up. These physiological reactions set the tone for how people feel, think, and behave in response to leadership.

This immediate physiological response to leadership is foundational, shaping everything from team dynamics to individual performance. By understanding how the body reacts to leadership cues, leaders can become more intentional about the signals they send and the environments they create.

The Ripple Effect of Stress: How Leadership Shapes Team Tension

Stress is one of the most pervasive biological responses in leadership situations, and it can either propel teams to high performance or push them into dysfunction. Research shows that stress can be contagious within teams, spreading from one individual to others almost like a virus. A leader's ability to manage stress, both their own and their team's, is a critical factor in determining overall team effectiveness. When a leader is calm and composed, they can help regulate the physiological responses of their team members, keeping stress at manageable levels. Conversely, when a leader is anxious or tense, they can exacerbate stress within the team, leading to poor decision-making, miscommunication, and reduced performance.

The biological impact of stress in leadership situations is largely driven by the hormone cortisol. When faced with a stressful situation, the body releases cortisol, which triggers the "fight-or-flight" response. This prepares the body either to confront the stressor or to escape from it, increasing heart rate, elevating blood pressure, and sharpening focus. According to research conducted by Dirk Hellhammer of the University of Trier,[1] while this response is useful in short bursts, chronic stress and constant exposure to cortisol can lead to burnout, anxiety, and a host of negative physical and mental health outcomes. This is why leaders who can regulate their stress responses, and that of their teams, are often better equipped to handle challenges with clarity and resilience.

Consider the example of a leader walking into a chaotic office environment where tensions are high due to a looming deadline. The leader's presence alone can influence the team's physiological responses. If the leader enters the room calmly, speaking in a measured tone, and with a relaxed posture, the team members may unconsciously mirror that calmness. Their heart rates might lower, their breathing may slow, and they'll likely become more focused and composed. In contrast, if the leader is visibly stressed—speaking rapidly, showing signs of frustration, or making sudden, abrupt movements—the team will likely mirror that stress. They'll feel more anxious, their stress hormones will increase, and their ability to think clearly and perform well will be compromised.

In fact, the spread of stress within teams has been well-documented in studies, including one by Hatfield, on emotional contagion, which show that stress can be transferred from leaders to followers through nonverbal cues and tone of voice. Leaders who fail to manage their stress effectively not only risk their own health but also undermine the performance and well-being of their teams.

Additionally, heart rate variability (HRV) plays a crucial role in understanding the biological impact of stress in leadership contexts. HRV refers to the variation in time between each heartbeat and is a key measure of how well the body is managing stress. Research by Julian Thayer of the National Institute of Aging/Gerontology Research Center,[2] tells us that high HRV indicates a flexible, resilient stress response, while low HRV suggests the body is stuck in a heightened state of stress. Rollin McCraty, researcher at the HeartMath Institute, adds that individuals with higher HRV are better able to handle stressful situations and recover more quickly from stressful events.[3]

Leaders can influence their team's HRV by managing their own stress responses! How amazing is that? The way we show up and stand out will influence the HRV of our team members. When leaders display calmness and composure, they create a ripple effect that helps others regulate their physiological responses to stress. Over time, this contributes to a culture of resilience and high performance.

Heartbeats and High Stakes: The Role of HRV in Leadership Resilience

HRV is a powerful tool for understanding and managing stress, both for leaders and their teams. By measuring the balance between the sympathetic (fight-or-flight) and parasympathetic (rest-and-recover) nervous systems, HRV reveals how well the body adapts to challenges. High HRV indicates balance and readiness, while low HRV signals heightened stress or difficulty recovering.

For leaders, HRV offers insight into resilience. Much like a coach managing a sports team's energy during a game, leaders can regulate their team's emotional and physiological energy. A calm, grounded leader helps maintain a team's HRV, fostering balance and focus. Conversely, an anxious or overwhelmed leader may unintentionally lower their team's HRV, creating tension and stress.

Practices like deep breathing, mindfulness, and exercise are ways to improve HRV and build resilience.[4] By managing their own stress responses, leaders set an example, creating environments where teams feel calm, focused, and capable of performing at their best.

HRV can also serve as an early warning system. Leaders who monitor their HRV can recognize signs of stress before feeling them consciously, allowing proactive steps like brief breathing exercises or moments of reset. Over time, this awareness fosters emotional resilience and a balanced approach to leadership.

Wearable technology, like a smartwatch, makes tracking HRV accessible. These devices provide real-time insights into physiological states, offering leaders a way to tune into their body's signals and make informed adjustments. Monitoring HRV isn't just about numbers—it's about using feedback to lead with greater awareness and effectiveness.

Breathe to Lead: The Power of Controlled Breath in Managing Stress

Controlled breathing is one of the simplest and most effective tools for leaders to regulate their physiological responses and influence their teams. Breathing techniques can calm the nervous system, lower cortisol levels, slow heart rate, and increase HRV. By practicing mindful breathing, leaders not only calm their own bodies but also send signals of safety and stability to those around them.

Research let by Ravinder Jerath of the Augusta Women's Center[5] shows that deep, slow breathing activates the parasympathetic nervous system, which counters the fight-or-flight response and promotes relaxation and focus. Leaders who adopt these techniques improve their ability to think clearly under pressure and help stabilize their teams' physiological states.

One effective method is the 4-7-8 technique: inhale for four seconds, hold for seven, and exhale for eight. This simple exercise quickly calms the nervous system, making it an excellent tool before high-pressure meetings or decisions. Leaders who use this approach ensure they are in the best state to lead effectively.

By incorporating controlled breathing into their routines, leaders can manage stress more effectively and create environments where their teams feel supported, calm, and ready to perform.

Emotion and Leadership

Leadership is as much about emotions as it is about decisions and strategies. Emotions shape the atmosphere of a team, often spreading without conscious awareness. This section explores how emotions manifest physically, why they're contagious, and how leaders can harness emotional awareness to foster thriving teams—even in high-pressure situations.

Harnessing the Power of Emotion

Emotions aren't fleeting; they are deeply physiological. The word "emotion," derived from the Latin *emovere* ("to move out"), reflects how emotions are energy in motion. Our bodies respond to emotions physically—our hearts race when excited, and our muscles tense when stressed—before we even articulate those feelings.

Imagine entering a meeting where calm prevails, only for a stressed leader to rush in. Without uttering a word, their energy shifts the room, creating tension and unease. This isn't just social dynamics—it's biology. Leaders influence emotional energy, setting the tone for focus or frustration.

Emotional Echoes: How Feelings Spread in Teams

Emotional contagion describes how one person's emotions spread to others. Leaders, given their role, significantly impact team mood and performance. When calm, leaders foster focus and resilience.

Conversely, visible stress from a leader can heighten team anxiety, diminishing morale and productivity.

I once faced a project deadline, and though I didn't vocalize my stress, my rushed communication and tense demeanor affected my graduate students. They mirrored my anxiety, rushing their work and making errors. This ripple effect occurred silently but powerfully.

The science of emotional contagion, according to neuroscientist Giacomo Rizzolatti of the University of Parma,[6] hinges on mirror neurons, which allow us to "mirror" others' emotions. A composed leader activates calmness in their team, while visible frustration or panic can elevate collective stress.

Steadying the Ship: Emotional Regulation

Emotional regulation—the ability to manage emotions in high-stress situations—is critical for leaders. Research led by Britta Hölzel[7] helps us see that a calm leader inspires stability, while a reactive one breeds chaos. Techniques like mindfulness encourage leaders to pause and observe emotions before reacting, promoting thoughtful responses.

Another strategy is emotional labeling, which involves naming emotions to reduce their intensity. Simply acknowledging feelings— "I'm anxious"—creates distance, making them easier to manage. Fred Rogers (aka "Mr. Rogers) captured this idea: "Anything that's mentionable is manageable."[8] By modeling this approach, leaders create a transparent, resilient culture where emotions are addressed, not suppressed.

Imagine a leader facing a crisis. By pausing, taking a deep breath, and addressing the team calmly, they maintain focus and morale. Reactive behavior, by contrast, escalates stress and impairs problem-solving. Strong emotional regulation anchors teams, fostering resilience and productivity.

Inside-Out Leadership

Understanding the biology behind leadership has shown us that it's not just about making decisions or motivating others—it's about mastering our own physiology to improve the way we show up. The biology of leadership is rooted in how our bodies and minds respond to challenges, and by leveraging these insights, leaders can better navigate the complexities of modern organizational life. The way you manage your own physiology directly affects how your team functions. Your calm, focused presence will have a compounding effect, helping your team regulate their own stress levels, focus their own energy, and maintain their own resilience in the face of challenges.

As a reminder, when you regulate your HRV and stay composed under pressure, it helps your entire team feel more secure. As we discussed, physiologically, we humans are wired to mirror the emotional and physical states of those around us. Emotional contagion helps explain why your calmness and resilience will be mirrored by your team members, helping them stay focused and calm as well. Just as we discussed earlier, the release of oxytocin can create trust and bonding within a team—this starts with how you show up and extends to how your team responds.

Leading by Example

As a leader, your presence is one of the most powerful tools you have. How you show up physically and emotionally sends signals to your team. Whether it's through nonverbal communication, tone of voice, or emotional regulation, you set the tone for how others respond. When you manage your own physiology, through techniques like mindfulness, controlled breathing, and meditation, you will be better able to lead your teams with clarity and composure.

This inward mastery extends outward. When you are fully present, your team members will feel more supported, safe, and empowered. Your steadiness under pressure will reassure them that they can rely on you. If you practice mindfulness and remain calm in a crisis, you signal to your team that the situation is manageable. This will prevent stress from escalating and encourage your team to maintain their focus and work toward solutions rather than succumbing to panic. The physiology we've explored—lowered cortisol, balanced heart rate variability, and the calming influence of gravitas—demonstrates how your leadership presence can regulate the emotional and physical states of your team.

Case Study: Leading Through Calm in a High-Stress Product Launch

Alex, a senior project manager at a tech company, is leading a team through the final phases of a high-stakes product launch. The team has faced delays and unexpected challenges, resulting in heightened stress and tension. Deadlines are looming, and the atmosphere in the office has grown increasingly frantic.

Alex notices that stress levels are impacting team performance— meetings are less productive, communication is strained, and errors are becoming more frequent. Recognizing the need for a change, Alex decides to apply principles from the biology of leadership to address the situation.

- **HRV Monitoring and Self-Regulation:** Each morning, Alex uses a wearable device to track HRV. On days when HRV readings are lower, Alex incorporates additional breathing exercises before work, ensuring they start the day in a calm state. By practicing the 4-7-8 breathing technique before entering high-pressure meetings, Alex reinforces a steady and grounded presence.

- **Creating a Ripple Effect of Calm:** In team meetings, Alex consciously slows their speech, softens their tone, and maintains open, approachable body language. These deliberate actions help regulate the team's collective stress response. Alex also schedules brief, daily check-ins, offering reassurance and emphasizing progress over remaining challenges to boost morale.

- **Building Trust Through Oxytocin Triggers:** Alex takes time to personally acknowledge individual contributions, offering sincere gratitude for specific achievements. These interactions, such as a brief "Thank you for stepping up on this task" accompanied by eye contact and a warm tone, foster trust and connection within the team.

- **Addressing Emotional Contagion:** During one particularly tense moment, a team member voices frustration about an unrealistic timeline. Instead of reacting defensively, Alex names the emotion: "I hear your frustration, and it's valid." By labeling the emotion and proposing a practical solution, Alex defuses tension and redirects focus. This approach demonstrates emotional regulation, encouraging the team to adopt a more solution-oriented mindset.

Over the next two weeks, the team's performance steadily improves. Errors decrease, collaboration strengthens, and meetings regain their productivity. Feedback from team members highlights how Alex's calming presence helped them stay focused and confident. The product launches successfully, with Alex's leadership style noted as a key factor in navigating the challenges effectively.

Practical Steps for Integrating Biology into Leadership

The key takeaway is that mastering your own physiology is the first step to becoming a more effective, resilient leader. But it doesn't stop there—by taking control of your energy, stress responses, and resilience, you are actively shaping the environment for your team. The way you manage yourself directly impacts the way others feel and perform. To put this into practice, consider adopting some of the simple strategies outlined in this chapter:

- **Breathing exercises** to regulate heart rate and manage stress in real-time
- **Mindfulness practices** to enhance focus, presence, and emotional regulation

- **Heart rate variability training** to build physiological resilience and stay composed under pressure
- **Meditation** to lower cortisol and improve overall well-being

As you integrate these practices into your daily leadership routine, remember that the benefits extend far beyond your own performance. By modeling energy management and resilience, you are setting an example for your team, helping them develop their own resilience, and creating a culture where both individual and collective well-being are prioritized.

Connecting Biology to Movement: Setting the Stage for Biomechanics in Leadership

In this chapter, we've uncovered the often hidden yet profoundly impactful biological processes that underpin leadership. From HRV as a window into our stress and resilience, to the silent language of nonverbal cues that shape how we connect and communicate, it's clear that our bodies play a pivotal role in how we lead. Leadership is not just a psychological or social activity; it's a biological one, driven by the signals we send and receive at a physiological level. Understanding these dynamics empowers us to fine-tune our presence, influencing not just how we are perceived, but also how our teams feel and perform.

However, biology is only part of the story. While the signals we emit are deeply rooted in our physiological states, how we move and physically engage with the world around us further defines our leadership presence. Our next chapter, "The Biomechanics of Leadership," builds on the biological foundation by exploring the critical role of movement, posture, and physicality in effective leadership.

Chapter 3 will take us deeper into the mechanics of presence, where we'll draw parallels between leadership and the art of physical expression often seen in performance and athletics. We will examine how deliberate movements—how we stand, walk, and gesture—can communicate authority, approachability, and confidence, shaping the way others perceive and respond to us. Just as an actor uses physical cues to bring a character to life, leaders can intentionally use biomechanics to amplify their presence, create connection, and inspire action.

By integrating the insights from biology with the tangible actions of movement, we can more fully understand how leaders can harness the power of their entire selves—not just their words—to lead with impact. This next chapter will provide practical strategies and actionable insights to help you align your body language with your leadership intentions, making your presence not only visible but also felt.

Let's move from understanding the biological signals of leadership to mastering the art of physical expression, setting the stage for a leadership style that is both authentically embodied and profoundly effective.

Chapter 3

The Biomechanics of Leadership

Imagine stepping into a room where a conversation has turned tense, the air charged with unspoken emotions. You've likely experienced this: subtle shifts in body language, changes in tone, or the way people suddenly sit straighter or lean back. Conversely, you may have seen the opposite—a surge of excitement and energy as everyone leans in and engages. In both cases, you sense the shift before you fully understand it. These are the invisible forces of leadership at work—the silent biological and physical signals that influence how we connect and engage.

In the previous chapter, we uncovered how biology shapes leadership. Hormones like cortisol, released under stress, ripple through a team, while oxytocin fosters trust and connection. These biological responses are not fleeting; they define how others perceive you and impact critical interactions.

But biology is just the foundation. The true impact of leadership emerges through deliberate physical actions—the gestures, posture, and presence that speak louder than words. This is where biomechanics comes into play, focusing on how physical movements align with leadership intentions. Leadership becomes a performance, not inauthentic but mindful—a physical embodiment of purpose. Like an athlete or actor who commands attention, leaders must use their presence to communicate intention and inspire action.

Vsevolod Meyerhold, an innovative theater practitioner, provides a compelling lens through his concept of *theatrical biomechanics*. Meyerhold argued that an actor is both a "player" and an "instrument"—the first conceives ideas, while the second executes them.[1] Unlike traditional methods that focus on inner emotion to drive external action, Meyerhold's biomechanics start with deliberate, precise physical movements to shape inner states. For leaders, this "outside-in" approach offers a transformative insight: leadership presence is not just about feeling confident or inspired internally; it's about using intentional physicality to project alignment, authenticity, and purpose. By mastering this alignment, leaders can influence the room as powerfully as any actor on stage, shaping the invisible forces that drive connection and engagement.

Meyerhold's concept of biomechanics in theater offers a compelling parallel. His approach flips the traditional narrative: instead of starting with internal emotions, he emphasizes deliberate physical movements to shape inner states. For leaders, this "outside-in" method transforms how intentions become visible, creating alignment between internal thoughts and external actions.

This concept mirrors Sir Ken Robinson's insights on education. Robinson critiques traditional systems for overemphasizing cognitive skills while neglecting physical expression and creativity.[2] Similarly, leadership development often focuses too heavily on strategy and decision-making while overlooking how these elements come to life through presence and action.

By integrating inside-out and outside-in approaches, the biomechanics of leadership offers a holistic view. It's not just about thinking like a leader; it's about embodying leadership. This alignment creates a dynamic presence that bridges the gap between the leader you envision and the one others see in action.

The Two Selves in Leadership

Leadership requires aligning your "two selves"—the internal thinker and the external doer. Without this harmony, even the best ideas may falter if the delivery lacks impact. Your ability to convey ideas through intentional actions ensures your brilliance doesn't remain locked away, unseen and unheard.

This challenge extends beyond yourself. Great leaders foster environments where their teams align their own internal and external selves. Solving complex challenges requires surfacing diverse contributions and linking them into a cohesive whole. The biomechanics of leadership helps unlock this collective potential, aligning individual strengths with organizational goals.

In the following sections, we'll explore how biomechanics enables leaders to connect through warmth, contribute with competence, and collaborate with gravitas. We'll examine how storytelling and conversation amplify these elements, turning small, deliberate actions into transformative leadership tools. Together, we'll uncover how these techniques help you show up, stand out, and empower others to do the same.

Biomechanics on the Court and on the Stage

Before I thought about the biomechanics of leadership, I was captivated by the biomechanics of basketball. Growing up, I idolized Julius "Dr. J" Erving, the iconic forward for the Philadelphia 76ers. A poster of Erving soaring through the air, mid-dunk, adorned my bedroom wall. He embodied grace and power, turning physical action into art. Each leap, pivot, and slam was intentional, confident, and controlled—an example of biomechanics in action, where efficient movement enhances performance and minimizes injury. Erving wasn't just a player; he was a performer.

I spent hours on the court, mimicking those moves, hoping my above-average height would grow into something closer to my heroes. But I eventually leveled out at 5'6". Dunking was out of reach. Yet what fascinated me was how players with vastly different physiques dominated the game. It wasn't just height or raw athleticism; it was how they used their bodies. Players like Allen Iverson, considered small at 6'0", excelled by leveraging agility, balance, and biomechanics. Iverson's quick shifts and low center of gravity allowed him to outmaneuver taller opponents, demonstrating that success relied on adapting movements to maximize strengths and minimize weaknesses.

Through this lens, basketball became more than plays; it was a dynamic expression of physical presence and strategy. Biomechanics shaped not just performance but perception—how players communicated through movement, from a subtle feint to an explosive drive. These lessons about the interplay of body and mind, reflected in theories of embodied cognition, would later resonate with me in unexpected ways.

From Gym Rat to Theater Nerd

In college, I planned to become a teacher and basketball coach. Then, on a whim, I auditioned for a play. Theater, I discovered, shared parallels with basketball: the need for focus, dedication, and teamwork. But it also demanded deeper collaboration, with technicians, designers, and crew all critical to success. Theater wasn't just performance; it was co-creation, where every movement and gesture told a story.

Hooked, I changed my major and dove into theater. One memorable production, *The Merchant of Venice*, cast me as Gratiano, a flamboyant character full of energy. To embody him, I didn't just memorize lines—I experimented with movement and physicality. Our director encouraged us to explore different shoes, believing they could transform how we carried ourselves. When I put on Gratiano's shoes, my posture changed, my stride became animated, and the character came alive. This experience mirrored embodied cognition research, which shows how external changes, like footwear, can influence internal states.

Theater taught me that physicality drives performance. Just as basketball players use biomechanics to influence the game, actors use deliberate movements to shape emotions and connect with audiences. Meyerhold's outside-in methodology emphasizes this idea: intentional physical actions unlock internal emotions, enhancing authenticity and impact.

Both sports and theater share a common truth: How we move shapes how we perform and how others perceive us. Whether on the court, on the stage, or in leadership, aligning physical expressions with intentions is a powerful tool for influence and connection.

Applying Biomechanics to Leadership

In leadership, as in acting, there is a duality: the internal self and the external self. I call these the "two selves" of leadership. The first self is the thinker, the originator of ideas and emotions—the internal world where vision and strategy are born. It's the source of leadership potential, the seat of thoughts and beliefs.

The second self is the doer, the executor, and the self that others see. This is the external world of actions, behaviors, and physical presence. It's not just about decisions or words; it's how you stand, move, and engage with others. This external self constantly communicates, often more powerfully than words, through your presence, energy, and confidence—or the lack of it.

I was reminded of these two selves when my last book, *Strategic Doing: Ten Skills for Agile Leadership*,[3] was released. Readers seemed split into two groups: those drawn by "strategic" and those by "doing." The first group loved deep dives into strategy and complexity theory. They were energized by discussing ideas but often stayed in the realm of theory, with limited tangible impact.

The second group, like a sales engineer I met, said, "I love Strategic Doing because it helps me get stuff done!" These action-oriented readers focused on outcomes, using the tools to navigate complexity and make things happen. This difference underscored the tension between the inner thinker and the outer doer. Both are valuable, but real leadership impact comes when these two selves align.

For leaders, misalignment between internal intentions and external actions creates confusion and distrust. A confident internal self, undermined by uncertain body language, sends mixed messages. In contrast, leaders who align their internal vision with their external presence project authenticity and clarity.

Leadership is an embodied experience, where external actions must reflect internal intentions. This is where biomechanics becomes essential. By developing your second self—the doer—you transform your internal leadership vision into visible, impactful actions that resonate with those you lead.

Outside-In Leadership

Traditionally, leadership development has focused heavily on the inside-out approach: developing self-awareness, building emotional intelligence, and cultivating a strong internal compass. We addressed this inside-out dynamic in the previous chapter. These elements are undoubtedly important, but they represent only half of the equation. The outside-in approach, which emphasizes physicality and external actions, is equally vital yet often overlooked. This perspective is rooted in the idea that how we move and present ourselves externally can shape how we feel and perform internally.

The outside-in approach aligns closely with Meyerhold's biomechanics, where the external actions of the body inform the internal state. In leadership, this means recognizing that your posture, gestures, and expressions can influence not only how others see you but also how you feel and behave. Imagine a leader walking into a meeting with a slouched posture, avoiding eye contact, and shuffling their feet. Even if they feel confident and prepared internally, their external actions communicate the opposite. Their team may perceive them as disengaged, unsure, or uninterested, affecting the dynamic of the entire interaction.

In contrast, leaders who adopt an outside-in mindset actively use their physical presence to convey their internal state. This can be as simple as standing tall, maintaining open body language, or making deliberate eye contact. These physical adjustments, while seemingly minor, can significantly impact both the leader's self-perception and the perception of others. Research in embodied cognition supports this idea, showing that our physical posture and movements can influence our mood, confidence levels, and decision-making processes.

Outside-in leadership encourages you to be mindful of the signals your body sends, not just to others but to yourself. It's about using your physical presence as a tool to align your external actions with your internal intentions. This approach doesn't replace the importance of emotional intelligence or self-awareness; rather, it complements these qualities by translating them into visible, tangible actions that enhance your leadership impact.

Throughout this chapter, we've explored how deliberate physical actions can amplify leadership presence. It's a reminder that the external signals we send—through posture, gestures, and movement—are deeply connected to our internal states. This interplay between the inside and the outside is at the heart of executive presence, making it imperative for leaders to cultivate both their mental approach and their physical expression.

Leaders from Day One

When you walk into a room, long before you say a word, people begin to form impressions of you. Your posture, your movements, and even the way you make eye contact communicate volumes about who you are as a leader. For many, these physical cues can either reinforce or undermine the message they want to convey. This is why presence matters—it's not just about what you think or what you know, but how you show up and make others feel in every interaction. Leadership presence, particularly from the outside in, is about mastering these external expressions so they align with your internal intentions. In her book *The Silent Language of Leaders: How Body Language Can Help—or Hurt—How You Lead,* Carol Kinsey Goman points out that nonverbal behaviors, including posture and gestures, are closely linked to perceptions of leadership effectiveness, often overshadowing verbal communication in their impact.

In my work with Purdue students, we began to see firsthand how the outside-in approach could transform our students. Many of our students were entering the workforce with leadership courses on their transcripts, but recruiters weren't just looking for academic credentials; they wanted to see leadership in action. Companies like PepsiCo, Amazon, and Nestlé were eager to hire students who could demonstrate leadership presence—students who looked, sounded, and acted like leaders from day one. This observation aligns with research by Willis and Todorov indicating that first impressions, often formed within the first seven seconds of an interaction, heavily influence how individuals are perceived and remembered.[4]

We realized that to prepare our students for this expectation, we needed to teach them more than just theory; we had to help them develop a tangible leadership presence. This meant coaching them on everything from how they walk into a room, to how they engage in a conversation, to how they project confidence and competence. The focus was not on changing who they were but on aligning their internal understanding of leadership with their external expression. By doing so, they could show up not just as job candidates, but as emerging leaders ready to contribute from day one. This approach reflects findings from Antonakis and House, which emphasizes the importance of visible competence and relational warmth in effective leadership.[5]

This approach wasn't about faking it; it was about becoming conscious of the signals they were sending and making deliberate adjustments to align their actions with their intentions. For those of us who naturally live in our heads—especially the scientists and engineers I teach at Purdue—this shift can be a revelation. It's about realizing that leadership isn't just something you know; it's something you do. By developing presence from the outside in, leaders can immediately elevate how they are perceived, making the invisible qualities of leadership visible and impactful. This aligns with the concept of embodied leadership, which suggests that physical expressions of leadership behaviors can influence others' perceptions and enhance a leader's ability to inspire and guide.

Practical Techniques

While leadership presence can feel like an abstract concept, it ultimately comes down to actions—specific, intentional actions that consistently demonstrate who you are as a leader. To put it simply, leadership is a verb. This idea parallels a phrase often associated with relationships: "Love is a verb." We know we are loved not because of what someone says, but because of what they do. They listen, they show up, they take care of us. Leadership works the same way; it's not what you say, but what you consistently do that defines you as a leader. The notion that leadership is action-oriented is supported by empirical evidence by Robert Kaiser suggesting that observable behaviors are the most significant predictors of leadership effectiveness.[6]

I often share this concept with my students by asking them to think of the person who loves them most and then consider how they know they are loved. Inevitably, their answers focus on actions: "They support me," "They listen to me," "They are always there for me." Love, like leadership, is demonstrated through behaviors, not just intentions or words. The same holds true in professional settings. You may have the best strategic ideas, but if your actions don't reflect your words—if you're not showing up, not engaging, not acting in ways that demonstrate your commitment—your leadership presence will fall flat. This aligns with the research by Simons on behavioral integrity, which shows that a leader's actions must match their words to maintain credibility and trust.

Practical techniques to embody leadership as a verb include making deliberate choices about how you present yourself and engage with others. It starts with small adjustments: standing tall, making eye contact, using open and inviting gestures, and speaking clearly and confidently. It means being present in the moment—putting away your phone during conversations, actively listening, and responding thoughtfully. It's about making sure your actions are congruent with your words, reinforcing your message through every gesture and movement. These small adjustments align with Mark Knapp's work at the university, showing that nonverbal cues, like body language and eye contact, significantly affect interpersonal trust and communication effectiveness.[7]

Consistency is key. Just as in a relationship where sporadic expressions of love are less convincing than consistent, thoughtful actions, your leadership presence is built through repeated behaviors. Showing up prepared, following through on commitments, and being visible in moments that matter all contribute to a sense of reliability and trustworthiness. People need to see you leading, not just hear you talking about leadership. Research by Dirks supports this by highlighting that consistent, dependable actions are critical in building and maintaining trust in leadership.[8]

To embody leadership as a verb, consider every interaction as an opportunity to reinforce your presence. Ask yourself, "How am I showing up today? What signals am I sending through my actions?" By approaching leadership from the outside in, you harness the power of deliberate actions to create a presence that inspires, influences, and leads others to follow. This is not about being perfect; it's about being intentional, consistent, and visible in your commitment to leading through action. By aligning your internal mindset with your external behaviors, you not only enhance your leadership impact but also create a more authentic, engaging, and effective leadership presence.

Embodied Cognition: The Science Behind the Biomechanics of Leadership

Leadership biomechanics is deeply rooted in the scientific theory of embodied cognition, which posits that our thoughts, emotions, and behaviors are intrinsically linked to our physical bodies. This section explores the theory, research evidence, and practical applications of embodied cognition to enhance your leadership effectiveness.

Embodied cognition challenges the traditional separation of mind and body. It suggests that our cognition is influenced by the body's interactions with the environment. In their book *Philosophy in the Flesh: The Embodied Mind and Its Challenge to Western Thought,* Lakoff and Johnson argue that physical experiences shape how we think, feel, and understand concepts, including leadership and confidence. This means your posture, movements, and physical states don't just reflect your mental state—they actively shape it.[9]

For instance, in an article in *Motivation and Emotion,* Riskind and Goty explained that adopting an upright posture can increase confidence and positively influence decision-making.[10] Similarly, physical actions like standing tall or gesturing assertively can generate feelings of authority even when those emotions aren't initially present. This aligns with Wilson's idea that mental processes are deeply connected to the motor system, providing a basis for the outside-in approach to leadership: Physical behaviors shape internal states.[11]

Research Evidence Supporting Embodied Cognition

Studies reveal that physical postures and expressions significantly impact emotions and cognition. For example:

- **Power Posing:** According to Carney and colleagues, standing with open, expansive postures can increase feelings of confidence and reduce stress, enhancing psychological readiness for challenges.[12]

- **Gestures and Communication:** Goldin-Meadow and Bellock found that gestures improve cognitive processing and communication clarity, helping leaders articulate complex ideas persuasively.[13]

- **Facial Feedback:** Strack and colleagues demonstrated that facial expressions like smiling influence mood, suggesting that maintaining positive expressions can create a ripple effect of optimism within teams.[14]

- **Mirroring and Rapport:** Barsalou showed that mimicking others' gestures fosters trust and alignment, enhancing team dynamics.[15]

This body of research underscores how intentional physical actions can amplify a leader's presence, clarity, and connection with others.

Applications for Leaders

Understanding embodied cognition provides actionable insights for leadership. Here are key strategies:

- **Adopt Confident Postures:** Use open, expansive stances to enhance self-assurance before high-pressure situations. These postures project authority and help you command attention in the room.

- **Leverage Gestures:** Deliberate gestures emphasize key points and make communication more engaging. For example, aligning hand movements with verbal cues can enhance understanding and persuasion.

- **Smile to Set the Tone:** Maintaining positive facial expressions influences your emotions and those of your team, fostering a constructive, focused environment.

- **Mirror for Connection:** Subtly mimicking others' body language builds rapport and trust. This is especially useful in negotiations or tense discussions.

- **Incorporate Movement:** Walking or pacing during problem-solving sessions can stimulate creativity and cognitive flexibility.

Embodied Leadership in Action

By aligning your physical presence with your intentions, you amplify the authenticity and effectiveness of your leadership. Each deliberate movement or gesture becomes a tool to communicate confidence, inspire trust, and foster collaboration. Leadership, at its core, is an embodied experience where your physical actions resonate as powerfully as your words.

Embracing embodied cognition transforms leadership from a conceptual idea into a lived reality, ensuring that how you think and act aligns with how you're perceived by others. As you engage with the biomechanics of leadership, remember that your body is not just a vessel for thought—it's an active participant in shaping your leadership identity and influence.

From the Stage to the Boardroom: More Leadership Lessons from the Theater

For several years, I served on the board of Black Box, a children's theater focused on creativity and storytelling. Its tagline, "Teaching character to build character," perfectly encapsulated the transformative power of theater. Watching my youngest son, Oliver, perform on stage reminded me of the invaluable lessons the arts offer—not just for actors but for leaders too.

Theater teaches presence, adaptability, and connection—skills vital in leadership. Just as actors develop characters and command attention, leaders must embody their roles, adapting to different challenges while inspiring confidence. The transition from stage to boardroom is closer than it seems; the principles of performance directly enhance how leaders engage and inspire.

Character Development Techniques

Character development in theater requires understanding motivations, emotions, and intentions, aligning internal reflection with external expression. Leaders similarly navigate roles requiring confidence, empathy, and decisiveness to guide their teams effectively.

One key theater technique is objective-driven actions, where every movement or line serves a purpose. Leaders benefit by entering interactions with clear objectives, ensuring focus and alignment with goals. Subtext awareness, another essential skill, helps leaders read the unspoken elements of communication—tone, body language, and what's unsaid—building trust and addressing underlying concerns.

Physical presence is equally powerful. Just as actors use posture and movement to express character traits, leaders communicate confidence and accessibility through their body language. Research highlights how open postures and intentional gestures enhance both self-perception and how others perceive you.[16] Emotional recall, drawing on personal experiences, deepens authenticity, allowing leaders to connect empathetically with their teams.

47

The Biomechanics of Leadership

Practical Exercises

To integrate these techniques, try the following:

- **Objective-Driven Interactions:** Define clear goals before meetings or conversations. This sharpens your focus and ensures purposeful actions.

- **Subtext Reading:** Pay attention to tone and body language during interactions, reflecting afterward on unspoken messages to improve connection.

- **Mirror Exercises:** Practice postures and expressions that convey confidence and openness, incorporating them into daily interactions.

- **Emotional Recall Journaling:** Reflect on personal experiences that shape your leadership, drawing on them to lead with empathy and resilience.

- **Role Reversal Simulations:** Switch roles with team members to gain new perspectives and refine your leadership approach.

- **Walking the Space:** Familiarize yourself with key environments, practicing purposeful movements and gestures to command attention.

- **Breath Control and Voice Modulation:** Use deep breathing and varied tones to communicate authority or warmth, matching the situation.

- **Character Journals:** Regularly document and reflect on the leadership traits you aspire to embody, ensuring alignment between intention and action.

These exercises help leaders consciously develop and embody their roles, enhancing presence, connection, and impact. Leadership, like acting, is an ongoing process of refinement. By practicing these techniques, you can bring the best version of your leadership to every moment.

Aligning the Two Selves: Coaching for Biomechanical Mastery

Effective leadership requires more than just understanding one's internal motivations or setting strategic goals; it demands that the internal self (the thinker) and the external self (the doer) be fully aligned. Coaching plays a crucial role in this alignment, helping leaders refine their physical presence and behaviors to match their intentions. Through targeted coaching, leaders can master the biomechanics of their presence, ensuring that their actions consistently reinforce their words and ideas.

Coaching Leaders

Coaching leaders in biomechanical mastery involves guiding them to recognize how their physical actions shape their leadership presence. It goes beyond teaching basics like standing straight or maintaining eye contact, though those are essential. The focus is on developing awareness of how gestures, movements, and posture communicate with others.

Coaches help leaders identify misalignments between internal states and external expressions. For instance, a leader who feels confident may unknowingly project uncertainty through slouched posture or closed-off gestures. Video analysis is a powerful tool in these sessions, offering leaders a clear view of how they appear to others. Seeing themselves from an external perspective helps them align their presence with their intentions.

Rehearsing scenarios, much like actors on stage, is another key component. Practicing responses, refining gestures, and adjusting posture enables leaders to navigate high-stakes situations with confidence and intentionality. Exercises targeting voice modulation, pacing, and use of space help leaders command attention without overwhelming others. Experimentation with physical cues allows leaders to discover what feels authentic while enhancing their impact.

Feedback Loops

Central to coaching is the concept of feedback loops—cycles of action, observation, reflection, and adjustment that continually refine a leader's presence. Feedback is dynamic, involving input from coaches, peers, and team members. For instance, a leader may learn that their assertive stance reads as confident to some but overly aggressive to others. Such nuanced insights allow for tailored adjustments.

Biofeedback tools, like heart rate monitors or voice analysis software, provide immediate data on physical and emotional states. A leader who speaks too quickly under stress, for example, can use this feedback to develop more deliberate pacing. This continuous process mirrors athletic training, where each action informs the next refinement.

Aligning the two selves through coaching and feedback is an ongoing practice, not a one-time event. Leaders who master their biomechanics consistently align their internal vision with external actions, cultivating a presence that is both impactful and authentic.

Small Changes, Big Impacts: The Power of Subtle Adjustments

In leadership, the most impactful changes often come from the smallest adjustments. These seemingly minor shifts, known as micro-behaviors, can dramatically alter how you are perceived and how effectively you connect with others. Micro-behaviors—small, intentional actions such as the way you nod, maintain eye contact, or adjust your posture—are the building blocks of executive presence. They may be subtle, but their cumulative effect can be profound, influencing how your message is received and how your leadership is experienced.

Micro-Behaviors

Micro-behaviors are the tiny, often unconscious actions that shape our interactions. These include nonverbal cues like a brief smile, the direction of your gaze, or the subtle tilt of your body toward a speaker.

Though small, these behaviors carry significant weight in communication. Research by Ambady and Rosenthal shows that micro-behaviors can influence perceptions of trustworthiness, competence, and warmth within seconds.[17] For leaders, mastering these small actions can be the difference between inspiring confidence and sowing doubt.

Consider something as simple as eye contact. In Western cultures, maintaining eye contact conveys attentiveness and engagement. A leader who consistently makes eye contact during conversations signals that they are present and interested, which fosters trust and connection. Conversely, avoiding eye contact, even unintentionally, can come across as disinterest or insecurity. Similarly, micro-behaviors like nodding slightly while listening can encourage the speaker and convey that you are actively engaged in the dialogue.

Posture is another critical micro-behavior. Standing or sitting with an open, upright posture communicates confidence and approachability. On the other hand, slouching or crossing your arms can create an impression of defensiveness or disinterest. By making conscious adjustments to your posture, you can subtly shift the energy of a room, making others feel more comfortable and willing to engage.

Even small vocal adjustments, such as modulating your tone or pace of speech, can have a big impact. A leader who speaks in a calm, steady voice during a crisis can provide a sense of stability and control, while a frantic or hurried tone may amplify anxiety. Though often overlooked, these micro-behaviors are powerful tools for influencing the emotional climate of any interaction.

The key to mastering micro-behaviors is mindfulness—being aware of how your small actions affect those around you. This doesn't mean overanalyzing every gesture, but rather developing an awareness of your habitual behaviors and their impact. By tuning into these subtleties, you can make small, deliberate adjustments that enhance your leadership presence and effectiveness.

Case Study: Sarah and Tom

To see the power of micro-behaviors in action, consider the case of Sarah, a mid-level manager in a tech company. Sarah was technically skilled and well-respected for her knowledge, but she struggled with commanding attention in meetings. She often found that her ideas were overlooked, and her presence in the room felt muted compared to her peers. After working with a leadership coach, Sarah learned that her physical presence—particularly her tendency to avoid eye contact and to speak softly—was undermining her authority.

Through targeted coaching, Sarah made a series of subtle adjustments. She practiced maintaining eye contact when speaking, using more deliberate hand gestures to emphasize her points, and slightly lowering the pitch of her voice to project more confidence. These changes were small, but their impact was immediate. Colleagues began to notice her more, and her ideas started to gain traction. Sarah's experience highlights how even the most nuanced adjustments can transform how a leader is perceived.

Another example comes from Tom, a senior executive who was known for his strategic thinking but often came across as distant and unapproachable. His team felt that he wasn't engaged during meetings, as he frequently checked his phone and maintained a closed-off posture. Recognizing the need to adjust his micro-behaviors, Tom made a conscious effort to put his phone away during discussions, sit with an open posture, and use more affirming gestures like nodding and smiling when others spoke.

The results were transformative. Team members reported feeling more connected to Tom, and his increased engagement fostered a more collaborative atmosphere. What seemed like small changes— eye contact, nodding, and open body language—created a ripple effect that improved team dynamics and overall morale.

These cases demonstrate that leadership isn't always about grand gestures or major overhauls; sometimes, the most significant shifts come from the smallest actions. By being intentional about micro-behaviors, you can make subtle but impactful adjustments that enhance your presence and influence.

As a leader, you are constantly sending signals, even in moments when you're not speaking. By refining your micro-behaviors, you can ensure that the signals you send are aligned with your leadership intentions, making every interaction a little more effective and every message a little more powerful.

52

Biohacking Leadership

The Biomechanics of Leadership as a Continuous Practice

Leadership is not a static skill but a dynamic practice that evolves with experience, feedback, and self-awareness. Just as an athlete refines their movements or an actor perfects their performance, effective leaders must continually develop, adapting their physical and behavioral cues to align with their leadership roles. The biomechanics of leadership is more than mastering techniques; it's about embracing a mindset of growth and adaptation.

The journey toward impactful leadership doesn't have a final destination. It's an ongoing process of learning, experimenting, and recalibrating. Biomechanics—how you move, engage, and present yourself—should be seen as an evolving toolkit. A gesture that feels natural in one setting might not in another. The key is maintaining curiosity and openness to change, adjusting your behaviors as you gather feedback.

This development process requires being self-aware and receptive to feedback, both from others and through your self-observations. Biomechanics isn't just about how others perceive you; it's about understanding your own body language, tone, and energy. It's an iterative cycle: act, observe, adjust, and repeat. This continuous evolution helps you stay authentic, ensuring your actions align with your values.

Think of leadership as an ongoing performance—each moment, meeting, and conversation provides an opportunity to refine your skills. These small, intentional changes compound over time, enhancing your presence and influence.

As we conclude this chapter, it's important to recognize that the physical aspects of presence are just one part of executive presence. The upcoming chapters will dive deeper into specific elements—warmth, competence, and gravitas—and how they manifest in leadership. You'll learn how to use warmth to build connections, project competence through your actions, and cultivate gravitas to guide collaborative spaces.

Coming Attractions

The next four chapters explore the essential elements of a new science-based approach to executive presence by breaking down the specific behaviors that define each quality. These chapters provide practical strategies for aligning the leader in your head—the originator of ideas—with the leader others see—the executor of those ideas, a concept rooted in Meyerhold's notion of our dual selves. You'll find insights on the challenges associated with demonstrating these behaviors, on-the-job examples of individuals who embody them, and how these behaviors impact teams. Each chapter also profiles leaders whose actions exemplify these traits, offering guidance on how to cultivate executive presence in your own development as a leader. We'll start first with an introduction and a critique of traditional notions of executive presence, present our updated model of leadership biodynamics, and then further examine the three characteristics of our model: warmth, competence, and gravitas.

Chapter 4

From Executive Presence to Leadership Biodynamics

When I first heard the term *executive presence*, I was reminded of my theater days. Back then, we spoke often of *stage presence*—that almost indescribable quality of an actor who commanded attention. A person with stage presence held the audience captive, their every movement and word impossible to ignore. But as I reflected on the traditional model of executive presence, it struck me that while it bore similarities to stage presence, it wasn't the full picture of leadership. This realization took me back to my time working with castmates who may not have commanded the spotlight on stage but instead had what I've come to think of as *backstage presence*.

These individuals were the glue that held the production together, creating an environment where everyone could excel. Often, the same standout actor who shone under the lights also worked tirelessly behind the scenes, ensuring the team functioned as a cohesive whole. It was this duality—the ability to shine in public and to strengthen others in private—that began shaping my understanding of what true executive presence entails.

In the chapters leading to this point, we've explored the unseen forces that shape leadership. We've examined how the biology of leadership influences our ability to connect, contribute, and collaborate, as well as how biomechanics—the deliberate use of physical actions—can enhance a leader's presence. These concepts converge in executive presence. It's not merely about commanding attention in a room; it's about aligning internal intentions with external expression to inspire trust, foster collaboration, and create shared value. Building on this foundation, we'll reimagine executive presence as a blend of stage and backstage presence, showing how leaders can simultaneously command attention and empower others to shine. This chapter begins with that redefinition, charting a path to help you cultivate both forms of presence in your leadership journey.

Rethinking Executive Presence

Leaders often face serious challenges: markets that never stop changing, attracting and retaining top talent, and the constant need to make quick, smart decisions. The old-school models of executive presence, focusing on command-and-control, assertiveness, and a "take charge" attitude, just don't cut it anymore. They miss the mark on the real skills that matter now: connecting, collaborating, and staying resilient when things get tough.

That's why we decided to rethink what executive presence should look like in today's world. Working with a team of researchers in the Netherlands and Matt Jones, currently a doctoral student at Purdue and author of one of the chapters in this book, we dove into the literature and the data. We didn't just pull ideas out of thin air—we poured over the existing research, validated our concepts with experts, and made sure our framework held up to rigorous scientific testing. The result? A robust, practical model informed by the biology of behavior. We call this new framework leadership biodynamics. Before we get to this updated model, let's review the more traditional one.

The Traditional Understanding of Executive Presence and Its Limitations

Executive presence has often been seen as that "it" factor that sets standout leaders apart, but it's been a bit of a mystery—typically linked to traits like confidence, assertiveness, and the knack for commanding a room. These qualities, often rooted in charismatic leadership theories, shaped the corporate world of the 20th century. Cultural norms and business traditions elevated these visible behaviors as the gold standard for leadership. But let's be honest:

this traditional model has its flaws. It's been criticized for being narrow, male-centric, and not very well backed by solid research. To understand why this old-school view falls short of today's leadership needs, we need to look at how it all started and why it's stuck around.

The concept of executive presence traces its roots to charismatic leadership, as introduced by sociologist Max Weber in the early 20th century. Weber described charisma as a form of influence based on a leader's personal magnetism and extraordinary qualities, rather than tradition or formal authority.[1] Charismatic leaders were seen as visionaries, inspiring loyalty through boldness and eloquence—an early blueprint for what we now consider executive presence.

By the mid-20th century, these ideas merged with transformational leadership theories from thinkers like James MacGregor Burns and Bernard Bass. Burns emphasized vision and inspiration as key drivers of leadership,[2] while Bass linked charisma directly to leadership success.[3] This shift brought executive presence into the corporate realm, highlighting traits observed in boardrooms and beyond.

Figures like Winston Churchill and Margaret Thatcher helped solidify the image of executive presence. Churchill's stirring speeches during World War II and Thatcher's assertive leadership style set enduring benchmarks, equating leadership with authority and command. Their ability to project strength and confidence reinforced the belief that leadership relied on outward displays of control.

As the business world evolved, executive presence became associated with visible traits such as posture, appearance, and speech. By the late 20th century, it was a recognized but narrowly defined quality, rooted in high-stakes environments like boardrooms and political stages. This focus on external attributes, however, left little room for the nuanced relational skills critical for today's leaders.

Cultural Influences: Media, Business Schools, and Corporate Culture

Media has played a significant role in shaping perceptions of executive presence. Hollywood films like *Wall Street* and *The Wolf of Wall*

Street glamorized the image of the charismatic, assertive CEO who dominates every room, reinforcing a larger-than-life ideal of leadership centered on control and boldness.

Business publications such as *Forbes* and *Fortune* amplified this narrative, spotlighting not only the decisions of top CEOs but also their style, communication, and overall demeanor. Business schools and executive training programs adopted similar frameworks, emphasizing public speaking, negotiation, and personal branding. Aspiring leaders were encouraged to emulate high-profile figures like Steve Jobs or Jack Welch, further cementing a narrow definition of what leadership should look like.

Even height has been rewarded, a particularly worrisome phenomenon for someone like me who is only five foot six! Timothy Judge and Daniel Cable conducted a study exploring the relationship between physical height and workplace outcomes.[4] Their research revealed a significant correlation between an individual's height and their career success, including higher income levels. The findings suggest that height may play an influential role in how individuals are perceived in professional environments, potentially affecting their opportunities for advancement and financial rewards. These biases have created barriers for diverse leadership approaches, privileging traits associated with dominance over collaboration or empathy.

As these norms spread globally through multinational companies and business education, they sometimes clashed with local leadership values. In many cultures, leadership emphasizes humility, consensus, or community rather than assertiveness and charisma. These tensions highlight the limitations of traditional executive presence models and underscore the need for a more inclusive and adaptable approach to leadership.

Characteristics of the Traditional Model

The traditional model of executive presence emphasizes a narrow set of visible traits and behaviors, often celebrated as indicators of leadership potential. These characteristics—centered on confidence, control, and charisma—reflect an outdated understanding of leadership, increasingly criticized for its biases and lack of inclusivity.

Visible Traits: Commanding Appearance, Assertiveness, and Charisma

At the heart of the traditional view of executive presence are visible traits—how leaders look, speak, and carry themselves. These outward signals often serve as quick judgments of competence and authority. A commanding appearance, defined by confident body language, professional attire, and physical presence, is frequently viewed as a hallmark of effective leadership. Judge's research confirms that leaders who stand tall, make direct eye contact, and exude confidence are perceived as more capable and trustworthy.

Assertiveness plays a significant role as well. Leaders who speak decisively and hold their ground are often seen as in control and authoritative. However, Eagly and Carli find that this focus on assertiveness can overshadow critical skills like listening, collaboration, and empathy—qualities essential for fostering productive workplaces.[5]

Charisma, the ability to inspire and captivate, has long been celebrated in leadership circles. Charismatic leaders often rally teams around their vision with compelling words and magnetic personalities. Yet charisma has its pitfalls, including a tendency toward overconfidence and impulsiveness, which can sideline valuable input and lead to poor decision-making, according to Conger. Charisma, however, doesn't inherently equate to sound judgment or ethical behavior, revealing the limitations of relying solely on visible traits as indicators of leadership success.

Top-Down Leadership: Command-and-Control and Hierarchical Norms

Traditional executive presence is frequently tied to a command-and-control leadership style rooted in clear hierarchies. Originating in military and industrial settings, this approach values decisive authority and firm control. In corporate environments, this has translated into leaders who guide from the top, maintaining a clear divide between themselves and their teams. While effective in certain contexts, this model often stifles collaboration, limits the flow of ideas, and creates disconnects between leaders and their teams.

The model is also deeply male-centric, prioritizing traits stereotypically associated with masculinity, such as dominance and assertiveness. Women and underrepresented groups often face double standards, being penalized for displaying assertive traits while simultaneously criticized if they don't project authority, according to Eagly. These biases exclude diverse leadership styles and discourage authenticity, narrowing the pool of potential leaders.

Leadership research by Nembhard and Edmondson highlights the flaws of these rigid hierarchies, advocating instead for inclusive and participative leadership styles that foster teamwork, innovation, and trust.[6] The traditional model, with its emphasis on top-down authority, struggles to adapt to today's demands for agility and collaboration.

Critiquing the Traditional Model

The traditional framework, focused on visible traits and command-oriented leadership, falls short in meeting the needs of modern organizations. Its heavy reliance on masculine-coded behaviors, like assertiveness and control, marginalizes inclusive approaches and overlooks critical relational skills such as empathy and active listening, according to Herminia Ibarra at London Business School and Anne Scoular at Oxford University.[7]

In a global business environment, the traditional model often clashes with culturally diverse leadership styles. Many non-Western cultures value traits like humility, patience, and collective action over individual assertiveness and charisma. This mismatch underscores the need for a broader, more adaptable approach to leadership.

Outdated norms like the command-and-control style stifle innovation, teamwork, and psychological safety—qualities essential for thriving in today's dynamic workplace. Furthermore, Kaiser and colleagues find that the focus on outward appearance risks prioritizing

60

Biohacking Leadership

performance over substance, leading to burnout, impulsive decision-making, and strained relationships.[8]

The traditional model of executive presence no longer aligns with the complexities of modern leadership. A shift toward a more inclusive, evidence-based framework is essential to meet the evolving demands of organizations today.

Criticism from Leadership Scholars: A Call for Change

Contemporary leadership scholars have criticized the traditional executive presence model as outdated, narrow, and unsupported by robust research. By prioritizing traits like charisma and assertiveness, the model fails to meet the needs of today's complex, team-driven organizations. While confidence and poise can make strong first impressions, these visible traits often prove inadequate for predicting long-term leadership effectiveness, particularly in collaborative environments.

Amy Edmondson's research highlights relational skills, emotional intelligence, and psychological safety as critical components of effective leadership.[9] Leaders who foster inclusive, safe environments consistently achieve higher team performance, innovation, and retention. However, these attributes are undervalued in traditional executive presence assessments, which remain skewed toward command-and-control behaviors.

A significant critique from Bass is the lack of measurable criteria within the traditional model. Unlike validated frameworks like transformational leadership's Multifactor Leadership Questionnaire, executive presence lacks standardized assessment tools.[10] This absence hinders consistent training and development, leaving leaders without clear guidance on how to cultivate presence effectively.

The model's reliance on Western, masculine ideals—emphasizing assertiveness and dominance—excludes diverse leadership styles. Leaders who favor humility, collaboration, or reflection often struggle to fit the mold. This cultural and gender bias makes the model increasingly irrelevant in a globalized, diverse workforce where leadership demands flexibility and inclusivity.

61

From Executive Presence to Leadership Biodynamics

Leadership scholars advocate for redefining executive presence to reflect a more inclusive, evidence-based approach. They call for a framework that prioritizes relational skills, emotional intelligence, and collaboration, moving beyond superficial traits to align with the realities of modern leadership. Such a model would empower leaders to connect authentically and lead effectively in today's fast-evolving, interconnected environments.

The traditional executive presence model's reliance on subjective assessments and weak research foundations diminishes its credibility. Addressing these critiques is essential to developing a more relevant framework—one that equips leaders with the tools they need to meet contemporary challenges.

A New Model: Leadership Biodynamics

Leadership Biodynamics offers a fresh, evidence-based approach to redefining executive presence. Moving beyond outdated, surface-level traits, this framework is rooted in the biology of behavior and draws on the principles explored earlier in this book. At its heart, Leadership Biodynamics views leadership as a dynamic interplay of behavioral signals—actions, expressions, and presence—that influence how others perceive and respond to you.

To better illustrate this concept, imagine a soundboard with three adjustable channels: warmth, competence, and gravitas. Each channel represents a biodynamic quality essential for effective leadership. Just as a sound engineer adjusts these channels to create the perfect mix, leaders must balance and modulate these elements based on their environment and objectives. Mastering this "biodynamic mix" enables leaders to project a presence that is not only authentic but also adaptable to the needs of diverse teams and organizational challenges.

This section introduces the development, validation, and refinement of the Leadership Biodynamics framework, created to address the gaps in traditional models of executive presence. By blending scientific rigor with practical application, this framework equips leaders to navigate complex environments with clarity and purpose.

Building Leadership Biodynamics: A Holistic Approach

The Leadership Biodynamics framework emerged to address critical shortcomings in traditional executive presence models, which often relied on superficial traits and subjective assessments. Instead, this new framework reimagines leadership as a dynamic process, drawing deeply from biological and behavioral sciences covered earlier in this book. Through extensive research and validation, three core channels—warmth, competence, and gravitas—were identified as the foundation for effective leadership.

Evidence-Based Foundations: From Research to Practice

The journey to create Leadership Biodynamics began with a comprehensive review of leadership literature. Traditional models often emphasized visible traits, such as charisma and assertiveness, while neglecting relational and collaborative skills vital to today's organizational success. By synthesizing insights from psychology, organizational behavior, and neuroscience, the framework centers on three dimensions critical to effective leadership: warmth, competence, and gravitas. Each dimension was selected for its strong empirical foundation and practical relevance.

Warmth: The Power of Connection

Warmth emerged as a cornerstone of leadership effectiveness. Research underscores its critical role in building trust, fostering psychological safety, and encouraging collaboration. Leaders who demonstrate empathy, active listening, and genuine connection are more likely to inspire loyalty and engagement, making warmth an indispensable element of the Leadership Biodynamics framework.

Competence: Strategic Action Under Pressure

Competence extends beyond technical skills to encompass strategic thinking, prioritization, and execution under pressure. Insights by Thaler and Sunstein from behavioral economics highlight the importance of managing biases and leveraging data-driven strategies.[11]

Within this framework, competence represents the ability to inspire confidence not just through expertise, but by consistently delivering results.

Gravitas: Influence Through Collaboration

In contrast to traditional notions of gravitas centered on authority, Leadership Biodynamics redefines gravitas as the ability to foster shared value through influence and collaboration. Drawing on systems thinking and collaborative leadership research by Uhl-Bein and colleagues, gravitas emphasizes aligning and empowering others, creating a gravitational pull that unites teams around a common purpose.[12]

Filling the Gaps: Redefining Executive Presence

Traditional executive presence models have been criticized for their narrow focus on visible traits and command-oriented leadership styles. Leadership Biodynamics addresses these gaps by integrating relational and strategic dimensions often overlooked in previous frameworks. By shifting attention to actionable behaviors across warmth, competence, and gravitas, this inclusive model reflects the complexity of modern leadership.

In the sections that follow, we explore how this evidence-based framework was validated and refined, ensuring its relevance across diverse leadership contexts and challenges.

Methodological Rigor: Construct Validation and Refinement

Developing the Leadership Biodynamics Framework was a rigorous, multiphase process designed to ensure it was not just theoretical but highly applicable across diverse leadership contexts. We aimed to create a reliable, evidence-based model rooted in the biological and behavioral sciences while providing leaders with practical tools for real-world use. The process involved expert consultation, iterative refinement, and robust psychometric assessments.

Expert Consultation: Insights from the Field

To validate our approach, we assembled a panel of leadership scholars, organizational psychologists, and practitioners from various industries. These experts were instrumental in bridging academic theory with practical application, ensuring the framework resonated with real-world challenges.

- **From Five Dimensions to Three:** Early workshops and focus groups revealed that our initial five-dimension model lacked clarity. The experts challenged our assumptions, guiding us toward a streamlined, three-dimension model: warmth, competence, and gravitas.
- **Highlighting Warmth:** Scholars like Amy Edmondson emphasized the importance of warmth in fostering psychological safety, which we refined into actionable behaviors such as active listening and empathetic engagement.[13]
- **Modernizing Gravitas:** Traditionally seen as authority-driven, gravitas was reimagined as the ability to create shared value through influence and collaboration.
- **Strategic Competence:** Feedback highlighted the need to expand competence beyond technical skills, incorporating strategic thinking, prioritization, and the ability to lead under pressure.

This collaborative effort ensured the framework addressed modern leadership demands while maintaining scientific integrity.

Iterative Refinement: Testing and Adjusting

The framework's development was an iterative process, guided by continuous feedback and real-world testing. We piloted the model across industries—including healthcare, education, and business—using self-assessments and peer evaluations to refine its components.

- **Behavioral Clarity:** Early feedback revealed that some descriptions under gravitas were too abstract. These were refined into clear, actionable behaviors like "standing one's ground with conviction and diplomacy."

- **Real-World Scenarios:** Practitioners emphasized the need for practical examples, leading us to incorporate real-life applications of warmth, competence, and gravitas. This shift made the framework relatable and easier for leaders to implement.

- **Accessibility:** Language and examples were refined to resonate with diverse cultural and organizational contexts, ensuring inclusivity and relevance.

Psychometric testing played a critical role, employing factor analysis to confirm that the dimensions were distinct yet interconnected. Statistical methods validated the internal consistency and reliability of the framework.

Psychometric Assessment: Ensuring Reliability and Validity

To establish the framework's credibility, we conducted rigorous psychometric evaluations, focusing on face validity, construct validity, and internal consistency.

- **Face Validity:** Panels of experts and leaders reviewed the framework to ensure it intuitively captured the qualities essential for leadership. Feedback confirmed that warmth, competence, and gravitas reflected real-world leadership needs.

- **Construct Validity:** Exploratory and confirmatory factor analyses demonstrated that the three dimensions were empirically sound and distinct. Adjustments clarified overlaps, particularly between warmth and gravitas.
- **Internal Consistency:** High Cronbach's alpha values across all dimensions confirmed the framework's reliability, ensuring consistent results across varied contexts.

Cross-Cultural Adaptability: A Global Perspective

To validate the framework's global applicability, we tested it with leaders from North America, Europe, Asia, and the Middle East.

- **Cultural Nuances:** Warmth was expressed differently across cultures, from humility in collectivist societies to active engagement in individualistic settings.
- **Adaptable Gravitas:** The gravitas dimension was expanded to include culturally sensitive behaviors, emphasizing respect and diplomacy in non-Western contexts.

Intervention Development: Translating Research into Practical Application

To bridge the gap between theoretical constructs and actionable leadership development, we designed interventions to bring Leadership Biodynamics to life. This process involved creating programs, tools, and assessments that leaders could use to develop warmth, competence, and gravitas in real-world contexts. Our interventions included a two-day Leadership Biodynamics Training and the use of tailored self-assessment and feedback tools.

Designing the Two-Day Leadership Biodynamics Training

The two-day Leadership Biodynamics Training program was developed to immerse participants in the core principles of the framework while providing actionable strategies for immediate application. The program blended theory with experiential learning, including:

- **Workshops on Warmth, Competence, and Gravitas:** Participants engaged in interactive sessions to explore each biodynamic channel, practicing behaviors such as active listening, strategic decision-making, and projecting confidence.
- **Role-Playing Scenarios:** Tailored exercises allowed participants to test and refine their ability to modulate their biodynamic channels in diverse leadership situations.
- **Real-Time Feedback Loops:** Participants received peer and facilitator feedback, enabling iterative improvement during the program.

Leveraging Self-Assessments and Feedback Tools

We developed customized tools to measure leadership growth in warmth, competence, and gravitas. These tools included:

- **Self-Assessments:** Participants rated their behaviors across the biodynamic channels, identifying strengths and growth areas.
- **Feedback Assessments:** Colleagues and team members provided evaluations, offering external perspectives on leadership presence.

Measurable Impact

The combined use of these interventions demonstrated tangible improvements in leadership effectiveness. Analysis of feedback assessment scores across multiple cohorts revealed:

- **20–30% Improvement in Feedback Scores:** Participants showed significant growth in peer-rated perceptions of warmth, competence, and gravitas.

- **Sustained Behavioral Change:** Follow-up assessments three months post-training indicated retention of skills and continued application in professional contexts.

By developing targeted interventions, we translated the Leadership Biodynamics Framework from theory to practice, ensuring it could be adapted to diverse settings while delivering measurable, lasting results.

Case Study: Improving Performance in a Complex, Collaborative Environment

In one of our engagements with a company we used these interventions to address some key performance issues. This organization, known for its cutting-edge work, faced several leadership hurdles. Despite their technical brilliance, leaders struggled to communicate effectively with external stakeholders, to align autonomous teams, and to foster collaboration across disciplines. The organization's cross-functional projects were often siloed, with fragmented communication and a lack of cohesion threatening their ability to innovate and deliver results.

Key Challenges

- **Communication Gaps:** Leaders had difficulty translating technical jargon into accessible language for stakeholders and cross-functional teams.
- **Siloed Teams:** Independent working styles created barriers to collaboration, limiting innovation and efficiency.
- **Leadership Presence:** Leaders lacked the ability to project confidence, trustworthiness, and unifying influence—traits necessary to inspire and align their teams.

Implementing Leadership Biodynamics

The organization partnered with the Leadership Biodynamics team to pilot the framework and address these challenges. Through a

69

From Executive Presence to Leadership Biodynamics

structured process combining training, coaching, and feedback, leaders were guided to develop and apply the biodynamic channels of warmth, competence, and gravitas

- **Enhancing Communication:** Leaders learned to structure complex ideas for diverse audiences, ensuring clarity without sacrificing technical precision. By incorporating storytelling techniques and displaying warmth, they improved their ability to connect with stakeholders emotionally and intellectually.
- **Building Collaboration:** Workshops emphasized creating psychological safety within teams, helping leaders foster trust and break down silos. They practiced signaling approachability and empathy, encouraging team members to share ideas openly and engage in meaningful dialogue.
- **Strengthening Leadership Influence:** Through deliberate practice, leaders refined their ability to project gravitas, balancing authority with approachability. Exercises in voice modulation, posture, and deliberate messaging helped them unify teams and inspire confidence in high-pressure situations.

Measuring Impact

The results of this field test were both measurable and transformative:

- **Improved Stakeholder Engagement:** Leaders reported increased success in securing project support and funding by simplifying and humanizing their communication.
- **Stronger Team Collaboration:** Collaboration across disciplines increased by 20%, driving innovation and reducing inefficiencies in cross-functional projects.
- **Enhanced Leadership Presence:** Peer and team feedback reflected a 30% improvement in perceptions of leadership presence, with leaders demonstrating greater alignment of warmth, competence, and gravitas in their actions.

Lessons Learned

This real-world application of the Leadership Biodynamics Framework validated its practical utility and adaptability. Leaders discovered that their ability to modulate their biodynamic channels—adjusting their behaviors to suit diverse audiences and situations—was a critical factor in achieving success. Moreover, the framework's focus on actionable behaviors provided a clear path for leaders to develop their presence and influence intentionally.

These insights reinforced the framework's versatility, making it a powerful tool for leaders in diverse environments.

A Commitment to Rigor and Relevance

The Leadership Biodynamics Framework reflects a commitment to creating a model that is both scientifically validated and practically useful. By integrating expert feedback, iterative refinements, robust psychometric assessments, and field testing we've ensured the framework meets the needs of modern leaders. This comprehensive process lays a strong foundation for an adaptable, inclusive, and actionable approach to leadership.

What's Next?

As we've explored, Leadership Biodynamics is much more than a set of visible traits or a mere ability to command a room. It's about harmonizing the internal and external aspects of leadership—aligning warmth, competence, and gravitas to create an authentic and influential presence. This chapter laid the foundation for understanding how the traditional model of executive presence falls short in addressing the dynamic, inclusive, and relational demands of modern leadership. Instead, we offer an updated model based on the biology of behavior: leadership biodynamics.

In the chapters that follow, we will delve deeper into each of the three critical elements of the model. First, we'll examine how warmth builds trust and connection, fostering environments where teams feel psychologically safe to collaborate and innovate. Next, we'll explore competence, highlighting its role in strategic decision-making, execution, and inspiring confidence in others. Finally, we'll redefine gravitas as the ability to bring people together, create shared value, and influence through collaboration. Together, these elements form a comprehensive and actionable framework to optimize your impact as a leader.

Chapter 5

Biohacking Warmth

In this chapter and the two that follow, we'll explore the biodynamic leadership channels of warmth, competence, and gravitas through six specific behaviors—or biomarkers—that signal each of these qualities. These biomarkers are like leadership diagnostics: when demonstrated consistently, they provide the visible cues that others recognize as hallmarks of effective leadership. By understanding and intentionally cultivating these biomarkers, you can biohack your leadership presence, creating a more profound and immediate impact.

Each of these chapters also offer examples of leaders, both current-day and those from the past, who consistently signal these behaviors. We'll also offer a few examples from some of my favorite fictional leaders.

Think back to a moment of uncertainty or vulnerability—perhaps during a professional challenge or a personal crossroads. You reached out for support, unsure how your concerns would be received. Instead of being dismissed or met with rushed solutions, someone listened with care, asked thoughtful questions, and made you feel truly understood. This experience is at the heart of warmth: the ability to make others feel seen, valued, and understood.

Warmth isn't just an interpersonal skill—it's a biodynamic tool that leaders can hone and wield with intention. By biohacking warmth, leaders create environments of psychological safety, empowering individuals to share ideas, take risks, and collaborate freely. Warmth sets the foundation for the leadership trifecta: competence that demonstrates capability and gravitas that unites people toward shared goals.

73

Why Warmth Matters

In today's dispersed and often uncertain work environment, warmth becomes a strategic asset. Just as warmth builds trust in personal relationships, in the workplace it fosters resilient, high-performing teams by creating spaces where people feel empowered to share ideas and challenge assumptions. This inclusivity drives innovation and creativity, encouraging diverse voices to contribute without fear of judgment.

Warmth also builds loyalty and trust, enhancing engagement and retention. It shifts leadership from transactional to relational, allowing competence to be recognized and gravitas to resonate deeply. Far from being just a "soft skill," warmth is a powerful leadership capability that drives performance, collaboration, and growth.

Warmth as the First Step in Leadership Biodynamics

In our Leadership Biodynamics model—comprised of warmth, competence, and gravitas—warmth comes first for a reason: it is the essential doorway to meaningful relationships and trust. Leaders who integrate warmth into their style inspire collaboration and build inclusive, high-performing teams. By making others feel valued and respected, warmth lays the foundation upon which competence and gravitas can flourish. It's the quality that elevates leadership from functional to impactful.

The Biodynamics of Connection: Tangible Actions That Generate Warmth

The purpose of warmth is to create connection. But what does that look like? What signals do we send that, when picked up by others, help create that warmth-enabled connection? How do we show up and stand out with warmth? Through our research, we've identified six key behaviors, or biomarkers, that actively cultivate warmth, transforming how leaders connect with their teams. In the sections that follow, we will explore each behavior in depth—defining it, examining its importance, and illustrating it through real-world scenarios and leader profiles. Let's get started with the first behavior: listening well.

Behavior One: Listening Well

At the core of warmth is the ability to listen—not just to the words being spoken, but to the emotions and intentions behind them. Listening well means showing others that their thoughts and perspectives are valued. It's an act of engagement that signals care, empathy, and genuine interest. However, listening is not just an internal process; it must be expressed outwardly through visible cues that others can perceive. When we align our internal attention with clear external signals, we build stronger connections and communicate our engagement effectively.

Listening goes beyond simply waiting for your turn to speak; it involves actively absorbing, reflecting, and responding to what's being communicated. Yet, even when we believe we are listening well internally, we may not always project those signals outwardly. Misalignments between our internal focus and external expressions can undermine the connection we are trying to build.

Challenges of Listening Well

Listening well is deceptively difficult. There were times when my now-grown sons were little guys, eagerly sharing with me detailed stories about Minecraft or Pokémon. Although I cared deeply about my sons, the topics were less engaging to me, leading my mind to wander. Even in those times when I made a conscious internal effort to listen well, my outward actions were limited to semi-distracted nods and absent-minded responses. Even when I got the inside part of the listening well equation right, my outward expressions of listening fell short. These were missed opportunities for deeper connection, where my internal listening was not visibly aligned with my outward signals.

I still struggle to listen well in professional settings. When a graduate student stops by with a concern while I'm deep into a writing project, or when a client starts processing a technical challenge aloud, it's easy for my internal listening to falter—and my external signals to follow. Recognizing this gap and actively working to close it is key to listening well.

Biohacking Listening Well

Listening well is one of the clearest demonstrations of warmth because it requires an alignment between internal engagement and external cues. These outward signals help others see that we are present, attentive, and genuinely invested in the conversation. The biodynamics of listening include specific actions that can help synchronize what we feel inside with how we are perceived:

- **Eye Contact and Open Body Language:** Maintaining steady eye contact and an open, relaxed posture shows that you are focused on the speaker. Even if you're fully engaged internally, failing to exhibit these outward cues can send mixed signals, undermining trust and connection.

- **Reflective Responses:** Reflecting and paraphrasing the speaker's words—such as saying, "It sounds like you're feeling…"— validates their experience and shows you're processing their input. This outward signal of understanding bridges your internal listening with visible acknowledgment.

- **Verbal Affirmations and Small Gestures:** Simple verbal affirmations like "I see" or "Go on," combined with nods and smiles, signal active engagement. These small outward expressions align your internal focus with what the speaker perceives, reinforcing connection.

- **Pausing and Thoughtful Responses:** Pausing before you respond demonstrates that you are considering what's been said, rather than rushing to reply. This outward behavior visibly acknowledges your internal reflection and shows respect for the speaker's input.

- **Managing Distractions:** Actively removing or minimizing distractions, such as silencing devices or turning away from screens, shows that you are prioritizing the conversation. These actions visibly align your intent to listen with your external presence.

This Behavior in Action

- **Healthcare:** In a busy hospital, a nurse manager makes it a practice to engage fully with her team during shift debriefs. She maintains eye contact, listens actively, and asks reflective questions, ensuring that every team member feels heard. This approach not only addresses immediate concerns but also builds trust and improves team cohesion, enhancing patient care outcomes.

- **Tech Start-Up:** At a tech start-up, a product manager listens attentively during a feedback session with junior developers. Rather than dominating the conversation, he uses active listening techniques, asking clarifying questions and validating their input. This approach helps the team feel valued and leads to innovative adjustments in the product development process.

- **Sports:** A basketball coach sits with her players after a tough loss, listening to their frustrations and anxieties without interrupting. By reflecting back their emotions and asking thoughtful questions, she creates a supportive environment that helps the team process their feelings and strategize for future games, turning a difficult moment into a learning opportunity.

Listen Like Lincoln

"I don't like that man. I must get to know him better." Although the exact setting in which Abraham Lincoln said this is not well documented, it perfectly captures Lincoln's approach to leadership and listening. One of the most notable examples of this mindset was his relationship with Edwin Stanton, his secretary of war. Stanton was known for his brusque manner and sharp criticisms; he even once publicly insulted Lincoln, calling him a "long-armed ape."

For many leaders, dealing with a Stanton-like team member might prompt anger or dismissiveness. However, Lincoln didn't respond that way. Instead of reacting with hostility or avoiding Stanton, Lincoln chose to listen deeply. He asked thoughtful questions, sought to clarify Stanton's concerns, and consistently reflected back what he was hearing. Through this process, Lincoln gained respect for Stanton's expertise, eventually transforming a former critic into one of his most trusted allies.[1]

Lincoln's example teaches us that listening isn't just a passive act; it's an intentional effort to understand others at a deeper level, even those who challenge us. By prioritizing listening over reaction, Lincoln demonstrated how outward signals of understanding—through questioning, reflecting, and engaging empathetically—can turn potential conflicts into opportunities for collaboration. Approaching disagreements with the mindset of listening and learning, rather than judging, transforms how we engage with others.

Listening like Lincoln means prioritizing understanding over reaction, empathy over ego, and collaboration over conflict. This approach aligns with intergroup contact theory, which suggests that engaging with individuals from different perspectives can break down biases and foster empathy.[2]

Behavior Two: Connect on a Personal Level

When we describe a leader as "warm," it often reflects a sense of personal connection. While listening well, as we discussed earlier, is a critical component of this, connecting on a personal level takes it a step further by ensuring that these connections are genuinely human. This connection can sometimes extend to leaders we've never met; it's the feeling of relatability, like the common sentiment that a political candidate seems like someone you'd want to have a beer or cup of coffee with. As a leader, connecting with others on a personal level—human to human—creates a foundation of trust and respect that deepens relationships and enhances collaboration. Leaders who connect personally foster a sense of belonging that makes teams more cohesive and resilient.

78

Biohacking Leadership

I've met a few presidents in my lifetime, mostly in receiving lines, limited to handshakes and brief greetings. One interaction with George H.W. Bush stands out because, even in just 15 seconds, he made a personal connection. During a campaign stop in my college town, amid a crowd clamoring for his attention, he noticed my striped nylon Brooks Brothers watchband and pointed out that he was wearing the same one. That small moment of connection stuck with me, demonstrating how even brief interactions can create lasting impressions when they feel personal.

Biohacking Personal Connection

Personal connection isn't about charisma or charm; it's about showing genuine interest in people beyond their roles or responsibilities. The biodynamics of connecting on a personal level involve specific outward actions that align with our internal intent to connect. These external signals help others feel valued and seen as individuals, not just as contributors to a task. Here are key actions that leaders can take to align their internal desire to connect with the external signals they project:

- **Genuine Interest and Engagement:** Expressing genuine interest in someone's personal life—asking about their family, hobbies, or weekend plans—signals that you value them as a person, not just an employee. This external demonstration of interest reinforces internal intentions and builds rapport.

- **Personal Acknowledgments:** Recognizing personal milestones like birthdays, work anniversaries, or individual achievements shows attention to the person beyond their professional role. These small but meaningful gestures align internal appreciation with outward acknowledgment, strengthening bonds within the team.

- **Customize Connections:** Customizing your interactions by noticing specific details about individuals and making personalized comments helps to create a sense of uniqueness and recognition. For example, George H.W. Bush's brief acknowledgment of my striped watchband during a crowded campaign event made a lasting impression. According to Daniel Cable of the London Business School, this outward signal of observance and personalization can deepen the sense of connection with others.[3] Leaders who take the time to tailor their approach to each individual demonstrate that they are paying attention, making their connections more memorable and meaningful.

- **Sharing Your Own Stories:** When leaders share their own experiences, they humanize their leadership. Sharing personal stories—whether about overcoming a challenge or celebrating a personal victory—invites others to see you as more than just a leader, encouraging reciprocal openness and deeper connection.

- **Empathy and Presence:** Demonstrating empathy involves not just understanding others' perspectives but also responding with validation and acknowledgment. Being fully present—putting away distractions, maintaining eye contact, and actively engaging—sends a clear signal that you are invested in the person in front of you, aligning internal empathy with outward behavior.

- **Consistent Check-Ins:** Regular, informal check-ins—whether during breaks, meetings, or casual encounters—provide opportunities to connect on a personal level. These brief interactions signal ongoing interest and create a space where team members feel comfortable sharing what's important to them.

This Behavior in Action

- **Corporate Sales:** A sales manager regularly engages with her team members on a personal level, asking about their lives outside of work. She knows each person's motivations and personal goals, which allows her to tailor her coaching approach. These personal connections foster loyalty and help the team perform better, even during high-pressure periods.

- **Manufacturing:** A plant manager starts each day with a walk around the factory floor, chatting with employees about their families, hobbies, and weekend plans. These informal conversations help him build strong personal connections and gain insight into the workforce's morale, which he uses to make better management decisions that improve productivity and team spirit.

- **Military:** A commanding officer makes a point to learn about the personal lives of his enlisted personnel. By showing interest in their families and backgrounds, he builds a strong rapport that translates into higher morale and a more cohesive unit. This personal connection strengthens the bonds within the team, making them more effective in their missions.

The Impact on Your Team

When you connect with your team on a personal level, the effects are profound. Research by Richard Boyatzis shows that employees who feel personally connected to their leader are more engaged, motivated, and loyal.[4] This sense of being seen and appreciated fosters trust, loyalty, and commitment, enhancing team performance and morale. Personal connections also strengthen team cohesion, encouraging collaboration and mutual support. When team members feel connected to their leader, they are more likely to connect with each other, fostering a culture of warmth and trust.

Personal connections make difficult conversations easier. When trust is established through personal connection, team members are more likely to approach conflicts constructively, knowing their leader values them as individuals and will approach challenges with empathy and respect. According to Zenger and Folkman, this reduces defensiveness, making conflict resolution smoother and more effective.[5]

Connect Like Mr. Rogers

Fred Rogers, known to millions as "Mr. Rogers," was a master of making personal connections. Whether on his television show or in his everyday life, Rogers took the time to understand and acknowledge the emotions of those around him. His ability to connect personally was evident in his interaction with a young boy named Jeff Erlanger, who appeared on *Mister Rogers' Neighborhood* in 1980. Jeff, a quadriplegic, joined Rogers on set to discuss his electric wheelchair. Rogers didn't just acknowledge Jeff's disability; he engaged in a conversation that focused on Jeff's experiences and feelings, creating a moment of profound connection. Their interaction was so impactful that years later, Jeff surprised Rogers during his Television Hall of Fame induction, bringing Rogers to tears and the audience to a standing ovation.[6] His authentic connections made people feel deeply seen and valued, exemplifying the power of empathy and personal connection.

Behavior Three: Validate Others

Validation is another powerful way to convey warmth. When you validate others, you acknowledge their contributions, ideas, and feelings, reinforcing their value within the team. Validation goes beyond recognizing someone's work; it's about affirming their worth as individuals. This behavior fosters an inclusive, supportive environment where people feel respected and appreciated. When individuals feel validated, they are more likely to engage fully, share ideas, and contribute meaningfully.

At its core, validation makes others feel seen and heard. Leaders who validate their team members create a culture where people feel comfortable expressing their thoughts, knowing that their input is valued. This leads to higher levels of engagement and job satisfaction, because employees who feel recognized are more motivated and loyal.[7] By validating others, you reinforce a sense of belonging and trust that strengthens team dynamics.

Biohacking to Validate Others

Validation is one of the clearest signals of warmth. It sends the message that people are important, building confidence and fostering deeper connections. Validation isn't just a passive acknowledgment;

it requires outward expressions that align with your internal appreciation. Here are key actions that leaders can take to align their internal desire to validate with the external signals they project:

- **Intentional and Consistent Validation:** Don't wait for formal settings to offer validation; find moments throughout the day to offer praise, express gratitude, or acknowledge hard work. Consistent validation reinforces that people's efforts are noticed and appreciated regularly, not just during scheduled reviews.

- **Specific Praise:** Instead of generic compliments like "Good job," offer specific validation that acknowledges the unique value someone brings. For example, saying, "I really appreciated the way you handled that client issue today; your calm approach helped resolve the situation quickly and professionally," shows that you are paying attention to details and recognize their specific contributions.

- **Acknowledge Effort, Not Just Results:** Validation isn't only about outcomes—it's also about recognizing effort. Even when the results aren't immediately visible, acknowledging dedication and persistence reinforces a person's sense of worth. Phrases like, "I know this project has been challenging, but your persistence is making a difference," validate the effort put forth, not just the final outcome.

- **Emotional Acknowledgment:** Leaders who validate not only efforts but also the emotions of their team members create stronger connections. If someone is struggling with a difficult project, acknowledging their frustration validates their feelings. Saying, "I can see how frustrating this has been, and I appreciate how you've stayed focused," shows that you recognize their emotional experience, not just their work.

- **Nonverbal Validation:** Nonverbal cues—like a warm smile, nod, or engaged posture—can communicate validation without words. Open body language and eye contact reinforce that you value what someone is saying, creating a welcoming space for open communication. These small gestures make people feel seen and respected.

- **Customize Validation:** Personalizing your validation to the individual can make it more meaningful. Whether it's referencing a specific skill, past achievement, or personal challenge they've overcome, tailored validation shows that you see the person behind the work. Leaders who customize validation create connections that feel authentic and deeply personal, reinforcing the idea that each team member's contributions are uniquely valuable.

This Behavior in Action

- **Corporate Finance:** During a strategy meeting, a senior finance leader openly acknowledges a junior analyst's suggestion, saying, "That's a great idea, and I think it could really streamline our workflow." This public validation encourages the analyst and others in the room to continue sharing ideas, fostering a culture of openness and innovation.
- **Public Service:** At a city council meeting, a council member publicly recognizes the efforts of community volunteers who have contributed to a local park renovation. By highlighting their work, she validates their contributions, boosting their morale and encouraging further community engagement in local projects.
- **Engineering:** During a project review, an engineering manager makes a point to validate a team member's unique approach to solving a complex problem. By specifically highlighting what was effective, the manager reinforces the value of creative thinking, encouraging the team to explore innovative solutions in future challenges.

The Impact on Your Team

Validation profoundly impacts team dynamics. When people feel that their contributions, ideas, and efforts are acknowledged, they are more likely to be engaged and committed. Research shows that validation increases job satisfaction and emotional well-being because individuals who feel recognized are more motivated and loyal. Validation fosters an environment where people feel safe to express themselves, take risks, and contribute fully.[8]

Validation also plays a critical role in building psychological safety within teams. Edmondson finds that when team members know that their ideas and contributions will be validated, they are more likely to participate actively and share creative solutions. This creates a culture of openness and trust, enhancing engagement and productivity.[9]

Validation reinforces positive behavior and encourages continuous improvement. It creates a long-term impact by affirming the behaviors and attitudes that contribute to success. Meaningful validation is about creating a culture where people feel valued and respected, strengthening the bonds that hold the team together and inspiring greater collaboration and innovation.

Validate Like Atticus Finch

In Harper Lee's *To Kill a Mockingbird*, the character of Atticus Finch embodies integrity and validation. As a lawyer defending Tom Robinson, a Black man wrongly accused of a crime, Finch treats his client with respect and dignity, validating Robinson's humanity in every interaction despite societal prejudice. Beyond the courtroom, Atticus teaches his children to see the world through others' eyes, validating their emotions and encouraging empathy. He even extends validation to Mayella Ewell, Robinson's accuser, recognizing her as a victim of her circumstances. Through Finch's actions, Lee demonstrates the profound impact of validating others, showing how it fosters respect, empathy, and deeper understanding even in the face of opposition.[10]

Behavior Four: Being Other-Oriented

Warmth moves front and center when you shift the focus from yourself to others during conversations and interactions. Being other-oriented means that you are fully present in the moment, prioritizing the perspectives, ideas, and needs of others over your own. When you engage with an other-oriented mindset, you create an environment of care, empathy, and trust—essential qualities of warmth.

At its core, being other-oriented is about valuing the thoughts, contributions, and emotions of others. It involves listening with the intention of understanding, asking thoughtful questions, and ensuring the conversation centers on the person in front of you rather than yourself. Leaders who master this behavior foster deeper connections and cultivate an atmosphere where people feel respected, valued, and empowered.

Biohacking an Other-Orientation

Being other-oriented in conversation signals that you care about the speaker's needs and experiences. This behavior fosters trust because it demonstrates that you're not just waiting to speak or looking to assert your own perspective. Instead, you're genuinely focused on the other person. Here are key actions that leaders can take to align their internal desire to be other-oriented with the external signals they project:

- **Shift Your Mindset:** Move from "What do I need to say?" to "What do they need from me in this moment?" This mental shift sets the foundation for being other-oriented and helps you approach conversations with curiosity and empathy.

- **Active Listening:** Active listening means giving your full attention—putting aside distractions, maintaining eye contact, and showing through your body language that you are engaged. These outward signals help others feel heard and valued, reinforcing your internal focus on them.

- **Ask Thoughtful Questions:** Questions like "Can you tell me more about that?" or "What's your perspective on this issue?" demonstrate genuine interest in the other person's thoughts. These questions shift the focus away from your own agenda and invite deeper dialogue, making the conversation truly other-oriented.

- **Manage Your Response:** Resist the urge to immediately respond with solutions or counterpoints. Pausing before you speak allows you to process what the speaker has said, ensuring that your response reflects their needs rather than just your own. This careful consideration strengthens the connection and keeps the focus on the other person.

- **Nonverbal Engagement:** Use nonverbal cues like nodding, smiling, and maintaining open body language to show that you are engaged and receptive. Even small gestures, like leaning in when someone is speaking, signal that you are fully focused on the other person.

- **Practice Humility:** Being other-oriented involves recognizing that your perspective isn't the only one that matters. Admitting when you don't have all the answers and actively seeking input from others demonstrates that you value their expertise and insights, fostering a culture of shared leadership.

- **Customize Your Engagement:** Tailor your approach to each individual by acknowledging specific contributions or referencing past conversations. For instance, referencing someone's past idea during a current discussion shows that you've been paying attention and value their input. This personalized approach strengthens connections and builds trust.

This Behavior in Action

- **University Leadership:** A university president listens attentively to faculty concerns during a meeting about curriculum changes. Rather than pushing his own agenda, he asks open-ended questions to understand their perspectives, demonstrating an other-oriented approach that leads to meaningful reforms incorporating input from multiple stakeholders.

- **Product Development:** In a brainstorming session, a senior executive consciously shifts the conversation from her own ideas to those of the team members. By encouraging everyone to share their thoughts and validating their input, she fosters a collaborative environment that results in a more innovative product design.

- **Hospitality:** A hotel manager listens closely to feedback from frontline staff about guest complaints and service improvements. By taking action based on their insights, she not only improves guest satisfaction but also empowers her team, demonstrating an other-oriented approach that enhances overall service quality.

The Impact on Your Team

Being other-oriented profoundly impacts team dynamics. When leaders focus on others in conversations, they create environments where people feel valued, respected, and heard. This builds trust and encourages open communication, essential for high-performing teams. Research by Gino shows that teams led by other-oriented leaders are more collaborative, innovative, and engaged.[11] By prioritizing others' needs and perspectives, you cultivate a culture where everyone feels empowered to contribute.

Being other-oriented also enhances psychological safety, which is critical for fostering innovation and collaboration within teams. When team members feel their ideas are valued, they are more likely to participate actively, share creative solutions, and engage in constructive problem-solving.

Additionally, focusing on others helps build emotional intelligence within the team. When you model empathy and attentiveness, it encourages others to adopt these behaviors, creating a ripple effect of emotional intelligence that strengthens relationships and team performance.

Oriented Toward Others Like Julius Rosenwald

Julius Rosenwald, a prominent philanthropist and former president of Sears, Roebuck & Co., exemplified being other-oriented through his deep commitment to improving educational opportunities for African Americans in the segregated South. Inspired by his partnership with Booker T. Washington, Rosenwald established the Julius Rosenwald

Fund, which supported the construction of over 5,000 schools across 15 Southern states during the early 20th century. Known as Rosenwald Schools, these institutions played a crucial role in educating a generation of Black leaders, including figures like Medgar Evers and Maya Angelou.

Rosenwald's approach was distinctly other-oriented; he required local communities to contribute funds alongside his own, fostering shared responsibility and collaboration. This approach demonstrated Rosenwald's belief in empowering communities rather than imposing solutions, aligning closely with the principles of being other-oriented. By listening to and addressing the needs of marginalized communities, Rosenwald helped bridge significant educational gaps, leaving a lasting legacy of empowerment and inclusivity.[12]

Behavior Five: Being Approachable and Relatable

Warmth is closely linked to approachability. Leaders who are approachable create an environment where people feel comfortable coming forward with ideas, concerns, or feedback. Demonstrating approachability signals openness and accessibility, encouraging direct communication and fostering stronger connections with your team. Approachability isn't about being overly familiar or informal—it's about genuinely being open to what others have to say and creating a space where people feel they can be themselves without judgment.

Relatability, on the other hand, involves being seen as a leader who understands and empathizes with the experiences of others. Relatable leaders make others feel at ease, sharing stories or perspectives that connect on a human level. When you are both approachable and relatable, you break down hierarchical barriers, allowing your team to engage with you more openly. This combination fosters a culture of trust, collaboration, and psychological safety.

Biohacking Approachability and Relatedness

Being approachable and relatable enables you to build authentic relationships with your team. Here are key actions that align your internal desire to be open and relatable with external signals:

- **Create an Atmosphere of Openness:** Approachability starts with making yourself accessible, such as through an open-door policy, regular check-ins, or simply being available for conversations. Leaders who are approachable invite more meaningful interactions, leading to stronger relationships and a more connected team.

- **Be Fully Present:** Approachability is demonstrated through presence. This means putting aside distractions, like phones or laptops, and giving your full attention to the person speaking. Full engagement in conversations signals that you value what the other person has to say and are approachable and willing to listen.

- **Share Personal Stories:** Relatability is built by sharing personal experiences that resonate with your team. This doesn't mean oversharing but offering insights that show empathy and shared humanity. For example, discussing how you overcame a similar challenge can make team members feel understood.

- **Maintain Open Body Language:** Nonverbal cues such as smiling, nodding, and maintaining eye contact create a welcoming presence. Leaders who use open body language are perceived as more approachable. Research shows that nonverbal communication significantly influences perceptions of approachability.[13]

- **Use Inclusive Language:** Phrasing like "What do you think?" or "How can we improve this?" signals that you value others' input and foster an environment of collaboration. Inclusive language encourages participation and strengthens team cohesion.

- **Set Regular Times for Feedback:** Scheduling regular feedback and one-on-one conversations provides consistent opportunities for team members to voice their thoughts. These interactions show that you're invested in hearing from your team, reinforcing your approachability.

- **Demonstrate Humility:** Humility is key to being approachable. Leaders who admit they don't have all the answers and are open to learning from others create a more approachable and collaborative environment. This openness helps reduce intimidation and fosters a culture of shared leadership.

This Behavior in Action

- **Corporate Law:** A managing partner at a law firm regularly holds informal check-ins with associates, creating an open line of communication. Her approachable demeanor encourages associates to bring up challenges or ask for advice, fostering a supportive work environment that reduces stress and increases engagement.

- **Police Force:** A police chief holds informal coffee sessions with officers to discuss departmental concerns in a relaxed setting. His approachable nature helps break down barriers, making it easier for officers to voice their opinions and collaborate on improving community relations.

- **Media Production:** On a film set, the director encourages crew members to share their ideas freely, often engaging in casual conversations during breaks. His relatability and open demeanor break down hierarchical barriers, creating a collaborative and creative environment that enhances the production process.

The Impact on Your Team

Approachability and relatability significantly impact team dynamics. When people feel they can approach you without fear of judgment, it creates a culture of trust and openness, fostering psychological safety and encouraging team members to take risks and share new ideas. Relatability humanizes leadership, enhancing team cohesion and collaboration. Leaders who are both approachable and relatable build resilient, adaptable teams where members feel supported and valued.

Be Approachable and Relatable Like George Bailey

George Bailey, the central character in Frank Capra's *It's a Wonderful Life*, exemplifies approachability and relatability. Throughout the film, George's willingness to help others, often at personal cost, makes him a beloved figure in Bedford Falls. His approachable demeanor, from giving his savings during a bank run to offering a compassionate ear, bridges the gap between leader and community. In his darkest hour, the community rallies to support him, demonstrating the reciprocal power of warmth and connection. George Bailey's approachability and relatability remind us that true leadership is grounded in human connection and empathy.[14]

Behavior Six: Being Thoughtful

Thoughtfulness is our final essential expression of warmth. It reflects your awareness of and care for the needs, feelings, and experiences of others. When you are thoughtful, you demonstrate that you are paying attention not just to tasks, but to the people around you. This behavior goes beyond daily responsibilities—it shows that you are willing to anticipate what others may need and respond with kindness, consideration, and respect.

Thoughtfulness involves being intentional in how you interact with others. It can be as simple as remembering a team member's birthday, following up on a concern they raised, or offering support during a challenging time. These seemingly small gestures significantly impact team dynamics by showing that you see your team members as individuals who matter. When you act thoughtfully, you foster a culture of care and connection, strengthening relationships and boosting team morale.

Biohacking Thoughtfulness

Thoughtfulness signals warmth because it shows that you are mindful of others and their well-being matters to you. Here are key actions that align your internal desire to be thoughtful with external expressions:

- **Targeted Recognition:** This emphasizes acknowledging individual achievements and contributions in a specific and meaningful way. Rather than offering broad praise, focus on the details that highlight the person's unique efforts, such as saying, "I appreciate the innovative approach you took in solving that problem—it really made a difference." Targeted recognition is about reinforcing positive behavior by connecting your acknowledgment directly to the individual's specific actions.

- **Follow-Up on Conversations or Concerns:** Thoughtfulness involves following up on what team members share with you, whether it's a personal story or a professional challenge. Asking questions like, "How did that issue resolve?" or "Are you feeling better about the situation now?" shows that you listen and care enough to check in.

- **Anticipate Needs:** Look for opportunities to offer support before being asked. If you notice someone struggling, saying, "I've seen you carrying a lot lately—how can I help?" shows attentiveness and willingness to step in, aligning your internal empathy with outward action.

- **Create Opportunities for Growth:** Thoughtful leaders take time to identify ways their team members can grow. Offering mentorship, recommending resources, or providing feedback demonstrates that you are invested in their personal and professional development.

- **Tailored Thoughtfulness:** This focuses on adjusting your overall approach to meet the unique needs and preferences of each team member. It involves understanding what matters to each person and aligning your actions accordingly, whether it's accommodating their work style, supporting them during personal milestones, or recognizing them in a way that resonates. Tailored thoughtfulness goes beyond individual praise—it involves consistently adapting your leadership style to foster a deeper connection and show you are attuned to their personal and professional needs, according to research by Chapman and White.[15]

This Behavior in Action

- **Church Member:** A church member learns that a fellow congregant has been going through a tough time after a family loss. Instead of waiting for Sunday services to provide an encouraging word, she makes a personal visit to the person's home, bringing along a home-cooked meal and a listening ear. This thoughtful gesture goes beyond spiritual support, demonstrating that she cares deeply about the congregant's personal well-being, creating a lasting bond of trust and connection.

- **Emergency Services:** After a challenging emergency response, a fire chief organizes a debriefing session to address the mental strain on his team. He provides access to mental health resources and follows up individually, showing thoughtful concern for their well-being beyond their professional duties.

- **Agriculture:** A farm owner makes sure to provide meals during the long harvest season, recognizing the hard work of farmhands in a personal and thoughtful manner. These actions not only show appreciation but also create a supportive atmosphere that keeps morale high during strenuous periods.

The Impact on Your Team

Thoughtfulness deeply impacts team morale and cohesion. When team members feel seen and valued, they are more likely to be loyal, committed, and willing to go the extra mile. Thoughtfulness fosters psychological safety, making team members feel comfortable sharing ideas and taking risks. Edmondson's research also indicates that thoughtful leadership enhances engagement and collaboration, as team members are more likely to contribute in an environment where they feel supported.

Thoughtfulness also strengthens the emotional bonds within a team. Leaders who pay attention to both professional and personal aspects of their team members' lives create a culture of empathy and care. This culture not only improves morale but also enhances resilience because team members are more likely to support one another during challenging times.

Be Thoughtful Like Florence Nightingale

Florence Nightingale, known as "the lady with the lamp," revolutionized nursing during the Crimean War through her thoughtful approach to patient care. Nightingale's meticulous attention to the needs of her patients extended beyond medical treatment; she improved sanitary conditions, wrote letters home for soldiers, and provided personal comfort to those in her charge. Nightingale's dedication to thoughtful care changed lives and transformed public health, showing that thoughtfulness in leadership can have far-reaching effects.[16]

You've Connected with Warmth. Now What?

Recall the moment described at the beginning of this chapter, when you were truly listened to and felt understood, valued, and safe to share your thoughts. Now imagine yourself as the leader others turn to in times of uncertainty—the leader who consistently shows warmth through empathy, attentiveness, and care. This is the power of warmth: it creates lasting connections built on trust and respect.

As the first step in establishing yourself as a leader, warmth opens the door to deeper connections, inviting others to engage and share openly. It's the essential foundation upon which competence and gravitas can flourish. Without warmth, leadership can feel distant or transactional. With it, you build the emotional connection that empowers your team to perform at their best.

Looking ahead, we'll explore how competence amplifies the impact of warmth. Where warmth invites others in, competence shows that you can deliver results, solve complex problems, and guide your team with expertise. Together, warmth and competence create a powerful synergy that defines much of what it means to be an effective leader. In the next chapter, we'll dive into the skills and strategies that will help you demonstrate competence, reinforcing the trust and connection established through warmth.

Chapter 6

Biohacking Competence

As in the previous chapter, this chapter addresses one of three channels in our leadership biodynamics model. Here, we delve into the channel of competence, presenting six specific behaviors or "biomarkers" that signal this critical leadership quality.

Imagine stepping into a high-pressure negotiation room. The details are intricate, the stakes are high, and the situation demands a precise, thoughtful approach. Amid the intensity, you stand out—not by overshadowing others, but by biohacking your competence to create trust, clarity, and actionable insights. This deliberate approach transforms complexity into progress and inspires confidence in your abilities and decisions.

Competence, as a biodynamic leadership trait, is about more than knowledge or expertise. It is the practical application of these skills to solve problems, drive decisions, and generate tangible value. Leaders who master the art of biohacking competence cultivate a dynamic set of behaviors that consistently reinforce their credibility and influence.

In this chapter, we explore how competence operates as an intentional practice, rooted in six foundational behaviors: setting priorities, managing workload, avoiding impulsiveness, being punctual, staying prepared, and maintaining organization. By biohacking these behaviors, leaders refine their ability to contribute effectively and inspire trust, ensuring that their impact is both immediate and enduring.

Competence is more than a marker of capability—it is the substance that sustains leadership credibility and propels teams toward sustainable success. Through the lens of biohacking, this chapter demonstrates how leaders can harness and enhance their competence to navigate challenges and drive impactful outcomes.

97

Competence versus Confidence

While competence and confidence are closely linked, confidence alone can fall short without demonstrated competence. The six core behaviors of competence ensure credibility and reinforce trust in leadership. Unlike confidence, competence reflects the substance behind the presence—skills, knowledge, and reliable execution that are visible through deliberate actions.

- **Competence Leads the Way:** Competent leaders possess the deep expertise needed to make sound decisions. They have a strong understanding of their field, allowing them to approach complex problems with a clear, strategic mindset. This expertise translates into effective problem-solving, strategic thinking, and decision-making. For example, a leader who sets the right priorities and manages their workload effectively demonstrates competence through their ability to focus on what matters most, reducing overwhelm and improving outcomes. Research shows that competence is often linked to higher levels of team performance because competent leaders can guide their teams with clarity and precision.[1] While confidence can draw initial attention, it is competence that sustains leadership credibility over time.

- **Credibility Matters:** Competence breeds credibility. When you consistently deliver results and demonstrate expertise, your team and peers naturally trust your judgment. This trust is the foundation of strong, collaborative teams. Credibility is not built on words alone but through actions and outcomes that reflect a deep understanding of the organization's goals and challenges. Leaders who avoid impulsivity, for example, are seen as thoughtful and deliberate, reinforcing their credibility through careful decision-making.

- **Performance over Perception:** Confidence can create an immediate impression, but competence sustains long-term trust and success. Leaders who rely solely on confidence may struggle when the substance behind their words doesn't match their capabilities. Over time, this erodes trust within the team, leaving the leader's credibility vulnerable to scrutiny. Competence, by contrast, ensures that a leader's performance aligns with the expectations they set, building trust and confidence in their leadership over the long haul. Punctuality and preparation are key behaviors that visibly reinforce competence, signaling respect for others' time and demonstrating a commitment to being well-informed.

- **Resilience in Tough Times:** Competent leaders are better equipped to handle challenges and crises because they draw on their experience and expertise. In turbulent times, competence allows leaders to make informed decisions, demonstrating to their teams that they can navigate the organization through difficulties. This competence, combined with thoughtful decision-making, instills confidence in others during periods of uncertainty.[2] A leader who uses organizational skills effectively, for instance, can keep their team focused and aligned during chaotic situations, further enhancing their perceived competence.

- **Long-Term Success:** Organizations thrive under the guidance of competent leaders. Competence ensures that strategies are well-informed, decisions are rational, and results are consistent. Over time, competence leads to sustainable success, because it builds a foundation for trust, collaboration, and growth. Research shows that competent leaders foster environments where teams feel supported and aligned with the organization's goals, leading to higher levels of engagement and performance.[3]

A Tale of Two Leaders

To better understand the distinction between confidence and competence, let's examine two contrasting leadership approaches. While both possess qualities that are commonly associated with strong leadership, their success—and the trust they build with their teams—hinges on more than just how they present themselves.

Meet John and Sarah—two leaders with distinctly different approaches. John is known for his charismatic and confident demeanor. He captures attention with his engaging presentations but often lacks the deep understanding required to provide meaningful solutions when issues arise. John's reliance on confidence without demonstrated competence gradually erodes the trust of his team, who begin to doubt his ability to lead effectively. For example, John frequently reacts impulsively to challenges, making quick decisions without fully considering the potential consequences. His lack of preparation often leaves him scrambling for answers in meetings, and his organizational skills are inconsistent, resulting in missed deadlines and overlooked details. Over time, his team recognizes that John's confident facade masks a lack of genuine competence, leading to frustration and decreased trust in his leadership.

Sarah, on the other hand, embodies the core behaviors of competence. She prepares thoroughly, ensuring she is well-versed in the details of every project. Sarah sets clear priorities, allowing her to manage her workload efficiently and avoid burnout while maintaining high productivity. She avoids impulsivity in her decision-making, taking the time to consider various perspectives before acting. Sarah's punctuality and organizational skills ensure that she is always reliable, meeting deadlines and maintaining a structured approach to her work. Her preparation extends to every interaction, whether it's a high-stakes presentation or a routine team meeting, demonstrating her commitment to excellence. When challenges arise, Sarah is quick to propose well-informed solutions, using her deep expertise to guide her team with confidence. Her deliberate and thoughtful approach instills trust in her team, reinforcing her credibility and solidifying her role as a competent leader.

Which Leader Would You Choose?

The contrast between John and Sarah highlights the crucial role that competence plays in sustaining long-term success. While John's confidence initially captures attention, it's Sarah's embodiment of the six core behaviors of competence—preparation, effective workload management, avoidance of impulsivity, punctuality, prioritization, and organizational skills—that truly inspires her team's trust and loyalty. As Warren Buffett wisely said, "It takes 20 years to build a reputation and five minutes to ruin it."[4] Competence is the cornerstone of a leader's reputation and the foundation on which trust sustained. Organizations face constant challenges and uncertainty, and competence is the trait that ensures consistent, thoughtful leadership.

The Complementary Role of Confidence

While confidence certainly has its place, it should complement competence, not replace it. The most effective leaders combine both traits. Confidence helps energize and inspire teams, but without the backing of competence, it can lead to empty promises and short-lived success. By prioritizing competence and consistently demonstrating the six core behaviors, leaders can build a future where knowledgeable, skilled, and capable individuals guide their organizations toward sustainable success.

Behavior One: Setting the Right Priorities

Competence starts with the ability to set the right priorities. If you're like most leaders, you are being constantly pulled in multiple directions by competing demands. The skill of prioritization goes beyond simple task management. You are expected to make strategic decisions that drive results, ensuring that your actions and those of your team align with the organization's broader goals. Setting clear priorities allows you to focus on what truly matters, directing your time and energy toward meaningful contributions.

- **The Challenges of Setting Priorities:** Setting priorities can be a balancing act. It requires distinguishing between what's urgent and what's important, navigating immediate pressures while keeping sight of long-term objectives. The challenge often lies in deciding not only what to address but also what to defer or eliminate entirely. Without clear priorities, both you and team risk becoming overwhelmed. This can lead to scattered efforts and diminished effectiveness. In contrast, when your priorities are well-defined, they act as a compass that guides decision-making, enhances focus, and propels the organization forward.

- **Biohacking Priority Setting:** Competence in setting the right priorities is not just about internal clarity; it's about projecting that clarity outwardly so that others see and understand your strategic focus. The biodynamics of aligning internal priorities with external signals involves specific tactics that communicate your commitment to effective decision-making:

  - **Using Data to Inform Decisions:** Prioritize based on evidence rather than intuition alone. When you visibly engage with data—referencing key performance metrics, citing customer feedback, or presenting market trends in meeting, you signal that your decisions are grounded in objective analysis. This transparency reassures others that choices are well-considered and strategically sound, fostering trust and confidence.[4]

  - **Clarify What's Urgent versus Important:** Using frameworks like the *Eisenhower Matrix*, which categorizes tasks by urgency and importance, demonstrates a methodical approach to prioritization.[5] Sharing this framework with your team and visibly sorting tasks into these categories sends a clear external signal that you are focused on high-impact work. By openly prioritizing in this way, you model a disciplined approach that encourages your team to do the same.

  - **Communicate Priorities Clearly:** Competent leaders don't just set priorities—they communicate them effectively. Holding regular briefings, clearly outlining the current focus areas, and explaining the rationale behind decisions make your priorities visible to others, as suggested by McChesney.[6] This external communication ensures alignment, keeps everyone on the same page, and reinforces the sense of shared direction.

  - **Adjust Priorities as Conditions Change:** When priorities shift, visibly acknowledge the change, including explaining why they've shifted.[7] This demonstrates your adaptability.

Whether through a team update or a quick meeting, discussing how new data or market shifts are influencing your priorities shows that you are responsive and flexible. This openness encourages your team to stay adaptable and focused on what's most relevant, enhancing collective resilience.

o **Balance Short-Term Wins with Long-Term Goals:** Leaders who consistently align their actions with both immediate and strategic objectives send a clear message about what matters most. Highlighting short-term successes in the context of long-term vision during meetings or progress updates reinforces the importance of sustained focus. This visible balance of priorities ensures your team understands how today's efforts contribute to tomorrow's goals.

This Behavior in Action

- **Energy Sector:** A senior project manager at a renewable energy firm uses data to prioritize high-impact solar projects over less profitable ones, reallocating resources to maximize the company's market share. By presenting this data-driven decision-making process in team meetings, the manager visibly demonstrates a strategic focus that builds confidence in the project direction.

- **Education:** A university president facing budget constraints prioritizes funding for student support services based on data showing their impact on retention rates. By sharing these priorities openly during faculty meetings, the president communicates a clear alignment with institutional goals, fostering buy-in and collaborative problem-solving.

- **Retail:** A retail chain CEO, confronted with declining sales, shifts focus from launching new products to enhancing the customer experience in existing stores. The CEO's visible focus on customer feedback sessions and frontline employee engagement makes the prioritization process clear to the entire organization, aligning efforts toward shared success.

The Impact on Your Team

Setting the right priorities doesn't just streamline tasks—it fundamentally transforms how your team operates. Clear priorities provide direction and reduce confusion, allowing team members to focus their efforts on what matters most. This focus boosts morale, reduces stress, and fosters a sense of purpose. When teams understand the rationale behind priorities, they feel more engaged and are better equipped to contribute effectively.

Prioritization also builds resilience. In fast-moving environments, conditions can change rapidly, but when priorities are clearly communicated, teams can adapt without losing sight of overarching goals. This agility enables them to navigate challenges confidently, knowing their work aligns with the organization's strategic direction.

Set Priorities Like Condoleezza Rice

Condoleezza Rice was respected for her strategic approach to setting priorities during her time as National Security Advisor and later as Secretary of State. Rice was known for her ability to filter through vast amounts of information and focus on what truly mattered—whether it was advancing U.S. foreign policy, managing complex international negotiations, or responding to crises. She prioritized clear communication and data-driven decision-making, often grounding her strategies in rigorous analysis. By consistently aligning her actions with the broader objectives of U.S. national security, Rice demonstrated how setting the right priorities can drive impactful even in the most complex and high-stakes environments.[8]

Behavior Two: Managing Your Workload Effectively

Your competence is also reflected in how you well you manage your workload. Balancing tasks, prioritizing responsibilities, and making efficient use of time are essential to ensure critical work gets done. Effective workload management is not just about staying busy; it's about structuring your approach to handle the most impactful tasks while avoiding burnout. When you manage your workload well, you maintain focus, drive productivity, and contribute meaningfully to your team and organization.

- **The Challenges of Managing Your Workload:** Managing workload effectively involves more than just creating to-do lists. The challenge lies in maintaining a balance between high-priority tasks and day-to-day responsibilities without becoming overwhelmed. When you lack effective workload management, productivity suffers, and stress levels rise. In contrast, mastering workload management means staying organized, setting boundaries, and consistently prioritizing tasks that align with your goals. By refining how you approach your workload, you set yourself and your team up for success.

- **Biohacking Workload Management:** Managing your workload effectively is not just about internal strategies; it's also about projecting those strategies externally. The biodynamics of managing workload involves visible actions that demonstrate your commitment to efficiency and balance:

  - **Time Blocking to Signal Focus:** Time blocking can include visibly allocating specific periods on your calendar for focused work, such as labeling blocks of time for strategic tasks or deep work. This not only helps you maintain focus but also sends a clear external signal to others that you are prioritizing your time intentionally. When colleagues see these dedicated blocks on your schedule, it communicates that you are managing your workload with purpose, guarding your most productive hours against distractions.[9]

  - **Task Batching as a Model of Efficiency:** Task batching, where you group similar tasks into a single work session, is another visible practice that demonstrates your ability to manage your workload effectively. Others see you handling emails only at specific times or dedicating a particular part of the day to meetings, which signals that you are in control of your workflow. This outward sign of structured work management helps set expectations and shows that you are strategic about how you allocate your energy and attention.[10]

o **Delegation as a Public Commitment to Teamwork:** Competence in workload management is often signaled through delegation. When you openly assign tasks to team members based on their strengths, it shows that you understand your own limits and trust others to contribute. This external action demonstrates that you are not overloaded and are focused on the most critical tasks. By visibly sharing the workload, you reinforce the message that leadership is a team effort and that you value collective contribution.

o **Visibly Maintaining Boundaries:** Setting boundaries, like not taking work calls during designated focus times or visibly stepping away from your desk for breaks, signals that you respect your own limits. These external behaviors show others that you are disciplined in your workload management and prioritize maintaining a sustainable pace. This not only enhances your performance but also sets a healthy example for the team, promoting balance and self-management.

o **Publicly Acknowledging Rest and Recovery:** Competence in workload management also involves visible signals of rest and recovery. Taking breaks and encouraging your team to do the same, or stepping out for a walk after a long meeting, for instance, shows that you value balance and understand the importance of recharging. These outward actions signal to your team that maintaining energy levels is a key part of effective workload management, promoting a culture of sustainability.[11]

This Behavior in Action

- **Entertainment:** A film producer uses time blocking to dedicate uninterrupted hours to overseeing production stages, ensuring that deadlines are met without overwhelming individual departments. By visibly setting these boundaries, the producer shows the team how to maintain focus and prioritize critical tasks.

- **Nonprofit:** A program director at a nonprofit employs task batching to handle routine grant applications in dedicated sessions, freeing time for strategic initiatives. The clear structure of her workflow is visible to the team, modeling efficient work habits that others are encouraged to adopt.

- **Manufacturing:** A shift leader at a manufacturing plant manages their workload by delegating routine maintenance checks and quality control tasks to experienced team members, allowing them to focus on coordinating production schedules and addressing urgent issues on the floor. This visible delegation shows the team that workload management is a shared responsibility and highlights the leader's focus on prioritizing high-impact tasks. By clearly distributing responsibilities, the shift leader fosters a collaborative environment that enhances overall productivity and operational efficiency.

The Impact on Your Team

Effective workload management doesn't just enhance your productivity—it positively impacts your entire team. When you manage your workload efficiently, you create a reliable, organized work environment that fosters trust and collaboration. Your ability to handle tasks with competence serves as a guide for your team, helping them adopt similar strategies and improve their own performance.

Teams benefit from clear workload management practices through reduced stress, fewer bottlenecks, and enhanced communication. By sharing workload management techniques, you contribute to a culture of efficiency and resilience. This not only boosts morale but also strengthens the team's ability to adapt to changing demands and priorities.

Manage Your Workload Like Cal Newport

Cal Newport, a computer science professor and author, is renowned for his disciplined approach to managing his workload and setting boundaries. Newport is a strong advocate for "deep work," where he focuses on high-impact tasks without distractions and strictly limits his availability outside of these sessions. He's known for not using social media and rarely checking email outside of designated times, visibly demonstrating his commitment to efficiency and balance. Newport's approach shows that setting clear boundaries and prioritizing focused work over constant connectivity leads to higher productivity and sustainable success.[12]

Behavior Three: Avoiding Impulsiveness

Competence involves maintaining control over your actions and responses, especially in high-pressure situations. Impulsiveness—whether it's making snap decisions, responding emotionally, or jumping into tasks without proper planning—can undermine your effectiveness and erode trust. Competent professionals exercise restraint, taking time to consider their options, gather information, and maintain composure.

- **The Challenges of Impulsiveness:** Impulsivity can manifest in various ways, such as reacting emotionally in meetings, making decisions without proper analysis, or jumping into tasks without a plan. These behaviors often lead to mistakes, strained relationships, and long-term setbacks. By contrast, those who avoid impulsiveness take a measured approach, aligning their actions with strategic goals and demonstrating reliability.

- **Biohacking Impulsiveness:** Avoiding impulsiveness is not just about internal restraint; it's about visibly signaling to others that your actions are thoughtful and deliberate. The biodynamics of controlling impulsive behavior involves specific strategies that communicate your commitment to measured decision-making:

o **Pause Before Reacting:** In meetings or conversations, taking a visible pause before responding signals that you're considering your words carefully. This moment of reflection shows others that you're not reacting impulsively but are thoughtfully weighing your response, which builds credibility and trust.[13]

o **Demonstrate Mindful Presence:** Practicing mindfulness, such as taking deep breaths or maintaining a calm demeanor, visibly conveys control and composure. When colleagues see you stay present and focused, even in stressful moments, it reinforces the perception that you are deliberate and composed in your actions.[14]

o **Communicate Thoughtful Decision-Making:** Articulate your reasoning when making decisions, especially in high-stakes situations. Sharing your thought process, such as referencing relevant data or consulting with key stakeholders, shows that your actions are not driven by impulse but by careful consideration of all factors.[15]

o **Maintain Consistent Nonverbal Cues:** Nonverbal signals, such as steady eye contact, measured gestures, and a relaxed posture, convey control. Avoiding impulsive body language, like fidgeting or abrupt movements, helps maintain an image of stability and thoughtful leadership.[16]

o **Reflect on Past Actions Publicly:** During team debriefs or meetings, openly reflecting on past decisions and discussing what you learned shows others that you value thoughtful consideration over impulsive actions. This visible reflection process models the importance of learning from experience, promoting a culture of careful decision-making.[17]

This Behavior in Action

- **Performing Arts:** A stage director faces unexpected challenges during a live performance. Instead of reacting emotionally to an actor's mistake, they stay calm and provide clear instructions, helping the production continue smoothly and maintaining the cast's confidence.

- **Manufacturing:** A shift leader in a manufacturing facility manages a sudden machinery breakdown without panic. By calmly coordinating the team's response and assessing the situation methodically, they prevent a small issue from escalating into a larger production delay.

- **Finance:** An investment manager is pressured to make a quick decision on a new opportunity but chooses to pause and conduct a thorough risk assessment first. This careful approach prevents the firm from making a costly investment mistake.

The Impact on Your Team

Avoiding impulsiveness creates a stable and reliable environment for your team. When you demonstrate thoughtful, measured actions, your team feels secure and confident in your leadership. This fosters trust and collaboration, because team members know that their ideas and concerns will be met with thoughtful consideration rather than impulsive reactions.

Teams led by individuals who avoid impulsiveness experience fewer conflicts and better communication. When leaders take time to reflect and respond thoughtfully, it sets a standard for everyone, promoting a culture of respect and patience. This approach enhances overall team performance, because careful decision-making leads to better outcomes and stronger relationships.

Control Your Impulses Like Angela Merkel

Angela Merkel, the former Chancellor of Germany, was known for her steady, deliberate decision-making process. Merkel approached political decisions with methodical analysis, often taking time to gather all relevant information before acting. Her calm, calculated response during the 2008 financial crisis helped stabilize Germany's economy and the broader European Union. Merkel's refusal to act hastily set her apart as a leader who valued thoughtful, evidence-based decisions over quick, reactive impulses.[18]

Behavior Four: Be Punctual

Punctuality might seem like a small detail, but it speaks volumes about your competence, respect for others, and commitment to your responsibilities. More than just arriving on time, punctuality reflects how you manage your time and prioritize your commitments. When you consistently show up punctually, you demonstrate discipline, reliability, and a clear understanding of how your actions impact others.

- **The Challenges of Being Punctual:** Punctuality signals respect for the time and efforts of your colleagues, clients, and team members. It shows that you value others' contributions and are committed to moving forward in an organized, efficient manner. Conversely, habitual lateness can signal disorganization, a lack of respect for others' time, and difficulty managing your responsibilities effectively. Chronic lateness erodes trust and damages credibility, making it harder to build strong professional relationships.

- **Biohacking Punctuality:** Punctuality may seem like an odd behavior to discuss on internal-external alignment. I mean, if you are late to a meeting, both the external you and the internal you is late, right? However, many people who struggle with punctuality don't lack the desire to be on time; rather, they often face underlying challenges that misalign their intentions with their actions. Research indicates that most people do want to be punctual but can struggle due to factors like poor time management skills, a tendency to underestimate how long tasks will take, or anxiety about certain situations.[19] This disconnect between intent and behavior highlights that punctuality isn't just about internal time management; it's about aligning your intentions with visible actions that signal respect and readiness to those around you. The biodynamics of punctuality involves outward actions that show others your commitment to being on time and fully prepared.

- **Visibly Prioritizing Buffer Time:** Adding visible buffer time between meetings or tasks on your calendar shows that you anticipate potential delays and value punctuality. By scheduling intentional gaps, you communicate that you are prepared to handle the unexpected without compromising other commitments. This visible prioritization sends a signal of foresight and careful planning, enhancing your reliability.[20]

- **Arriving Early and Preparing Ahead:** Consistently arriving a few minutes early to meetings or appointments visibly demonstrates that you are prepared and respectful of others' time. By being early, you signal reliability and readiness, allowing you to settle in and start on time. This behavior sends a clear message that you value punctuality and are proactive in managing your commitments.[21]

- **Visible Use of Reminders and Alerts:** Setting visible reminders or alerts for meetings and deadlines shows others that you take your commitments seriously. Whether it's a pop-up reminder on your phone during a meeting or a visible alert on your watch, these signals reinforce your proactive approach to staying on time and organized.

- **Publicly Acknowledging Timeliness as a Value:** Recognizing and praising punctuality within your team—whether in meetings, emails, or team debriefs—sends a message that you value and expect this behavior. This public acknowledgment reinforces punctuality as a team standard and aligns everyone with the expectation of being on time.

- **Handling Delays Transparently:** If you anticipate being late, visibly communicate in advance, whether through a quick call, email, or message. By acknowledging delays and adjusting schedules publicly, you demonstrate accountability and respect, showing that punctuality is a priority even when challenges arise.

This Behavior in Action

- **Hospitality:** A hotel manager ensures that all team meetings and staff briefings start on time, setting the tone for a disciplined and respectful work environment. By consistently being punctual and prepared, the manager visibly demonstrates reliability, which boosts staff morale and ensures that daily operations run smoothly without delays. This approach helps foster a culture of professionalism throughout the hotel staff, enhancing guest experiences and overall team efficiency.

- **Corporate Law:** A partner in a law firm makes it a point to arrive on time for client meetings, demonstrating respect for their schedules and ensuring that important discussions aren't rushed or cut short. This reliability strengthens client relationships and reinforces the firm's professional standards.

- **Higher Education:** A university professor consistently starts and ends lectures on time, providing students the full benefit of their scheduled class period. This punctuality sets a professional standard and shows respect for students' time, enhancing the learning environment.

The Impact on Your Team

Punctuality promotes trust, collaboration, and efficiency within teams. When everyone shows up on time for meetings and meets deadlines, it sets the stage for productive discussions and smooth workflows. Teams that operate on a foundation of punctuality stay on track, meet project timelines, and avoid the disruptions that lateness can cause.

Punctuality also fosters a culture of mutual respect. When team members can rely on one another to be on time, it builds trust and accountability. This mutual respect enhances collaboration, because people are more engaged when they know their time is valued. In contrast, chronic lateness can create frustration, erode team cohesion, and lead to disengagement.

Biohacking Competence

Be Punctual Like Tom Hanks

Tom Hanks, one of Hollywood's most respected actors, is known for his professionalism, including his commitment to punctuality. In an industry often criticized for its lack of discipline, Hanks consistently arrives on time, whether on set or in meetings, demonstrating his respect for everyone's time. His punctuality reflects a broader commitment to preparation and respect, setting a positive tone for his colleagues. Hanks's reputation for being reliable and professional highlights the importance of being punctual as a cornerstone of effective leadership.[22]

Behavior Five: Be Prepared

Preparation is one of the clearest signals of competence. It's not just about arriving on time; it's about showing up with all the necessary information, anticipating potential challenges, and having a clear plan of action. Being prepared distinguishes reactive professionals from those who consistently perform at a higher level. When you are always prepared, you demonstrate attention to detail and a commitment to excellence, setting yourself apart in any professional environment.

- **The Challenges of Being Prepared:** Preparation can be demanding. It requires time, foresight, and often a willingness to go the extra mile. In today's fast-paced environments, it's easy to fall into the trap of "winging it," but this approach rarely yields the best outcomes. Without adequate preparation, even the most capable professionals can falter under pressure. Preparation allows you to anticipate problems before they arise, respond effectively to unexpected challenges, and make informed decisions. Without it, you risk being caught off guard, undermining your credibility and performance.

- **Biohacking Preparedness:** Competence in being prepared is not just about what happens behind the scenes; it's about making that preparation visible to others. The biodynamics of being prepared involves outward actions that signal your readiness and dedication:

o **Use Checklists and Planning Tools:** When you visibly use checklists, project management software, or detailed notes during meetings, you signal that you've done your homework. These external signs of organization reflect your commitment to thorough preparation and help ensure that no details are overlooked.[23] When others see you working methodically, it builds confidence in your ability to handle complex tasks.

o **Arrive with Relevant Data and Insights:** Bringing well-researched data, market analysis, or detailed proposals to meetings demonstrates your depth of preparation. This outward display of readiness shows that you value the discussion and are fully equipped to contribute meaningful insights. By grounding your contributions in solid information, you reinforce your credibility and influence.[24]

o **Anticipate Questions and Challenges:** Demonstrating foresight by addressing potential questions or objections before they arise signals that you have thought through various scenarios. Whether it's having backup data or contingency plans, being visibly prepared for the unexpected shows others that you are proactive, not reactive. This approach builds trust, because it assures colleagues that you are ready for whatever comes next.[25]

o **Rehearse Key Presentations and Meetings**: Taking the time to practice and refine your delivery shows that you take your responsibilities seriously. Rehearsing allows you to anticipate timing, refine key messages, and adjust your approach. When your delivery appears polished and confident, it signals to your audience that you have invested time in preparation, enhancing your professional image.[26]

o **Share Preparation Efforts with Your Team:** Communicating how you've prepared—whether by sharing pre-meeting

Biohacking Competence

materials, providing context in advance, or outlining your preparation steps—sets a visible standard. This transparency encourages others to come equally prepared, fostering a collaborative culture of readiness and thoroughness.[27]

This Behavior in Action

- **Product Development:** A product manager consistently arrives at sprint planning sessions with updated data on user feedback and market trends, enabling the team to make informed decisions and adjust development priorities quickly. This visible preparation boosts team confidence and accelerates the product's success.

- **Special Events:** A conference center manager prepares for high-profile events by thoroughly reviewing guest preferences, coordinating with department heads, and running pre-event briefings. This attention to detail ensures that everything runs smoothly, visibly demonstrating her competence to both her team and the guests.

- **City Planning:** A city planner enters community meetings equipped with detailed maps, impact assessments, and answers to likely questions. By demonstrating such thorough preparation, the planner builds trust with stakeholders and guides discussions toward constructive solutions.

The Impact on Your Team

Being consistently prepared doesn't just enhance your own performance—it positively impacts your entire team. When you come ready with data, insights, and well-thought-out plans, you set the tone for a culture of excellence. Your readiness fosters a professional environment where team members feel motivated to rise to the same standard, increasing overall productivity and collaboration.

Preparation also drives efficiency. Teams that are well-prepared spend less time catching up and more time on meaningful work. Meetings are more productive, deadlines are met, and quality improves.

116

Biohacking Leadership

As a leader, your commitment to preparation becomes a model that encourages everyone to approach their work with the same level of thoroughness and care.

Be Prepared Like Jimmy Carter

Jimmy Carter's dedication to preparation was evident throughout his career, particularly in his post-presidential work with organizations like Habitat for Humanity and the Carter Center. Known for his meticulous attention to detail, Carter often arrived at negotiations and humanitarian missions armed with extensive research, strategic plans, and deep knowledge of the issues at hand. His thorough preparation was instrumental in achieving the Camp David Accords, where his detailed understanding of the political landscape enabled him to facilitate a historic peace agreement between Egypt and Israel. Carter's approach exemplifies how thorough preparation sets the stage for impactful leadership.[28]

Behavior Six: Be Well-Organized

Competence is closely tied to how well-organized you are. Being organized goes beyond maintaining a tidy workspace—it's about structuring your time, tasks, and resources to maximize efficiency and effectiveness. When you are organized, you not only manage your workload more effectively, but you also create clarity for yourself and your team, enabling everyone to focus on what matters most.

Being well-organized ensures that nothing falls through the cracks. Whether it's managing complex projects, staying on top of deadlines, or simply keeping track of day-to-day responsibilities, your organizational skills help you stay in control and ensure that tasks are completed efficiently. This foresight allows you to anticipate challenges, address issues proactively, and consistently meet your commitments.

- **The Challenges of Staying Organized:** Staying organized is essential but often challenging, especially when juggling multiple responsibilities. Without clear systems in place, it's easy to lose track of priorities, miss deadlines, or feel overwhelmed by competing demands. Disorganization can lead to missed opportunities, unnecessary stress, and reduced effectiveness. In contrast, a well-organized approach allows you to work smarter, not harder, and consistently deliver high-quality results.

- **Biohacking Being Organized:** Competence in organization isn't just about what happens behind the scenes—it's about making your organizational skills visible. The biodynamics of organization involves outward actions that show others your commitment to structure, efficiency, and reliability:

  - **Utilize Digital Tools for Organization:** Using project management software, digital calendars, and task management apps publicly signals that you have a structured approach to your responsibilities. When others see you actively engaging with these tools—assigning tasks, setting deadlines, and tracking progress—it shows that you have a clear plan and are committed to maintaining order.[29] This visibility helps build confidence in your ability to handle complex workloads.

  - **Break Down Large Tasks into Manageable Steps:** By openly discussing how you break down large projects into smaller, actionable tasks, you demonstrate your systematic approach to work. Sharing your process with your team— such as through project briefs or checklists—reinforces that you're not just looking at the big picture but are also attending to the details. This visible structure helps others understand the path forward and aligns their efforts with the project's goals.[30]

  - **Implement Clear and Consistent Organizational Systems:** Competent leaders establish and visibly maintain clear organizational systems for tasks, information, and communication. Using standardized processes, such as shared project management boards, structured agendas for meetings, or clearly labeled digital folders, signals to your team that there is a reliable method for managing work. This visible order enhances efficiency, reduces misunderstandings, and ensures everyone knows where to find necessary information, reinforcing a culture of organization and accountability.[31]

o **Maintain a Consistent Routine:** Routines provide a visible rhythm to your workday. When team members see you consistently start and end meetings on time, adhere to a structured schedule, or follow regular workflows, it signals that you have a reliable system in place. This outward consistency helps create a predictable and organized environment that others can rely on and model.

o **Regularly Review and Reflect on Progress:** Taking time to review your progress and adjust your plans is a critical part of staying organized. By visibly engaging in regular check-ins, status updates, or reflection sessions, you show your commitment to continuous improvement and accountability. This openness invites others to reflect on their own work and align their efforts with the team's overall objectives.

This Behavior in Action

- **Executive Chef:** An executive chef at a high-end restaurant meticulously organizes kitchen operations, from ingredient inventory to staff scheduling, using a digital management system. This structured approach ensures that the kitchen runs efficiently, reduces waste, and allows the team to focus on creating high-quality dishes. The visible organization of the kitchen creates a smooth workflow, enhances collaboration, and consistently delivers an exceptional dining experience.

- **School Principal:** A school principal uses a detailed calendar system to manage meetings, student activities, and staff evaluations. By keeping all stakeholders informed and ensuring that schedules are well-coordinated, the principal maintains a well-organized school environment that supports student learning and teacher productivity. This visible organization fosters a sense of stability and trust among students, parents, and staff, making the school run more efficiently.

- **Supply Chain Manager:** A supply chain manager uses advanced tracking software to monitor inventory levels, manage supplier schedules, and anticipate potential disruptions in the supply chain. This visible organization allows the manager to proactively address issues before they impact production, ensuring timely delivery of products. The structured approach not only improves efficiency but also builds confidence among team members, suppliers, and clients.

The Impact on Your Team

Being well-organized doesn't just benefit you; it significantly impacts your entire team. When you are organized, your team feels supported, knowing that tasks are clearly outlined and there's a plan in place to achieve goals. This structure fosters trust and collaboration, because team members can rely on you to maintain order and clarity.

An organized team is also a more productive team. When roles, responsibilities, and deadlines are clearly communicated and tracked, your team can focus on their work without confusion or delays. Teams that operate in an organized environment are better able to meet deadlines, deliver high-quality work, and maintain momentum on long-term projects.

Your organizational competence also sets a standard for your team. When team members see that you are organized and have a system in place, they are more likely to adopt similar habits. This creates a culture of organization and efficiency, where everyone understands the value of maintaining structure and staying on top of their responsibilities.

Ultimately, being well-organized is about creating an environment where you and your team can thrive. By staying organized, you ensure that tasks are completed efficiently, goals are achieved, and your team remains focused and engaged. Organization isn't just a personal skill—it's a cornerstone of effective leadership and team success.

Biohacking Leadership

Organize Like Marie Kondo

Marie Kondo, the renowned organizing consultant and author, has transformed the way people think about organization. Kondo's "Kon-Mari" method goes beyond tidying up spaces; it's about organizing one's life in alignment with what truly matters. Her approach emphasizes intentionality, helping people streamline their environments and, by extension, their minds. Kondo's personal life reflects her teachings; she runs a highly structured business, balancing her work with family life while maintaining a clear, organized approach to all aspects of her endeavors.[32]

Staying Competent

Competence is not a static quality; it is dynamic and evolves through continuous learning and reflection. Leaders must regularly assess and refine their behaviors, adapting to new challenges and environments. This commitment to growth is key to sustaining leadership biodynamics.

Throughout this chapter, we've explored the six core behaviors that signal competence: setting the right priorities, managing your workload effectively, avoiding impulsiveness, demonstrating punctuality, being prepared, and maintaining organization. These behaviors form the biodynamics of contribution, enabling you to make impactful decisions, solve problems, and guide your team with confidence.

Competence is not only about what you know—it's about how you apply that knowledge to consistently contribute in meaningful ways. As a leader, every action, decision, and interaction creates impacts your team and organization. Competence inspires trust, fosters collaboration, and sets the stage for sustainable success.

Competence also evolves. Just as you must adjust to the demands of a high-pressure negotiation room, your ability to grow, learn, and adapt keeps your leadership relevant. Embracing this growth mindset allows you to navigate today's challenges and anticipate tomorrow's, ensuring you and your team are always prepared to excel.

As we move into the next chapter, we'll explore gravitas—the final element of leadership biodynamics. Building on the foundations of warmth and competence, gravitas will enable you to inspire, influence, and create lasting impact. Understanding how to leverage gravitas will elevate your leadership, turning your skills and knowledge into a force that commands respect and drives meaningful change.

Chapter 7

Biohacking Gravitas

Gravitas, the third and final channel in the leadership biodynamics model, serves as the gravitational force that unites teams, fosters collaboration, and drives collective outcomes. In this chapter, we will explore six specific behaviors or "biomarkers" that signal gravitas, offering practical insights for leaders seeking to refine this essential quality.

Biohacking gravitas means intentionally developing the behaviors that stabilize and align teams, much like gravity holds celestial bodies in orbit. Effective leaders with gravitas act as the steadying center of collaborative efforts, creating environments where diverse perspectives converge to achieve shared goals. Gravitas is not about commanding attention or dominating dialogue; it is about fostering the conditions for others to thrive and aligning efforts toward meaningful outcomes.

Imagine gravitas as the invisible force that harmonizes collaboration. Leaders with gravitas don't rely on authority to control—they use their influence to guide, empower, and stabilize their teams. This stabilizing presence allows others to contribute dynamically and confidently, knowing they are supported by a leader who ensures alignment and clarity amidst complexity.

This chapter introduces six core behaviors of gravitas—effective message delivery, standing one's ground with conviction and diplomacy, making tough calls, maintaining composure when challenged, using silence strategically, and acting with decorum and grace. Through real-world examples and actionable strategies, we'll examine how these behaviors can be cultivated to strengthen collaboration, enhance team trust, and achieve impactful results. By biohacking gravitas, leaders can transform their ability to lead with calm authority, fostering the stability and alignment their teams need to excel.

Behavior One: Effective Message Delivery

Delivering messages effectively is at the heart of gravitas. It aligns teams and individuals, fostering collaboration and clarity in pursuit of shared goals. Effective message delivery is not just about conveying information—it's about ensuring that others understand the purpose and their role within the broader mission. When leaders communicate clearly and with intention, they eliminate confusion, inspire trust, and create a sense of unity that drives meaningful progress.

Challenges of Effective Message Delivery

Delivering clear and purposeful messages may sound straightforward, but it's deceptively difficult, especially in dynamic environments. Leaders often face challenges in distilling complex ideas into accessible language or in adapting their messages to diverse audiences. For example, cross-functional teams may include individuals with varied expertise and cultural perspectives, making precise and inclusive communication critical yet challenging.

Misalignment between verbal content and nonverbal cues can further muddy the waters. Leaders who fail to project confidence, trustworthiness, or authenticity risk undermining the very messages they aim to deliver. Addressing these challenges requires not only internal clarity but also external consistency in how messages are framed and delivered.

Biohacking Effective Message Delivery

Delivering messages with gravitas requires aligning internal clarity with external expressions of confidence and purpose. Leaders can achieve this through several key biodynamic actions:

- **Clarity and Simplicity:** Leaders with gravitas distill complex ideas into simple, actionable language that resonates with their audience. This is particularly important in interdisciplinary environments, where jargon or overly technical language can alienate team members. By focusing on essential points and eliminating unnecessary complexity, leaders ensure their messages are both accessible and impactful.

- **Adapting Communication to the Audience:** Adaptability is critical to effective communication. Leaders tailor their tone, language, and messaging to meet the needs of different audiences, ensuring alignment across diverse teams. Whether addressing senior executives, frontline staff, or external stakeholders, leaders adjust their approach to resonate with the audience while maintaining consistency in the core message.

- **Nonverbal Communication:** Nonverbal cues often speak louder than words. Leaders with gravitas understand that body language, tone of voice, and facial expressions must reinforce their verbal message. For example, maintaining eye contact, adopting open gestures, and using a steady tone convey confidence and authenticity, ensuring that the message is received as intended.

This Behavior in Action

- **Technology Company:** During a major merger, a CEO delivers a clear and consistent message about organizational changes. By tailoring the message to different departments (e.g., technical versus administrative teams) and ensuring alignment across the board, the CEO fosters collaboration and reduces uncertainty during a tumultuous transition.

- **Healthcare System:** A hospital administrator communicates policy changes to physicians, nurses, and administrative staff. They adapt their messaging to address each group's specific concerns, ensuring that everyone understands both the operational details and the broader organizational goals.

- **Manufacturing:** A plant manager rolling out new safety protocols reinforces the importance of the changes through clear communication and consistent nonverbal cues. By demonstrating commitment through their words and actions, the manager fosters trust and compliance among workers.

125

Biohacking Gravitas

Deliver Messages Like Satya Nadella

Satya Nadella exemplifies the power of effective message delivery. When he became CEO of Microsoft, the company faced significant cultural and strategic challenges. Nadella's ability to distill complex strategies into clear, relatable messages helped unite the organization around a renewed mission. By communicating Microsoft's shift to cloud computing as part of a broader vision to empower people worldwide, Nadella inspired alignment and collaboration across teams.[1]

His communication style—marked by clarity, humility, and adaptability—was a cornerstone of Microsoft's transformation into a global leader in cloud computing. Nadella's success highlights how effective message delivery fosters trust, innovation, and unity within diverse organizations.

Satya Nadella's approach to leadership communication underscores the importance of clarity, adaptability, and alignment. When he took the helm at Microsoft, he inherited a company with entrenched silos and a waning sense of purpose. Nadella's ability to articulate a clear, unifying vision—centered on empowering people and organizations—enabled him to rebuild trust and drive meaningful change.

Nadella tailored his messaging to resonate with employees at every level. He framed complex strategies in simple, relatable terms and ensured that his nonverbal cues—calm demeanor, open gestures, and steady tone—reinforced his verbal messages. By aligning his internal clarity with external expressions of confidence and purpose, Nadella demonstrated the true power of gravitas.

Leaders can learn from Nadella's example by focusing on three key principles:

1. Simplify complex ideas into actionable messages.
2. Tailor communication to diverse audiences without losing the core message.
3. Align verbal and nonverbal signals to project authenticity and inspire trust.

Delivering messages effectively is not just a leadership skill—it is the gravitational force that aligns people, fosters collaboration, and drives results. By mastering this behavior, leaders can ensure that their words resonate, inspire, and create lasting impact.

Behavior Two: Stand One's Ground with Conviction and Diplomacy

At the core of gravitas lies the ability to stand one's ground with conviction and diplomacy. Leaders with gravitas serve as stabilizing forces, holding firm to their principles while remaining open to constructive dialogue. This behavior enables them to navigate tension and conflict effectively, ensuring collaboration thrives even amidst differing opinions. Much like gravity keeping celestial bodies in orbit, this balance between conviction and diplomacy creates a sense of stability that keeps teams aligned and focused on shared goals.

Challenges of Standing One's Ground

Balancing conviction and diplomacy is no easy feat, especially in environments with diverse viewpoints and competing priorities. Leaders may struggle with appearing too rigid when standing firm or too accommodating when fostering dialogue. Missteps in this balance can lead to fractured teams, unresolved conflicts, or diminished trust.

For example, leaders who rely solely on conviction may alienate others, stifling collaboration. Conversely, leaders who overemphasize diplomacy without clear principles risk being perceived as indecisive or lacking authority. Achieving the right balance requires intentionality and skill, particularly in high-pressure situations.

Biohacking Conviction and Diplomacy

To effectively balance conviction and diplomacy, leaders must align their internal steadiness with external expressions of openness and adaptability. These biodynamic actions help achieve this alignment:

- **Clarity of Purpose:** Leaders with gravitas maintain unwavering clarity about their mission and principles. This clarity acts as an anchor during moments of tension, ensuring decisions remain consistent with long-term goals. For example, articulating a clear "why" behind decisions fosters alignment even when disagreements arise.

- **Active Listening and Reflection:** Diplomatic leaders excel at listening to diverse perspectives, validating input, and fostering constructive dialogue. By engaging actively with opposing views, leaders demonstrate respect and inclusivity, which strengthens trust within teams.

- **Constructive Conflict Management:** Leaders with gravitas harness tension as a tool for innovation rather than division. By framing disagreements around shared goals and focusing on solutions, they transform conflict into an opportunity for creative problem-solving.

- **Visible Steadiness:** Remaining calm and composed in the face of disagreement signals confidence and stability. Nonverbal cues like open gestures, steady eye contact, and measured tones reinforce a leader's conviction and create a reassuring presence.

This Behavior in Action

- **Corporate Merger:** A CEO overseeing a merger navigates conflicting interests by standing firm on the organization's new strategic values while diplomatically addressing operational concerns from both sides. This approach ensures stability and alignment during a transformative period.

- **Media Company:** A media executive balances creative integrity with investor demands by maintaining a clear vision for the company's artistic direction while engaging stakeholders in dialogue to address financial concerns.

- **Sports Team Management:** A sports team manager under pressure to prioritize profits over player development stands firm on long-term talent investment. Through diplomacy, they illustrate how nurturing young players benefits both performance and revenue, preserving team morale and ownership trust.

Stand Your Ground Like Mary Barra

Mary Barra, CEO of General Motors, exemplifies the balance between conviction and diplomacy. During GM's recall crisis, Barra stood firm on her commitment to transparency and accountability, ensuring the company addressed safety issues head-on. Simultaneously, she engaged diplomatically with stakeholders, including regulators, employees, and customers, fostering collaboration and rebuilding trust.[2]

Barra's leadership highlights key principles of standing one's ground with gravitas:

1. **Stay Anchored in Your Values:** Barra's unwavering focus on accountability provided clarity during uncertainty.

2. **Adapt Your Approach to the Audience:** She tailored her messaging to address the unique concerns of different stakeholders.

3. **Engage Conflict Constructively:** Barra maintained an open dialogue, turning a potential crisis into an opportunity for growth.

Barra's ability to balance assertiveness with openness allowed GM to navigate a tumultuous period while preserving its reputation. Leaders can learn from her example by aligning their principles with inclusive and adaptive communication strategies.

Behavior Three: Making Tough Calls

Making tough decisions is one of the most visible expressions of leadership gravitas. These decisions often carry significant consequences, requiring leaders to weigh competing interests, maintain empathy, and act decisively. Tough calls—such as layoffs, strategic pivots, or addressing safety concerns—highlight the leader's role as a gravitational center, holding the team steady while navigating uncertainty.

Leaders with gravitas understand that making tough decisions is not about detachment but about balancing the organization's goals with the well-being of those affected. Empathy and decisiveness are not opposing forces but complementary elements that create a foundation for thoughtful, impactful decision-making. When communicated with clarity and transparency, these decisions can strengthen trust and foster long-term resilience within teams.

Challenges of Making Tough Calls

Tough decisions are inherently challenging because they often involve trade-offs that impact both organizational success and individual well-being. Leaders may face resistance, emotional backlash, or even self-doubt when making these choices. Furthermore, the pressure to act quickly in high-stakes situations can lead to rushed or poorly considered decisions, compounding their consequences.

Balancing empathy and decisiveness is another critical challenge. Leaders who overemphasize empathy may struggle to make necessary but painful decisions, while those who lean solely on decisiveness risk alienating their teams and eroding trust. The ability to balance these dynamics is the hallmark of leadership gravitas.

Biohacking Tough Decision-Making

To navigate the complexities of tough decisions, leaders with gravitas focus on aligning their internal clarity with external actions. This involves three key biodynamic practices:

- **Decisiveness and Clarity: Anchoring the Team:** Decisiveness is essential when making difficult choices. Leaders must assess the situation, gather available information, and act swiftly to provide a clear sense of direction. Indecision can destabilize

130

Biohacking Leadership

teams, leading to confusion and diminished morale. Leaders with gravitas anchor their teams by making firm decisions, even under pressure, and communicating them with conviction.

- **Empathy: Balancing Organizational Goals and Human Impact:** Tough calls often have profound human consequences. Leaders with gravitas integrate empathy into their decision-making, ensuring that those affected feel respected and valued. Empathy doesn't negate the need for hard decisions but adds a layer of humanity that preserves trust and morale.

- **Transparency: Building Trust Through Honest Communication:** Trust is built when leaders communicate tough decisions openly and honestly. Transparency involves explaining the rationale behind decisions, the factors considered, and the anticipated outcomes. By fostering a sense of inclusion, transparency ensures that team members feel respected, even if they disagree with the decision.

This Behavior in Action

- **Technology Company:** A tech CEO faces a downturn and must implement layoffs. The leader makes the decision with empathy, offering severance packages and career transition support. Transparency is emphasized through town hall meetings where the rationale is clearly communicated.

- **Construction Industry:** A construction firm's director pauses a high-profile project due to safety concerns. Despite financial losses, the leader prioritizes safety, clearly explaining the decision to the team and stakeholders to maintain trust and credibility.

- **Entertainment Industry:** A film studio executive cancels a popular show over concerns about content that conflicts with the company's core values. The leader transparently communicates the decision's alignment with long-term brand strategy, fostering trust despite public backlash.

Make Tough Calls Like Ursula Burns

Ursula Burns exemplifies the power of decisive and empathetic leadership. When she took over as CEO of Xerox, the company was grappling with declining revenues and an outdated business model. Burns made tough calls, including workforce reductions and strategic pivots toward digital technologies.[3]

What set Burns apart was her ability to balance decisiveness with empathy. She ensured that those affected by the changes were treated with respect, offering support and resources to help them transition. Burns also communicated the rationale for her decisions clearly and openly, fostering trust and alignment within the organization.

Leaders can learn from Burns by focusing on three principles:

1. **Anchor Decisions in a Clear Vision:** Burns's focus on long-term strategy ensured her decisions aligned with organizational goals.

2. **Balance Empathy with Decisiveness:** She demonstrated care for those impacted while making the tough choices necessary for Xerox's future.

3. **Communicate with Transparency:** Her honest communication style built trust, even in the face of significant challenges.

Ursula Burns' leadership during Xerox's transformation underscores that making tough calls is not just about decisiveness—it's about navigating challenges with empathy, clarity, and a commitment to long-term success.

Behavior Four: Maintaining Composure When Challenged

In any collaborative effort, disruptions are inevitable. Challenges can arise from external pressures, interpersonal conflicts, or unforeseen crises. The fourth behavior of gravitas, maintaining composure when challenged, anchors teams in times of uncertainty. Leaders who remain composed act as a stabilizing force, reassuring their teams and enabling them to stay focused on shared goals. This ability is not merely about staying calm; it's about modeling resilience and clarity in the face of adversity.

When leaders lose composure, they risk spreading anxiety and uncertainty, which can erode team confidence and cohesion. Conversely, leaders who remain composed under pressure inspire stability and trust, setting the tone for how their teams respond to challenges. Their influence acts as gravity, holding the team together and preventing collective efforts from unraveling.

Challenges of Maintaining Composure

Maintaining composure during challenges is easier said than done. High-pressure situations often provoke strong emotional reactions—frustration, fear, or anger—that can be difficult to regulate. Leaders must also navigate the "emotional contagion" effect, where their emotional state influences the mood and performance of the team. This means that visible frustration or panic can quickly ripple through a group, amplifying stress and undermining morale.

Another challenge is balancing composure with authenticity. While staying calm is critical, leaders must avoid coming across as indifferent or detached. Effective composure involves both emotional regulation and genuine engagement, ensuring that leaders appear steady while remaining connected to their teams.

Biohacking Composure in Leadership

To maintain composure under pressure, leaders with gravitas focus on a combination of emotional regulation, resilience, and consistent communication. These practices create a foundation for stability, even in the most challenging situations.

- **Emotional Regulation: The Science of Staying Calm:** Emotional regulation involves recognizing and managing both positive and negative emotions to maintain clarity and control. Leaders with gravitas are skilled at managing their own emotional responses to prevent them from destabilizing the team. This self-control is especially critical during moments of conflict or crisis, where a leader's demeanor sets the tone for the group.

- **Modeling Composure: The Ripple Effect on Teams:** A leader's emotional state directly affects team morale and performance. Research on emotional contagion suggests that calm, composed leaders create a stabilizing effect on their teams, promoting focus and cohesion.[4] Leaders who model composure under pressure demonstrate resilience, reassuring their teams that challenges can be overcome.

- **Resilience: Bouncing Back from Setbacks:** Composure is closely tied to resilience—the ability to recover from setbacks and adapt to changing circumstances. Leaders with gravitas demonstrate resilience by maintaining focus on long-term goals, even when faced with immediate challenges. This forward-looking mindset ensures that adversity does not derail the team's momentum.

- **Mindfulness Practices: Strengthening Composure:** Leaders who practice mindfulness techniques, such as deep breathing or meditation, enhance their ability to stay present and regulate stress. Mindfulness reduces anxiety and improves decision-making, equipping leaders to respond to challenges with clarity and poise. A study by Hülsheger and colleagues found that mindfulness training improved leaders' emotional regulation, reducing stress-related symptoms and enhancing their effectiveness in high-pressure situations.[5]

This Behavior in Action

- **Manufacturing Company:** A CEO faces a sudden supply chain disruption that threatens to halt production. Amid mounting pressure, the CEO gathers the leadership team to assess the situation calmly, explore alternative solutions, and communicate transparently with stakeholders. By modeling composure, the CEO prevents panic and helps the team identify a temporary workaround.

- **Education Sector:** A school principal faces criticism from parents over a controversial curriculum change. During a tense PTA meeting, the principal remains composed, actively listening to concerns and providing clear, transparent explanations. The principal's calm demeanor deescalates the situation and fosters constructive dialogue.

- **Tourism Industry:** A hotel chain executive faces backlash over a controversial pricing policy. During a heated public meeting, the executive maintains composure, actively listening to stakeholders and guiding the discussion toward constructive solutions. The executive's steady leadership helps preserve trust and credibility during a difficult period.

Stay Composed Like Jacinda Ardern

Jacinda Ardern's leadership as prime minister of New Zealand during the Christchurch mosque shootings in 2019 exemplifies the power of composure under pressure. In the immediate aftermath of the tragedy, Ardern addressed the nation with calm resolve, offering empathy and reassurance. Her composed demeanor helped unify a grieving country and inspired swift legislative action to reform New Zealand's gun laws.

Ardern's leadership demonstrated three key principles of composure:

1. **Emotional Regulation:** She managed her own emotional response, projecting calmness and focus.

2. **Resilience:** She maintained a forward-looking perspective, emphasizing healing and systemic change.

3. **Transparent Communication:** She communicated openly and authentically, building trust during a time of crisis.

By balancing emotional regulation with empathetic action, Ardern exemplified how maintaining composure can inspire trust and resilience in teams and communities alike.

Behavior Five: Using Silence When Needed

Like the stillness in space that allows recalibration of gravitational forces, silence in leadership offers moments of reflection and alignment. The fifth behavior of gravitas, using silence when needed, empowers leaders to create space for reflection, dialogue, and the emergence of new ideas. Far from being passive, strategic silence is a deliberate leadership tool that recalibrates the flow of conversation, ensuring focus and balance.

Silence, when used effectively, is a form of presence. Leaders who wield this tool with intention signal authority, invite inclusivity, and create an environment where ideas can surface and mature. Just as gravity steadies the orbits of celestial bodies, silence helps maintain equilibrium in collaborative settings, fostering deeper engagement and thoughtful decision-making.

Challenges of Using Silence

The value of silence is often overlooked in fast-paced environments where verbal contributions are emphasized. Leaders may feel pressure to speak frequently to assert authority or provide constant direction, risking the loss of opportunities for reflection and balanced dialogue. Misinterpreting silence as disengagement or uncertainty can further complicate its use.

Additionally, diverse teams with varying communication styles may struggle to embrace silence as a productive pause rather than an awkward void. Leaders must intentionally use silence to encourage reflection without inadvertently creating discomfort or confusion.

Biohacking Silence in Leadership

- **Silence as a Form of Authority and Control:** Silence can project authority and influence when used intentionally. Silence, strategically placed, increases perceptions of power and control in conversations.[6] This stems from silence's ability to disrupt the natural flow of dialogue, creating a moment of anticipation and focus.

- **Encouraging Reflection and Deeper Engagement:** Silence creates space for reflection, enabling individuals to process information and contribute more thoughtfully. In fast-paced discussions, constant verbal exchanges can overwhelm team members, leading to superficial responses. Strategic pauses allow teams to digest complex ideas and arrive at more meaningful contributions.

- **Silence as an Invitation for Inclusivity:** Silence levels the playing field, creating space for voices that might otherwise be overshadowed in fast-moving discussions. This is particularly valuable in diverse teams where communication styles and cultural norms vary. Leaders who hold intentional pauses signal that all contributions are welcome, fostering inclusivity and balanced participation.

- **Preventing Information Overload:** In high-pressure environments, silence helps mitigate information overload, allowing teams to prioritize key issues and make informed decisions. Leaders with gravitas understand that constant verbal exchanges can dilute focus and clarity. By slowing the pace of conversation, silence enables teams to sift through competing priorities and approach decisions with greater precision.

This Behavior in Action

- **Technology Company:** A CEO leading a strategic planning session presents a bold new vision for the company's direction. Rather than seeking immediate feedback, the CEO introduces a moment of silence, giving the team time to reflect. This pause results in a more thoughtful and constructive discussion, ensuring alignment with long-term goals.

- **Law Firm:** During a high-stakes negotiation, a senior partner strategically pauses after presenting a key argument. The opposing counsel, filling the silence, reveals additional information that strengthens the firm's position.

- **Manufacturing Plant:** A plant manager addressing a product failure uses deliberate pauses during a crisis meeting. By allowing engineers to process the situation and offer solutions, the manager ensures a calm and collaborative approach to problem-solving.

Lead with Silence Like Nelson Mandela

Nelson Mandela's leadership during South Africa's transition from apartheid exemplifies the power of silence in fostering meaningful dialogue. In negotiations with allies and adversaries alike, Mandela's deliberate use of silence signaled his authority and encouraged reflection. By pausing after key statements, he invited others to consider their positions more deeply, often diffusing tension and opening the door to compromise.[7]

Mandela's approach demonstrated three key principles of using silence effectively:

1. **Signal Authority:** Strategic pauses emphasized Mandela's presence and command in negotiations.

2. **Encourage Reflection:** His use of silence created space for thoughtful dialogue, leading to more meaningful outcomes.

3. **Foster Inclusivity:** By not dominating discussions, Mandela allowed diverse voices to emerge, strengthening collaboration.

Mandela's example reminds leaders that silence is not the absence of communication but a deliberate act of presence. By integrating silence into their leadership toolkit, leaders can inspire trust, promote inclusivity, and create space for the collective intelligence of their teams to shine.

Behavior Six: Acting with Decorum and Grace

The final behavior of gravitas, acting with decorum and grace, embodies a leader's ability to maintain poise, professionalism, and dignity in every interaction—especially in challenging or emotionally charged situations. Like the harmonious motion of celestial bodies, leaders who demonstrate decorum and grace guide their teams with respect and composure, ensuring collaboration remains constructive and grounded in mutual understanding. This behavior signals inner strength and fosters an inclusive, respectful culture that elevates team morale and trust.

Decorum and grace are not passive traits; they are active demonstrations of leadership maturity. Leaders with gravitas remain composed under pressure, treating others with dignity while modeling the professionalism they expect from their teams. In doing so, they create a stabilizing force that enhances cohesion, trust, and resilience.

Challenges of Acting with Decorum and Grace

Acting with decorum and grace can be particularly challenging in high-pressure or emotionally charged situations. Leaders may feel compelled to react defensively or assert authority, risking the erosion of trust and professionalism. Additionally, maintaining grace under scrutiny requires emotional regulation and self-awareness, which can be difficult when facing criticism, setbacks, or conflict.

Cultural and interpersonal differences can further complicate this behavior. What one person perceives as respectful or dignified may vary across cultural contexts or personal expectations. Leaders must navigate these complexities with intentionality, ensuring their actions are interpreted as inclusive and professional while fostering collaboration.

Biohacking Decorum and Grace

Decorum and grace are active demonstrations of professionalism and dignity, especially in challenging or emotionally charged situations.

Leaders with gravitas embody these qualities to maintain trust, foster collaboration, and inspire respect within their teams. Here's how leaders can biohack their ability to act with decorum and grace:

- **Maintain Poise to Instill Confidence:** Poise under pressure signals steadiness and competence. Leaders with gravitas remain calm and composed even in the face of adversity, providing their teams with a stabilizing presence. Maintaining poise reassures team members that challenges are manageable, preventing panic and fostering trust.

- **Use Emotional Intelligence to Guide Interactions:** Grace in leadership is grounded in emotional intelligence. Leaders who manage their emotions while remaining sensitive to the feelings of others demonstrate care and build stronger relationships. Emotional intelligence allows leaders to approach difficult conversations with empathy, humility, and respect, ensuring interactions remain constructive.

- **Foster a Culture of Respect Through Dignified Leadership:** Leaders with gravitas create environments where respect and professionalism are the norms. Acting with decorum ensures that team members feel valued and safe to express their ideas, even during disagreements. By modeling respect, leaders encourage psychological safety, enabling deeper collaboration and innovation.

- **Resolve Conflicts with Patience and Composure:** Graceful conflict resolution involves listening carefully, acknowledging different perspectives, and guiding conversations toward solutions that respect everyone involved. Leaders with gravitas handle disagreements with patience and tact, ensuring that conflicts strengthen rather than fracture the team. Acting with decorum and grace allows leaders to create an atmosphere of dignity and mutual respect, ensuring collaboration and cohesion even in the most challenging circumstances. By integrating these behaviors into their leadership approach, leaders can inspire trust, maintain professionalism, and cultivate environments where everyone thrives.

This Behavior in Action

- **Technology Company:** A tech CEO faces backlash over a restructuring plan. Rather than reacting defensively, the CEO holds an open forum to address employee concerns. By listening empathetically and responding with grace, the CEO deescalates tensions and fosters a collaborative discussion about the company's direction.

- **Fashion Industry:** A fashion brand leader receives public criticism for a lackluster collection. In an interview, they defend their team's efforts while gracefully accepting feedback, emphasizing the company's adaptability and commitment to innovation.

- **Telecom Sector:** After a major outage, a telecom CEO handles a tense press conference with poise, responding to aggressive questions calmly and reaffirming the company's dedication to customer service. Their professional demeanor restores stakeholder confidence during the crisis.

Lead with Grace Like Fred Rogers

Fred Rogers exemplified how grace can transform leadership. Though his platform was a children's television show, his empathetic and composed demeanor influenced millions. Rogers's approach to addressing complex issues—through active listening, emotional intelligence, and unwavering respect—serves as a model for leaders in any context.[8]

Rogers demonstrated that grace is about treating others with dignity, especially during difficult conversations. Leaders can learn from his example by focusing on three key principles:

1. Listen with empathy and respond with care.

2. Acknowledge mistakes and prioritize humility.

3. Foster an environment of respect and inclusivity.

Fred Rogers reminds us that leadership is not just about driving results but about how we treat others along the way. By acting with decorum and grace, leaders inspire trust, foster collaboration, and create a lasting impact.

Gravitas as the Foundation of Collaborative Success

Ultimately, gravitas is the foundation upon which successful collaboration is built. Leaders who embody gravitas create spaces where diverse ideas converge into innovative solutions, where conflict leads to growth, and where every individual feels valued and respected. By mastering the behaviors of gravitas, leaders not only assert their own presence but create the conditions for collective excellence, allowing their teams to stand out through shared success.

Chapter 8

The Neuroscience of Storytelling

Once upon a time in a bustling tech startup...

All good stories start like that, right?

Once upon a time in a bustling tech startup, Sarah, the CEO, faced a set of daunting challenges. The market had shifted unexpectedly, forcing a detour in the company's scaling strategy. Her team sensed something was off, and uncertainty hung in the air, eroding morale. Traditional communication methods—data reports, strategic plans, motivational speeches—were unlikely to ignite the sense of urgency and purpose needed to move forward. So Sarah gathered her team in the office's breakout area and began to weave a narrative that transcended spreadsheets and PowerPoint slides.

Sarah shared recollections from the company's early days, painting a vivid picture of the passion and ingenuity that fueled their initial successes. She didn't just recount facts; she told a story that connected past triumphs to present challenges, illustrating how their collective efforts could redefine their future. She recalled stories of past setbacks they had overcome together, highlighting resilience, innovation, and collaboration as core elements of their journey. As Sarah spoke, she tapped into her team's emotions and aspirations, reigniting a sense of purpose and determination. It was as if she were using a bellows on barely glowing embers, causing them to flame with excitement once again. Her storytelling wasn't

143

just about sharing memories—it was a strategic act of leadership that galvanized her team with renewed confidence and clarity. And they lived happily ever after.

Sarah's approach demonstrates a fundamental truth about leadership: great leaders don't just communicate; they connect. They understand that storytelling is not just about sharing information—it's about creating an emotional connection, shaping reality, and inspiring action. For leaders, storytelling can serve as a magic time machine. Stories can help us revisit the past, reminding us of shared values and past victories over adversity, offering a sense of continuity and purpose. Stories can also transport us into the future, articulating a compelling vision of what's possible. And not only can stories help us time travel, but they also help us make sense of the here and now, reframing our current context in ways that reveal new choices that lie at our feet.

Whether you're the founder of a startup, a manager in a global company, leading a nonprofit, or any other sort of leader, your ability to tell the right story at the right time can become one of your superpowers.

This chapter delves into the science of storytelling: how stories work on biological and neuroscientific levels and how you can harness this power to enhance the way you lead. We'll explore storytelling as a practice as well, providing practical frameworks and techniques to help you craft narratives that resonate deeply with your audience. You'll learn about classic storytelling structures and discover how to use them to turn your experiences, values, and vision into compelling narratives.

We'll also examine the challenges leaders face when using storytelling as a tool, such as balancing personal vulnerability with professional authority and ensuring that stories remain authentic and aligned with your leadership goals. You'll gain insights into navigating these complexities, avoiding common pitfalls that can undermine your message.

Additionally, we'll explore how storytelling can bridge the gap between the leader inside you—the originator of ideas—and the leader others see. Just as Meyerhold's concept of biomechanics suggests that every action has both an internal intention and an external expression, storytelling is about aligning your inner narrative with the one you present to the world. By mastering this alignment, you can use storytelling to enhance your leadership biodynamics, building trust and inspiring those around you.

As you turn the pages of this chapter, remember that the stories you tell are more than just reflections of the past. They are tools for shaping the future. Your stories can connect, motivate, and lead. Let's explore how you can master the art of storytelling to turn every interaction into an opportunity to bring your leadership to life, ensuring your message not only informs but also inspires and unites.

The Science of Storytelling

Storytelling is more than just an art; it's a science deeply rooted in how our brains process information, form memories, and connect with others. Understanding the neurological, psychological, and emotional mechanisms behind storytelling can help you harness this tool more effectively, enhancing your ability to inspire, persuade, and unite your team. Here's a closer look at why stories have such a powerful impact.

The Neurological Impact of Storytelling

When you tell a story, you're not just communicating words. As a storyteller, you're engaging the brains of others in a unique way that goes beyond typical data processing. Research shows that storytelling activates multiple areas of the brain, including the sensory cortex, which processes smells, sights, and sounds; the motor cortex, which governs movement; and the frontal cortex, responsible for decision-making and empathy.[1] Unlike mere facts, which primarily engage the brain's language processing areas, stories stimulate the whole brain, creating a richer, more immersive experience.

For example, when you describe an experience of running through a forest, the listener's motor cortex is activated as if they were running themselves. This multisensory engagement allows listeners to live the story, not just hear it. It's a process called "neural coupling," where the storyteller's brain syncs with the listener's, creating a shared experience, according to Hasson and colleagues.[2] This connection enhances understanding and retention because the brain naturally stores stories in a way that is easier to recall.

Skilled storytelling also triggers the release of dopamine, a neurotransmitter associated with pleasure and reward. This chemical release not only makes the story more enjoyable but also reinforces memory formation, helping listeners retain key information. This is why stories can be far more memorable than straightforward presentations of data or dry explanations—our brains are hardwired to remember narratives that evoke strong emotions.

The Emotional Power of Narrative

The emotional pull of stories is one of their most powerful aspects. When a story is engaging, it triggers the release of oxytocin, a hormone linked to trust, empathy, and social bonding. Oxytocin is sometimes called the "trust hormone" because it creates a sense of connection between the storyteller and the listener, fostering a deeper bond. This is why stories are so effective in building rapport and trust, both crucial elements of leadership.

Imagine a leader who shares a personal story about overcoming adversity. This narrative doesn't just inform; it moves the audience emotionally, making them more likely to trust and connect with the leader on a deeper level. When former Apple CEO Steve Jobs told the story of being fired from Apple only to return and lead it to success, he wasn't just recounting his career ups and downs—he was building an emotional bridge with his audience, demonstrating resilience, humility, and vision.[3]

Stories that create emotional resonance are more likely to motivate action than stories that don't. When people hear emotionally charged stories, their brains release higher levels of oxytocin, which not only boosts feelings of empathy but also increases the likelihood that they will engage in prosocial behaviors, such as cooperation, trust, and generosity.[4] Leaders who can tap into this emotional power can inspire their teams to go beyond what they thought was possible.

Memory Retention and Storytelling

One of the reasons storytelling is such an effective communication tool is its impact on memory retention. Stories stick with us because they engage our brains in a way that traditional facts and figures simply don't. While we might forget a list of data points, we are far more likely to remember the narrative in which those data points are embedded. This is because stories activate parts of the brain associated with sensory experiences, making the information feel more real and tangible.[5]

Memory retention is particularly important for those who need to convey complex ideas or reinforce key messages. When you use storytelling effectively, you ensure that your audience remembers the core message long after your interaction with them is over. To maximize the retention impact, you can use vivid imagery, emotional contrasts, and sensory details within your stories. Here is a simple example. Instead of saying, "We need to cut costs," you might tell a story about how a small, thoughtful change helped a previous team achieve significant savings without sacrificing quality, painting a clear picture of what's possible.

Stories are 22 times more likely to be remembered than facts alone.[6] This underscores the importance of incorporating storytelling into leadership communication, particularly when the goal is to reinforce a message or motivate action over time.

Storytelling and Influence: Persuasion Science

Stories are not just memorable; they are also powerful tools of persuasion. Robert Cialdini, a leading expert on the psychology of influence, highlights storytelling as a critical mechanism for creating social proof and authority—two key principles of influence. A well-told story can serve as a powerful example that validates a leader's message and demonstrates credibility.[7]

One concept that explains the persuasive power of storytelling is "narrative transportation," where the listener becomes so engrossed in the story that they feel they are part of it. When this happens, the listener is more open to the messages embedded within the narrative, making them more likely to adopt new beliefs or take desired actions. This means that storytelling can be a highly effective tool for influencing attitudes, aligning teams, and driving change.[8]

In times of organizational change, a leader might use storytelling to address resistance by embedding the change narrative within a story of past successes or industry transformations. This technique not only makes the concept of change more relatable but also lowers psychological barriers because the audience feels guided rather than pushed toward a new perspective.

Real-World Applications: The Storytelling Advantage

The storytelling advantage is clear across various real-world scenarios. In business, leaders use storytelling to pitch ideas, align teams, and inspire action. During a crisis, storytelling can provide a narrative that helps employees make sense of uncertainty, boosting resilience and focus. In strategic planning, stories about past achievements can serve as a reminder of what's possible, reinforcing a shared sense of purpose.

Research consistently supports the idea that storytelling enhances leadership effectiveness. A study published in the *Harvard Business Review* by Gill found that executives who used storytelling were perceived as more authentic and credible than those who relied solely on data and directives. This perception translated into stronger team engagement and better organizational outcomes, reinforcing the value of storytelling as a key leadership skill.[9]

By understanding the science behind storytelling, you can leverage its power to create compelling narratives that resonate, persuade, and inspire. Whether it's motivating a team during a challenging project, aligning stakeholders around a new strategy, or simply building a stronger connection with your audience, storytelling gives you a distinct edge. In the next section, we'll explore how you can align the storyteller within you—the originator of ideas—with the storyteller others see, ensuring that your message not only informs but also inspires and unites.

Aligning the Storyteller Inside with the Storyteller Others See

Storytelling often begins within the mind of the storyteller—a vivid internal narrative that captures emotions, intentions, and visions of possibility. However, the challenge lies in effectively externalizing these inner stories to connect with and inspire others. This gap between the story we hold inside and the one we share outwardly can be difficult to navigate, particularly for leaders whose influence depends on their ability to communicate compellingly. This section delves into how you can better align your internal storyteller with the storyteller others see and experience, ensuring your narratives resonate powerfully in the real world.

The Internal Narrative versus External Expression

Inside your head, the stories you create are rich with meaning, detail, and intention. These internal narratives are shaped by your experiences, values, and aspirations, forming a detailed tapestry that guides your thoughts and actions. Translating these stories into words that capture their full complexity, however, can be surprisingly difficult. We often find ourselves grappling with how to convey the emotions, nuances, and intentions of our inner narrative in a way that resonates with others.

This disconnect between internal intention and external expression is common for most of us. You might know exactly what you want to convey, a message of resilience during a time of change, for instance. Maybe a call to action that inspires bold innovation. But when it comes time to share that story, it falls flat or misses the mark. This gap can leave your listeners unengaged or even misaligned with your intended message. It's a disconnect between the leader inside you, the originator of ideas, and the leader others see and experience.

149

The Neuroscience of Storytelling

Meyerhold's biomechanics idea speaks directly to this challenge. Meyerhold emphasized the importance of aligning the actor's internal intentions with their external expressions. As a leader, this concept is equally relevant: The stories you tell must reflect the full depth of your inner narrative to resonate authentically. This alignment requires a conscious effort to ensure your words, tone, and body language are in sync with the story you intend to tell, creating a seamless connection between your inner self and how others perceive you.[10]

Verbing: Clarifying Intention and Action

One powerful technique to help bridge this gap is "verbing," another concept borrowed from the world of theater. In acting, verbing involves assigning a specific action verb to lines of dialogue, clarifying the intention behind each line. Rather than simply delivering words, the actor knows they are "provoking," "reassuring," or "challenging" with each phrase. This intentionality sharpens the performance, bringing the character's motivations to life.[11] For a leader, verbing can be equally transformative, serving as a tool to clarify the purpose behind your storytelling and ensure it aligns with your goals.

Applying verbing in leadership means consciously choosing the verb that best captures what you are trying to achieve in a given interaction. Imagine you are sharing a story to "motivate," "warn," "celebrate," or "educate." This choice of verb shapes the entire narrative and helps you stay focused on your intention, ensuring that your internal motivation aligns with your external delivery.

Think back to the story of Sarah, the CEO who faced daunting challenges in her tech startup. Sarah knew she needed more than just data to steer her team through uncertain times—she needed to reconnect them with their shared purpose and reignite their drive. As Sarah prepared to speak, she might have chosen her verbs carefully, aligning her internal intention with the impact she hoped to achieve.

Sarah might have begun her narrative with the verb "reassure," aiming to calm the anxiety that had been building within her team:

"I want to take us back to where we started [reassure], to those early days when our vision was clear, and our determination was unbreakable. I remember when we faced that first market hurdle, and how we tackled it head-on [reflect]. We knew then, as we do now, that challenges are part of the journey."

Sarah's initial verb was "reassure," but as she continued, she might have shifted to "inspire" and "energize":

"This isn't the first time we've faced adversity. And it won't be the last. But every time, we've come out stronger. I see the same talent, the same grit, the same fire in this room that we had on day one [inspire]. This shift in strategy isn't a setback—it's a chance to redefine our path forward [energize]. We're not just reacting; we're leading. We're not just adjusting; we're innovating."

Finally, Sarah could have anchored her story with the verb "unite," bringing her team together with a clear call to action:

"Let's embrace this new direction together [unite], just as we've done before. I believe in this team. Let's turn this challenge into our next big success [rally]."

Sarah's careful choice of verbs—reassure, inspire, energize, unite—helped her to structure her message intentionally, aligning her inner confidence and conviction with the words she delivered. Each verb guided how she expressed herself, ensuring that her internal story of resilience and hope translated effectively to her team.

Before engaging in storytelling, consider Sarah's example. Take a moment to reflect on your objective. Ask yourself, "What am I trying to do here?" Identifying a clear verb can transform your approach. Are you aiming to "reassure" your team during a period of uncertainty? Then your story might highlight overcoming past challenges with a calm, confident tone. Are you seeking to "challenge" your team to reach new heights? Then your story might evoke a call to action with a sense of urgency and determination.[12]

For instance, consider a leader preparing to deliver a presentation on an upcoming organizational change. If the leader's internal intention is to "align" the team with the new strategy, the external story needs to reflect this clearly. The leader might choose to share a narrative about a previous time the team successfully adapted to change, drawing a parallel between past resilience and current opportunities. The verb "align" guides every element of the story—from its content to its delivery style—ensuring that the leader's internal narrative matches what the team experiences externally.

Meyerhold's Concept of Aligning the Internal and External Selves

As you'll recall, Meyerhold emphasized the alignment of an actor's internal motivations with their external physical expressions. He believed that the body's movements should reflect the character's internal state, creating a cohesive and compelling performance. This concept is highly relevant to leadership storytelling because it highlights the importance of synchronizing your internal narrative with your outward expression.

For Meyerhold, every action had to be intentional and purposeful, rooted in the actor's understanding of their character's inner world. This same principle applies when you, as a leader, step into the role of storyteller. Your ability to align what you feel and believe with what you convey ensures that your message is authentic and impactful. Misalignment—where your inner conviction doesn't match your delivery—can lead to disconnects that weaken your presence and undermine your influence.

Consider the scenario of a leader who internally feels deeply committed to a new strategic direction but delivers their message hesitantly or without conviction. The misalignment between the leader's internal commitment and external expression can create doubt and hesitation among team members. Conversely, when your internal storyteller is

152

Biohacking Leadership

fully aligned with the external, your stories carry the weight of authenticity and intention, resonating deeply with your audience.

You can achieve this alignment through conscious practice and reflection. Before sharing a story, take the time to connect with your internal narrative. What are the key emotions, values, and intentions driving your story? How do these elements manifest in your choice of words, tone, and body language? By consciously aligning these aspects, you ensure that your storytelling doesn't just inform but truly inspires.[13]

Overcoming the Challenges of Alignment

Aligning the storyteller inside with the storyteller others see and experience is not without challenges. It requires you to be mindful of how your internal state translates externally, paying attention not just to what you say but to how you say it. It's about bridging the gap between the leader you feel you are and the leader that others perceive.

One common pitfall is allowing external pressures, like the fear of judgment or the desire to be liked, to distort your storytelling. Leaders may be tempted to water down your narratives, avoid vulnerability, or shy away from expressing your true intentions, leading to stories that feel disingenuous or hollow. To counter this, embrace the technique of verbing and Meyerhold's principles as a guide, centering each story around a clear, authentic purpose.

Ultimately, aligning the storyteller inside with the one others see involves both self-awareness and intentional action. It's about closing the gap between your inner narrative and your external expression, ensuring that the stories you share are as rich, purposeful, and engaging as the ones you hold inside.

As we move into the next section, we'll explore specific techniques that can help you master this alignment, refining your storytelling to maximize its impact. You'll learn how to craft stories that resonate not only because of their content but because of the clear intention behind them. By aligning your internal storyteller with your external presence, you'll elevate your leadership narrative to new heights, ensuring that the stories you tell serve as powerful tools for connection, influence, and inspiration.

153

The Neuroscience of Storytelling

Narrative Structures: Crafting Stories that Move

Narrative structures are the frameworks that shape how we tell stories. Understanding these structures is crucial because the right framework can amplify your message, making it more engaging, memorable, and persuasive. Whether you're motivating a team, managing change, or inspiring innovation, having a few go-to storytelling frameworks can help you construct narratives that resonate deeply with your audience. This section explores some of the most effective narrative structures, including "The Hero's Journey" and Kurt Vonnegut's story shapes, and provides practical frameworks like ABT (And, But, Therefore) and FSA (Fact, Story, Ask) that leaders can use to craft compelling stories.

The Hero's Journey

One of the most well-known and widely used storytelling frameworks is "The Hero's Journey," popularized by Joseph Campbell in his work *The Hero with a Thousand Faces*.[14] This narrative arc follows a protagonist (the hero) as they embark on an adventure, face a crisis, overcome challenges, and ultimately return transformed. The Hero's Journey is powerful in leadership storytelling because it mirrors the challenges and transformations inherent in organizational and collective growth. However, for a leader, it's rarely effective to cast yourself as the hero. Instead, point to others—your team, your organization, your customers, or even your product—as the hero of the narrative. This approach not only elevates those around you but also positions you as the guide, mentor, or catalyst that supports the journey.

The journey typically begins with the "Call to Adventure," representing a problem or opportunity that necessitates action. This phase is followed by challenges and trials, where the hero encounters obstacles. The final stages—overcoming the crisis and returning transformed—highlight resilience, learning, and growth. Again, as a leader, you should rarely make yourself the central figure in this

154

Biohacking Leadership

journey. Instead, your role is to facilitate and shine a spotlight on the hero's transformative experience.

For example, imagine you're leading a team through a difficult project. Rather than positioning yourself as the hero who led the team to success, use the Hero's Journey to highlight your team as the protagonists. Start with the challenge they faced—the "Call to Adventure"—like an unexpected market shift or a demanding client request. Describe the obstacles they encountered along the way, such as tight deadlines, technical issues, or resource constraints. By emphasizing the skills, perseverance, and collaboration of your team, you frame them as the heroes of the story who ultimately overcame these trials. This approach not only makes your team feel valued but also reinforces the idea that their collective efforts are what drive success.

Another way to apply the Hero's Journey in leadership is by positioning your organization or product as the hero. If your company is undergoing a major transformation, you might tell the story of how the organization started in its "ordinary world" before the disruptive market forces or internal challenges—the "Call to Action"—required a strategic pivot. Highlight the "road of trials" your company faced, such as market resistance, financial pressures, or technological hurdles, and celebrate how the collective resolve and innovative thinking of your employees steered the company through. This narrative not only honors the hard work of your people but also aligns the company's story with the values and vision that propel it forward.

When storytelling about product development, you can make the product itself the hero. Tell the story of the problem the product set out to solve, the setbacks encountered during design or testing, and how the team's ingenuity led to a breakthrough. This positions the product not just as a solution but as a transformative force that overcame its own journey from concept to reality.

Positioning others as the hero in your storytelling achieves two critical outcomes: it boosts morale by recognizing contributions, and it builds trust by showing that you, as a leader, are committed to elevating those around you rather than claiming the spotlight. This approach also aligns with the servant leadership model, where the leader's primary

155

The Neuroscience of Storytelling

role is to support and empower their people, creating an environment where everyone feels capable of heroics, according to Greenleaf.[15]

The Hero's Journey is more than just a template for storytelling. It is a powerful way to shape narratives that inspire, validate, and motivate. By pointing to others as the hero—your team, your organization, or even your product—you create stories that celebrate collective effort and resilience. You establish your role as the guide or mentor, reinforcing your leadership presence without overshadowing those you lead. Use the Hero's Journey to craft narratives that resonate deeply, turning every challenge into an opportunity for collective triumph and shared success.

The Story Shapes

Kurt Vonnegut, known for his unconventional storytelling, famously mapped out the "shapes" of stories, illustrating how the protagonist's fortunes rise and fall over time. These shapes include "Man in Hole" (a character gets into trouble and gets out of it), "Boy Meets Girl" (two entities meet, face conflict, and reconcile), and "From Bad to Worse" (a series of unfortunate events). These structures are more than literary curiosities; they provide leaders with a way to align the emotional journey of a narrative with the message they want to convey.

For example, the "Man in Hole" shape can be used when sharing a story about overcoming adversity. It's a simple yet effective arc where a person (or organization) faces a problem, tackles it, and emerges stronger. This shape can resonate when motivating teams who are struggling because it emphasizes that difficulties are temporary and surmountable.[16]

Alternatively, the "Boy Meets Girl" shape could be applied to stories of partnership, collaboration, or merger. It highlights the initial meeting, the conflict or disagreement, and ultimately the reconciliation or alignment of goals. Leaders can use this shape to discuss how diverse teams came together to tackle a major challenge or how an organization forged a successful partnership after overcoming early differences.

The "From Bad to Worse" shape might be useful when preparing a team for a tough road ahead. While it may seem counterintuitive, sharing a narrative that acknowledges worsening circumstances can create a sense of solidarity and realism, preparing your team mentally and emotionally for the challenges to come. Leaders who acknowledge the "bad to worse" narrative demonstrate empathy and transparency, which can build trust, even when delivering difficult messages.[17]

Practical Frameworks

While classic narrative structures provide the overall arc of a story, practical frameworks like ABT (And, But, Therefore) and FSA (Fact, Story, Ask) offer simple, repeatable structures that leaders can use to construct compelling narratives quickly and effectively.[18]

The ABT framework, popularized by scientist and storyteller Randy Olson, is a simple but powerful structure that distills any message into three parts:

- **And:** Establish the context and current state.
- **But:** Introduce the problem or conflict that disrupts the status quo.
- **Therefore:** Present the solution or action that addresses the problem.

The ABT structure is effective because it mirrors how our brains naturally process stories—through setup, conflict, and resolution. This pattern creates a clear, logical flow that makes it easy for listeners to follow and engage with the narrative.

For instance, if Sarah, our earlier CEO, were using ABT to communicate a strategic pivot to her team, her story might sound like this:

> "We've been growing rapidly and expanding our market share [And], but the recent market shift has disrupted our scaling strategy [But]. Therefore, we need to adjust our approach and focus on this new opportunity to stay ahead of the competition [Therefore]."

157

The Neuroscience of Storytelling

This framework clearly outlines the situation, the challenge, and the necessary action, making it easy for the team to understand the rationale behind the pivot.

Another useful framework is "Fact, Story, Ask." This structure is particularly effective when you need to persuade or rally your audience around a specific action.[19] Here's how it works:

- **Fact:** Start with a compelling fact or data point that sets the stage.

- **Story:** Transition into a story that humanizes or contextualizes the fact.

- **Ask:** End with a clear call to action or request from your audience.

For example, imagine a leader aiming to inspire a team to improve customer service. They might begin with the fact that customer satisfaction scores have dipped. Then they share a story about a specific customer who had a poor experience and how that impacted their perception of the brand. Finally, the leader makes an ask: "Let's all commit to one small act of exceptional service this week to turn this around."

This framework turns data into a narrative, making it more relatable and actionable for the audience. By embedding the ask within a story, you're not just delivering information—you're creating a sense of urgency and purpose.

Using Narrative Structures

Narrative structures are versatile tools you can adapt to various contexts, from motivating teams to managing change. When crafting a narrative for change management, for instance, you might use the Hero's Journey to frame the organization's strategic shift as a transformative quest, positioning the team as co-heroes in the process. Similarly, Vonnegut's story shapes can help leaders navigate the emotional landscape of difficult conversations, acknowledging the highs and lows of the journey in a way that resonates.

In motivational settings, frameworks like ABT and FSA provide a streamlined approach to crafting stories that inspire action. Whether you're speaking at a team meeting, presenting to stakeholders, or addressing your organization in a time of crisis, these structures offer a clear pathway for creating narratives that move people emotionally and intellectually, according to Denning.[20]

By mastering these storytelling frameworks, you can transform your communication from transactional to transformational, making every message an opportunity to connect, persuade, and lead. The right narrative structure not only helps you tell a better story but also ensures that your message aligns with your leadership goals, amplifying your impact and effectiveness.

As you explore different narrative structures like the Hero's Journey and others, remember that the story you choose and how you tell it can elevate those around you, inspire action, and align your team with a shared vision. Crafting stories with intention allows you to position others as the heroes of your narrative, building trust, motivating your team, and creating a sense of collective ownership in the journey ahead.

Now that we've explored how to construct compelling stories, it's time to delve deeper into the practical side of storytelling: bringing your narratives to life in everyday leadership situations. In the next section, we'll look at how leaders can use storytelling to lead through change, inspire teams, and create a culture of shared success.

Leading Through Stories

For a leader, becoming a master storyteller will help you go far beyond merely sharing information. It can become a strategic skill that can shape perceptions, drive action, and build a sense of shared purpose. The key to leading through stories lies in choosing the right story for the right moment—one that aligns with your message, audience, and leadership objectives. A well-told story can inspire a team, navigate complex change, or reinforce values in a way that data or directives cannot. In this section, we explore how to harness the strategic power of storytelling, the importance of authenticity and vulnerability, and essential dos and don'ts to ensure your storytelling remains effective, ethical, and impactful.

The Strategic Use of Storytelling in Leadership

Effective leaders use storytelling strategically, selecting stories that resonate with the audience and the specific leadership challenge at hand. For example, when leading through change, a story about past transformations or overcoming adversity can provide reassurance and a roadmap for navigating uncertainty.[21] In moments when you need to inspire, stories that highlight success, innovation, or resilience can ignite the drive and commitment within your team. The strategic choice of story is about knowing what your audience needs to hear at that particular moment.

Think of a leader at a nonprofit organization faced with a sudden funding crisis. Instead of focusing solely on the data and budget cuts, the leader might share a story about the organization's founding—its original mission, the impact it has made, and the resilience it has shown in the past. This narrative not only provides context but also rekindles the passion and commitment that brought everyone together in the first place. By tapping into the collective memory and values of the organization, the leader creates a sense of continuity and purpose that motivates the team to persevere.

In a corporate setting, a CEO looking to shift company culture might tell the story of a competitor who successfully transformed by embracing new values. By framing the story as a lesson rather than a directive, the leader allows the team to draw their own conclusions and internalize the need for change. This approach is far more effective than simply outlining new cultural expectations; it invites the team to see themselves as part of the unfolding narrative.

The art of storytelling is knowing when to deploy these narratives and which stories will resonate most deeply. Whether you are trying to influence behavior, encourage innovation, or build resilience, the story you choose and how you tell it can make all the difference.

Leaving a Tip on the Table

Authenticity and vulnerability are key elements of powerful storytelling. In his memoir, *Still Foolin' 'Em*, comedian Billy Crystal reflects on the concept of "leaving a tip on the table," which he describes as the willingness to give a little more of yourself in every performance. For Crystal, this means showing the audience not just the polished jokes but also the personal moments—the struggles, the doubts, and the humanity that connects him with his audience.[22] In leadership, this principle translates into sharing stories that are honest, personal, and sometimes vulnerable.

Authenticity in storytelling doesn't mean sharing every detail of your life or airing personal struggles that may undermine your leadership. It's about finding the balance between professionalism and humanity, allowing others to see that you, too, have faced challenges, made mistakes, and learned along the way. Vulnerability, when used thoughtfully, builds trust and deepens connections. It signals that you are not just a distant authority figure but a leader who understands and shares in the experiences of those you lead.[23] Remember, you should not usually make yourself the hero of your story, but, like Crystal, offer a little piece of you, when appropriate.

Consider a leader managing a team through a tough project. Instead of presenting as if they have all the answers, they might share a personal story about a time they faced a similar challenge, how they felt, and what they learned from it. This type of storytelling fosters a culture of openness and resilience, where team members feel safe to take risks, admit mistakes, and grow.[24]

Vulnerability, however, should be approached with care. It's important to ensure that your stories are purposeful and aligned with the message you want to convey. Authenticity doesn't mean oversharing or shifting the focus onto yourself at the expense of your audience's needs. It's about creating a genuine connection that enhances your message and reinforces your leadership presence.

Storytelling Dos and Don'ts: Navigating Ethics and Avoiding Manipulation

While storytelling is a powerful tool, it also comes with responsibilities. The stories you tell, especially as a leader, have the power to influence, inspire, and sometimes manipulate. Navigating this fine line is crucial to maintaining trust and credibility.

- **Do: Choose Stories with Intention:** Always select stories that serve a clear purpose. Ask yourself: What am I trying to achieve? How does this story align with my leadership message? Avoid stories that are self-serving or that may come across as boasting. The goal is to use stories to connect, not to create distance.

- **Don't: Manipulate Emotions Unethically:** Stories can be deeply emotional, and leaders must be careful not to use them to manipulate or coerce. For instance, overly dramatizing a narrative to provoke fear or guilt can backfire, damaging trust and credibility. Use emotion honestly and ensure that your stories uplift and engage rather than manipulate or deceive.[25]

- **Do: Respect Privacy and Boundaries:** When telling stories involving others, be mindful of their privacy and boundaries. This is especially important when sharing stories from your team or organization. Seek permission when appropriate and avoid sharing sensitive information that could harm or embarrass others.

- **Don't: Overuse Vulnerability:** While vulnerability is powerful, it should not be the centerpiece of every story. Overusing vulnerability can make it seem insincere or self-indulgent. Balance personal stories with narratives that also highlight the achievements, strengths, and values of your team or organization.[26]

- **Do: Keep It Real:** Authentic stories are relatable and impactful. Stick to narratives grounded in reality and avoid embellishments that could undermine your credibility if exposed. Your audience is more likely to connect with a story that feels real and honest, even if it's imperfect.

- **Don't: Rely Solely on Stories:** While storytelling is a valuable tool, it shouldn't replace data, analysis, or strategic thinking. Use stories as a complement to other forms of communication, ensuring that your messages are well-rounded and substantiated.

- **Do: Make Your Stories Inclusive:** Craft stories that reflect the diversity of your audience and consider different perspectives.

Stories that are inclusive and resonate across different backgrounds will have a broader and more meaningful impact.

In navigating the complexities of storytelling, leaders must maintain a balance between being compelling and being ethical. By choosing stories with intention, remaining authentic, and respecting the power of narrative, you can lead through stories in a way that inspires trust, motivates action, and fosters a deeper sense of connection within your team.

Challenges of Storytelling in Leadership

While storytelling is a powerful leadership tool, it is not without its challenges. The art of crafting and delivering a story that resonates requires careful consideration, and even the most seasoned leaders can fall into common pitfalls. Missteps in storytelling can undermine credibility, cause misunderstandings, or, worse, alienate your audience. In this section, we'll explore some of these challenges and provide strategies for overcoming them to maintain the integrity and impact of your narrative.

Overembellishment: Balancing Truth and Engagement

One of the most common pitfalls in storytelling is the temptation to embellish details to make a story more compelling. While it might seem harmless to amplify certain aspects of a narrative for dramatic effect, over-embellishment can erode trust if discovered. Leaders who stretch the truth risk losing credibility because audiences today are highly attuned to authenticity. Research shows that audiences can detect when a story feels inauthentic or exaggerated, which can lead to skepticism and a breakdown in trust.[27]

To maintain credibility, it's essential to ground your stories in truth. Instead of embellishing, focus on finding the real, compelling moments that can stand on their own. Authenticity is more persuasive than dramatization because it allows your audience to connect with you on a human level. When crafting a story, ask yourself: Are

163

The Neuroscience of Storytelling

these details accurate? Am I presenting this experience honestly? By staying true to the essence of your experiences, you ensure your stories resonate genuinely with your audience.

Relevance: Ensuring the Story Fits the Context

Another challenge leaders face is ensuring their stories are relevant to the current context. A well-told story can quickly lose its impact if it feels disconnected from the audience's needs, the organizational culture, or the moment at hand. Irrelevant stories can appear self-indulgent, causing your audience to tune out or question your message's intent.

To avoid this, always align your stories with the current situation, the values of your organization, and the emotional state of your audience. Consider your purpose: Are you trying to motivate your team during a challenging project? Are you addressing change resistance? The right story will resonate because it speaks directly to the circumstances your audience is experiencing. Before telling a story, test its relevance by asking: Does this address the needs of my listeners? Does it reinforce the message I am trying to convey?

Cultural Insensitivity: Navigating Diverse Perspectives

In today's diverse work environment, cultural insensitivity in storytelling can create unintended barriers and misunderstandings. Stories that draw on culturally specific references, humor, or values might resonate strongly with some but alienate others. Leaders must be mindful of the diverse cultural backgrounds within their teams and ensure their narratives do not inadvertently exclude or offend.

Culturally attuned storytelling—where the storyteller considers the diverse backgrounds of their audience—can enhance engagement and team cohesion. When preparing to tell a story, consider the cultural context of your audience. Ask yourself: Does my story reflect inclusive values? Could it be misinterpreted due to cultural differences? Seek feedback from diverse perspectives to refine your story, ensuring it resonates across your team.

Strategies for Overcoming Storytelling Challenges

Navigating these challenges requires awareness and adaptability. Here are some strategies to ensure your storytelling remains effective and credible:

- **Stick to the Truth:** Ground your stories in real events and facts. If you need to add elements for clarity, ensure they do not distort the truth or mislead your audience. Trust is built on authenticity, and the power of your story lies in its reality.

- **Tailor Your Story to the Context:** Before sharing a story, take a moment to assess the situation and your audience. What are their current challenges? How can your story address their needs? Tailoring your narrative ensures it resonates and reinforces your message.

- **Embrace Simplicity:** Avoid overcomplicating your story with unnecessary details. Simplicity often enhances clarity and impact. Focus on the core message and let the narrative flow naturally. Simpler stories are more memorable and persuasive.[28]

- **Seek Feedback:** Don't hesitate to test your story on a trusted colleague or advisor. Their feedback can help you identify potential pitfalls, like cultural insensitivity or lack of relevance, allowing you to refine your narrative before presenting it to a broader audience.

- **Be Mindful of Language and Tone:** Pay attention to the language and tone you use, ensuring it's inclusive and respectful of your audience's diversity. Avoid jargon or colloquialisms that might not translate well across different cultures or contexts.

By staying aware of these common challenges and applying these strategies, you can refine your storytelling approach to maintain credibility, connect authentically, and inspire action. Remember, storytelling is not just about the narrative itself but also about the connection it fosters between you and your audience. As you develop your storytelling skills, you'll find that the right story, told in the right way, can be a transformative tool in your leadership arsenal.

As you refine your storytelling skills, remember that each story told thoughtfully can strengthen the bonds within your team, align them with your vision, and inspire them to take meaningful action. In the next section, we'll explore how effective storytelling not only influences individual perceptions but also impacts team dynamics. We'll look at real-world examples of leaders who have used storytelling to drive change, build trust, and enhance team performance, illustrating the profound impact that stories can have on collective success.

The Impact of Storytelling on Teams

Storytelling is not just a tool for individual influence; its power extends to the entire team, shaping culture, driving engagement, and fostering resilience. Effective storytelling can be a catalyst for team cohesion, motivation, and performance, providing a shared narrative that aligns everyone around common goals and values. This section delves into how storytelling influences team dynamics and offers examples of leaders who have used storytelling to transform their teams.

Enhancing Team Cohesion

One of the most significant impacts of storytelling is its ability to enhance team cohesion. Stories create a shared experience, allowing team members to see themselves as part of a collective journey. When leaders tell stories that reflect the team's shared challenges, values, and triumphs, they create a sense of belonging and unity. Storytelling fosters a sense of group identity, which is crucial for building a cohesive and motivated team.[29]

Consider a leader who tells the story of a past project where the team faced adversity but ultimately succeeded through collaboration and perseverance. This narrative not only reminds the team of their capability but also reinforces the idea that they are stronger together.

By celebrating collective wins and learning from shared setbacks, storytelling helps teams build a resilient, unified identity that can withstand future challenges.

Motivating Teams Through Shared Vision

Stories are also powerful motivators. A well-told story can energize a team, aligning their efforts toward a shared vision. Leaders who articulate a compelling future narrative can inspire their teams to go beyond the status quo, tapping into their intrinsic motivation. This is particularly effective in times of change or uncertainty, where a clear and inspiring narrative can provide direction and hope.

Consider Ratan Tata, former chairman of Tata Group, who used storytelling to inspire a shared vision during challenging times in India's automotive sector. When Tata Motors launched the Nano, the world's cheapest car, it wasn't just a business decision—it was part of a larger narrative about making safe, affordable transportation accessible to millions of Indians. Tata's storytelling wasn't just about a new product; it was about a broader social mission that connected deeply with both employees and customers. His narrative galvanized Tata Motors' workforce around a vision of innovation with purpose, motivating the team to embrace challenges and push boundaries in the automotive industry.[30]

Building Resilience and Trust

Storytelling also plays a crucial role in building resilience and trust within teams. When leaders share stories of their own vulnerabilities, setbacks, and recoveries, they model resilience, demonstrating that failure is not the end but a step in the journey. This transparency builds trust because team members see their leader as approachable and human, not infallible.

One powerful example comes from Ngozi Okonjo-Iweala, director-general of the World Trade Organization and former finance minister of Nigeria. Okonjo-Iweala often shares stories of the challenges she faced in combating corruption and navigating political

167

The Neuroscience of Storytelling

opposition in Nigeria. By openly discussing her setbacks, including threats to her personal safety, she highlighted her perseverance and commitment to public service. Her storytelling reinforced resilience not just in her own leadership but also in her teams, showing them that obstacles are part of the journey and that determination can lead to transformative outcomes.[31]

Driving Change and Innovation

In times of transformation, storytelling can be a powerful tool for driving change and sparking innovation. Leaders who can frame change as part of a larger narrative—one that connects the past, present, and future—can help their teams make sense of new directions and embrace the unknown. Stories make abstract concepts tangible, helping teams visualize what's possible and how their contributions fit into the bigger picture.

A striking example of this is Carlos Ghosn, the former CEO of Nissan and Renault, who used storytelling to drive change during Nissan's financial crisis in the early 2000s. Ghosn crafted a compelling narrative around Nissan's need for cultural transformation, moving away from traditional hierarchies to embrace a more agile, results-driven mindset. By framing the company's turnaround as a collective journey and consistently sharing stories of early successes, he motivated employees to buy into the changes and work collaboratively toward the company's revival. This strategic storytelling helped transform Nissan from near bankruptcy into one of the world's most profitable car companies at the time.[32]

Real-World Examples of Leadership Storytelling Impact

Storytelling has been a pivotal tool for leaders across various sectors, helping to drive change and build cohesive, motivated teams. One compelling example is Lee Kuan Yew, Singapore's founding prime minister, who used storytelling to unite a young, diverse nation. Lee often recounted stories of Singapore's early struggles, from poverty and racial tensions to limited natural resources. By framing Singapore's rapid development as a story of resilience, hard work, and strategic vision, Lee fostered a strong national identity and inspired his people to embrace transformation.[33]

Another compelling example is Ellen Johnson Sirleaf, the former president of Liberia and Africa's first elected female head of state. Sirleaf often told stories of Liberia's civil war, her time in exile, and the challenges of rebuilding a nation scarred by conflict. Her storytelling was deeply personal and resonated with the Liberian people because she drew on themes of forgiveness, hope, and collective action. By sharing these narratives, Sirleaf built trust and inspired her nation to work together toward a peaceful future.[34]

Becoming a Storytelling Biohacker

To biohack storytelling, you'll need to recognize that storytelling is as much science as it is art. You'll need to become a storytelling biohacker. This means you should continuously experiment with your narratives, observing their impact, and refining your approach based on what you learn. Just as a scientist tests hypotheses, you can test stories to see how they resonate, influence decision-making, and foster connections.

- **Experiment, Observe, Adapt**
  - Think of each story you tell as an experiment in influence and connection. Test different narrative structures, tones, and levels of vulnerability to see what lands most effectively. For instance, did your story engage your audience emotionally? Did it clarify your message or create confusion? Treat these outcomes as valuable data, approaching them with curiosity, not judgment.
  - Once you've shared your story, observe its impact. Pay attention to your audience's reactions—their body language, facial expressions, and level of engagement. Are they leaning in, showing signs of emotional resonance, or are they disengaged? These subtle cues are your data points, guiding you

toward more impactful storytelling techniques. Reflect on when your story moved the room and when it fell flat, using these insights to refine your storytelling craft.

o Finally, adapt your approach based on the feedback you gather. A storytelling biohacker is not rigid; they tweak narratives to fit the moment. This might mean adjusting the length of a story, focusing on a different character, or even dropping a narrative that no longer serves its purpose. Your goal isn't to deliver a perfect story but to create one that best connects with and inspires your audience at any given time.

- **Align Intent with Execution**

o To be effective, storytelling requires alignment between your internal intentions and your external delivery. This is where techniques like "verbing" and "physicality of intent" come into play. Before you tell a story, ask yourself: What am I trying to achieve? Are you aiming to reassure, motivate, challenge, or educate? The verb you choose shapes not only your narrative but also your delivery. It aligns your internal mindset with the external expression of your story, making your message more coherent and impactful.

o Beyond verbal intention, consider your body language, tone, and overall physical presence. Are your gestures open and engaging? Is your tone aligned with the emotional core of your story? This alignment ensures that your audience not only hears your message but also feels it. Physicalizing your intent means that your body language, facial expressions, and voice all work together to reinforce the story you're telling, enhancing the emotional and cognitive impact on your audience.

- **Foster a Culture of Storytelling and Continuous Learning**
o Becoming a storytelling biohacker also involves encouraging a culture of storytelling within your team. Create opportunities for your team members to share their narratives, whether celebrating successes, navigating challenges, or sharing personal experiences. This collective storytelling builds a

170

Biohacking Leadership

shared narrative, strengthens team cohesion, and cultivates a culture where everyone feels heard.

o Commit to ongoing learning and refinement of your storytelling skills. Stay curious about new storytelling techniques, evolving cultural contexts, and the latest insights into narrative science. By reading widely, engaging with other storytellers, and seeking feedback, you ensure your storytelling remains fresh, relevant, and engaging. This continuous learning mindset helps you grow as a leader and keeps your storytelling dynamic and effective.

The Storytelling Biohacker in Action

By embracing the mindset of a storytelling biohacker, you evolve beyond simply telling stories to strategically shaping your team's narrative. Use storytelling as a tool to connect, motivate, and lead with impact. As you transition to the next chapter on the neuroscience of conversation, consider how these principles apply to dialogue. Conversations, like stories, are collaborative narratives that shape the collective experience. By mastering both storytelling and conversation, you can elevate your leadership and foster a culture of connection, trust, and shared success.

Chapter 9

The Neuroscience of Conversation

In many ways, parenting is an ongoing conversation. Just when you think you've figured out what your children need from you, they grow. As infants, they require constant attention and care, and just as you settle into that rhythm, they become toddlers, demanding a whole new approach. Before long, you're adjusting again for preschoolers, then elementary schoolers, and then the teenage years hit, changing the relationship entirely.

I remember a pivotal conversation with my oldest son when he was 16 years old. At that age, he was beginning to step into adulthood, and it was clear to both of us that the kind of fathering he needed was shifting. So I sat down with him and asked, "What do you need from me now?" I was honest—I didn't know. I only knew that what worked when he was younger no longer applied, and I needed to hear from him what kind of support he needed at this new stage. That conversation was deeply impactful, allowing both of us to express what we were thinking and recalibrate our relationship.

We had a similar conversation a couple of years later when he left for college. Because we were no longer living under the same roof, our dynamic had to shift again. I found myself asking him once more, "What do you need from me now?" And once again, the conversation opened up new possibilities for how we would relate to each other.

Though sometimes difficult, these conversations have been a gift. They have allowed us to grow together and maintain a relationship built on respect, trust, and understanding. Every stage in life calls for a new conversation, and it is through these dialogues that we deepen our connection and adapt to the changes that life brings.

Leadership as a Constant Conversation

In my work with leaders, I've seen how important it is for them to ask the same question of their teams: "What do you need from me now?" Leadership, much like parenting, requires a constant reassessment of what people need as they grow and evolve. Conversations are the means through which leaders can adapt, connect, and guide effectively. But leading through conversation isn't just about knowing what to say; it's about being curious, observant, and willing to adjust your approach based on the feedback you receive—much like a scientist in a lab.

Think of each conversation as an experiment in leadership. Every dialogue is an opportunity to test your assumptions, refine your communication, and better understand those you are leading. Just as scientists observe outcomes, adjust variables, and try new approaches, leaders must constantly refine how they engage in conversations. It's not about having perfect conversations but about learning from each one and adapting your approach over time.

In this chapter, we'll explore the dynamics of great conversations and how you can become a conversation biohacker. We'll dive into the biology and neuroscience of how conversations work, including nonverbal cues and emotional dynamics that underpin every meaningful exchange. You'll learn how to create environments where deep, focused conversations can thrive, and we'll explore strategies for engaging in these dialogues with confidence and intention.

We'll also look at how leaders can tailor conversations to different contexts, whether in a fast-paced, high-stakes organizational setting or as an introverted leader navigating more intimate discussion. By the end of this chapter, I hope you will see conversations not only as a powerful leadership tool but as an evolving process that requires a mindset of curiosity, experimentation, and continuous improvement.

To truly master conversations, you must approach them with the same curiosity and adaptability you would bring to any new challenge. Becoming a conversation biohacker means seeing each dialogue as an opportunity to learn, connect, and refine your leadership practice. Let's dive in and explore how you can turn every conversation into a powerful moment of influence, growth, and connection.

The Science of Conversation

Conversations are more than just exchanges of words; they are collaborative narratives that shape the shared experiences and decisions within a team or organization. By understanding the underlying science of conversations, leaders can leverage these dialogues to build trust, drive engagement, and foster a deeper connection with their teams. In this section, we will explore the neurological and psychological foundations of conversations, examine how they function as emotional connectors, and uncover their critical role in decision-making dynamics.

The Neurology and Psychology of Conversations

Consider a time when you felt completely in sync during a conversation—where you seemed to understand each other perfectly, almost without effort. What do you think was happening in that moment that made it feel so connected? Conversations engage our brains in ways that go far beyond simple language processing. During a dialogue, the brain activates multiple regions, including those responsible for sensory experiences, emotions, and empathy, creating a rich, multisensory engagement that mirrors the holistic impact of storytelling. This is why conversations are more than just exchanges of information; they are powerful cognitive and emotional events that shape how we think, feel, and connect with others.

Neuroscientific research shows that when we engage in conversation, various areas of the brain light up, such as the language centers and the regions responsible for processing emotions and empathy. This dynamic interaction helps us connect deeply with others, allowing us to share not just words but experiences. For instance, mirror neurons—specialized brain cells that respond both when we perform an action and when we observe someone else performing the same action—play a significant role in this process. These neurons help us understand and empathize with others by allowing us to "mirror" their emotions and intentions subconsciously.[1] We previously touched on mirror neurons in the storytelling chapter, but in conversations, their role is even more pronounced due to the real-time, back-and-forth nature of dialogue.

A crucial aspect of this neurological interplay is active listening, a skill that significantly enhances the conversational bond. When we listen attentively, our brains work to decode both the spoken and the unspoken cues—from tone of voice to body language—further engaging our empathetic response. This type of listening strengthens connections by aligning our emotional states with those of the speaker, fostering a deeper sense of mutual understanding and trust.[2] Leaders who practice active listening not only enhance their leadership biodynamics but also create a more cohesive and motivated team dynamic.

The neurological effects of conversations underscore why they are such a vital tool for leaders. By understanding the cognitive and emotional impact of dialogues, leaders can leverage conversations to build stronger connections, improve team dynamics, and lead more effectively.

Conversations as Emotional Connectors

Think about a conversation that left you feeling emotionally closer to someone—perhaps a moment of vulnerability, shared joy, or profound understanding. How did that dialogue deepen your connection? Conversations do more than exchange information—they create emotional bonds that are essential for trust, resilience, and effective leadership. This idea is famously captured by a *New York Times* article that introduced the "36 Questions That Lead to Love," a set of prompts designed to create intimacy and closeness between two people.[3]

Now, getting someone to fall in love with you might not be your goal as a leader. If it is, you might get ready for that call from HR. But the principle behind the questions still applies: structured, meaningful conversations can break down barriers and foster deep emotional connections. At their core, conversations are about connection, serving as a bridge between individuals that allows emotions, intentions, and values to be shared and understood. Leaders who harness the emotional power of conversation can significantly enhance their influence and build stronger, more cohesive teams.

When we engage in meaningful dialogue, our conversations trigger the release of oxytocin, often referred to as the "bonding hormone."

This neurochemical is key in fostering trust and social connection, reinforcing the sense of psychological safety within teams. As we discussed in the storytelling chapter, oxytocin plays a crucial role in creating emotional resonance. In conversations, this hormone helps establish a foundation of trust, making it easier for team members to speak openly, share ideas, and collaborate more effectively.

Emotional connection through conversation is particularly vital during challenging times. Leaders who use conversations to express empathy, acknowledge fears, and provide reassurance can help their teams navigate uncertainty with greater confidence. For example, a leader who engages in open dialogue during a crisis, like Sarah did with her team, not only addresses the immediate concerns but also reinforces a sense of unity and shared purpose. This kind of engagement builds resilience because team members feel heard and valued, strengthening their commitment to the group's goals.

The way leaders converse can either build or erode trust. A transactional conversation—focused solely on getting things done—may achieve immediate goals but lacks the emotional depth that fosters long-term loyalty and engagement. In contrast, relational conversations that prioritize understanding, empathy, and mutual respect create a foundation for trust that can be drawn upon during more challenging interactions. This is why leaders who consistently invest in meaningful dialogue tend to cultivate more resilient and motivated teams.

Leaders who understand the emotional dynamics of conversation can use this knowledge to foster environments where team members feel connected, appreciated, and inspired. By prioritizing authentic, empathetic dialogue, leaders can create a culture of open communication that drives both individual and collective success.

Conversations and Decision-Making Dynamics

Reflect on a time when a conversation influenced a key decision—whether at work, in a community group, or in your personal life. What was it about the way the dialogue unfolded that swayed the outcome? Conversations play a pivotal role in decision-making within teams and organizations. The quality of these dialogues directly impacts the effectiveness of the decisions made, shaping how ideas are explored, debated, and ultimately acted upon. Leaders who are adept at facilitating productive conversations can significantly enhance their team's decision-making processes, ensuring that diverse perspectives are heard and considered.

Effective conversations promote better decision-making by encouraging open dialogue, reducing hierarchical barriers, and fostering a collaborative atmosphere. When team members feel safe to voice their opinions without fear of judgment, the collective intelligence of the group is fully utilized.[4] This dynamic allows teams to tap into a broader range of insights, leading to more innovative solutions and better outcomes.

Leaders influence decision-making through both verbal and nonverbal cues during conversations. The way a leader frames a discussion, asks questions, and responds to input can either open the dialogue or shut it down. For example, a leader who asks open-ended questions, listens actively, and acknowledges diverse viewpoints encourages a more inclusive conversation. This approach not only enhances the quality of the decisions made but also boosts team morale and engagement because members feel that their contributions are valued.

Conversational structures like strategic questioning, reflective listening, and Socratic dialogue are powerful tools for guiding decision-making. Strategic questioning helps leaders direct the conversation toward critical issues without dominating the discussion. Reflective listening, on the other hand, ensures that all voices are heard because it involves summarizing and reflecting what team members have said, validating their input and clarifying points of confusion. Socratic dialogue—where questions are used to stimulate critical thinking and draw out underlying assumptions—can be particularly effective in complex decision-making scenarios, helping teams challenge existing perspectives and consider alternative viewpoints.

In practice, leaders can use these techniques to guide conversations in a way that surfaces the best ideas and navigates potential conflicts. Imagine Sarah from our earlier story engaging her team in a strategic conversation about a new business pivot. By using reflective listening, Sarah could acknowledge concerns while highlighting the strengths of various proposals, steering the discussion toward a balanced and well-informed decision. Her role as a conversational guide—rather than a directive leader—would empower her team to contribute fully, enhancing the decision-making process and fostering a sense of ownership over the final outcome.

Becoming a Conversation Biohacker

To guide conversations effectively, think like a scientist, learn and leverage the science of dialogue to connect, influence, and inspire. Conversations are dynamic, interactive processes that engage our brains, foster emotional bonds, and drive decision-making. By exploring the neurological and psychological underpinnings of conversations, leaders can harness these insights to create deeper connections, build trust, and guide their teams toward shared success.

Like a scientist, you can approach conversations with curiosity, observation, and intention. You can understand that conversations are powerful cognitive and emotional events, shaping how your team thinks, feels, and collaborates. By tuning into the nuances of dialogue—from mirror neurons that help us empathize to the active listening that aligns emotional states—you cultivate a culture where open communication thrives.

Being a conversation biohacker also means recognizing the emotional power of dialogue. Just as structured questions can build deep bonds, as seen in the "36 Questions That Lead to Love," meaningful conversations in leadership can break down barriers, foster trust, and create resilient teams. While your goal may not be to make someone fall in love with you, the principle remains: conversations that prioritize connection over transaction are key to cultivating motivated and engaged teams.

Applying the principles outlined in this chapter you can guide dialogue with intention, and use strategic questioning, reflective listening, and inclusive practices to elevate the collective intelligence of the group. As our friend Sarah the CEO demonstrated, leading through conversation means facilitating rather than dictating—steering the

179

The Neuroscience of Conversation

dialogue toward collaborative solutions and empowering your team to take ownership of the outcomes.

As you move forward, embrace the role of a conversation biohacker. Experiment with dialogue, refine your approach, and observe the profound impact these conversations can have on your team. In the next section, we'll delve into the specific techniques that will equip you to master these dynamics, transforming everyday interactions into powerful leadership moments.

Conversational Structures: Crafting Dialogues that Drive Engagement

Conversations are not just exchanges of words; they are dynamic processes that underpin leadership and decision-making. Structured approaches to conversation can transform how leaders connect with their teams, navigate conflict, and drive engagement. By leveraging specific conversational frameworks, leaders can create more intentional and impactful dialogues that foster deeper connections, understanding, and collaboration. In this section, we will explore practical structures such as the Socratic method, reflective listening, and strategic questioning, and examine how these techniques can be applied in various leadership contexts.

The Socratic Method: Leading with Questions

The Socratic method, named after the ancient Greek philosopher Socrates, is a dialogical approach that uses open-ended questions to stimulate critical thinking, challenge assumptions, and draw out deeper insights. Rather than simply providing answers, this method encourages exploration and reflection, making it an invaluable tool for leaders who aim to empower their teams to think independently and develop their own solutions.

The Socratic method can be particularly effective in coaching and mentoring scenarios. For instance, rather than telling a team member how to solve a problem, a leader might ask questions like "What options have you considered?" or "What do you think the impact of each choice could be?" This approach shifts the focus from directive advice to a more collaborative discovery process, allowing the individual to engage more deeply with the issue and arrive at their own conclusions.[5]

Consider Sarah, our startup CEO, engaging with a team member who is struggling with a project deadline. Instead of immediately offering solutions, Sarah could use the Socratic method to guide the conversation:

- **Sarah:** "What challenges are you facing with this deadline?" (seeking understanding)
- **Team Member:** "I'm having trouble prioritizing my tasks; everything seems urgent."
- **Sarah:** "Which of these tasks, if completed first, would make the biggest impact?" (redirecting focus)
- **Team Member:** "Probably the client proposal—it sets the tone for everything else."
- **Sarah:** "How could prioritizing that task influence your overall workload?" (connecting actions to outcomes)
- **Team Member:** "It would probably help me streamline my approach to the other tasks."

Through this structured questioning, Sarah helps her team member identify a path forward, empowering them to take ownership of the solution. This method not only addresses immediate concerns but also fosters critical thinking skills, enhancing the team's ability to navigate future challenges independently.[6]

Reflective Listening: Building Trust Through Validation

Reflective listening is a conversational technique that involves actively listening to the speaker and then reflecting back what you've heard to validate their feelings and ensure mutual understanding. This approach not only clarifies the message but also builds trust and rapport, showing the speaker that their thoughts and emotions are acknowledged.[7] Reflective listening helps leaders pick up on underlying issues that might not be immediately apparent, allowing them to address concerns more effectively.

For a leader, reflective listening can be particularly valuable in conflict resolution and one-on-one feedback sessions. When team members feel heard and understood, they are more likely to engage constructively, reducing defensiveness and opening up the space for honest dialogue.

Imagine Sarah meeting with a team member who feels overwhelmed by recent changes in their workload:

- **Team Member:** "I'm really struggling to keep up with all these new tasks; it's just too much."

- **Sarah:** "It sounds like you're feeling overloaded with everything that's been added recently." (reflecting back)

- **Team Member:** "Yeah, and I'm worried I'm not meeting expectations."

- **Sarah:** "You're concerned that this might impact your performance and how others see your work." (validating and clarifying emotions)

Reflective listening here allows Sarah to connect with her team member on an emotional level, demonstrating empathy and understanding, which builds trust and provides a platform for finding solutions together.

Strategic Questioning: Guiding Conversations to Productive Outcomes

Strategic questioning is a technique that involves asking purposeful questions designed to guide conversations toward desired outcomes. This structure can be particularly effective in leadership scenarios that require alignment, problem-solving, or decision-making. Strategic questioning goes beyond basic inquiry; it's about using questions to lead the dialogue in a way that clarifies objectives, identifies barriers, and uncovers opportunities.

For example, during a team meeting, a leader might use strategic questioning to facilitate brainstorming:

- **Leader:** "What are the biggest challenges we're facing with this project?" (identifying barriers)
- **Team Member:** "We're struggling with communication across departments."
- **Leader:** "What strategies have worked well in the past to improve cross-department communication?" (exploring solutions)
- **Team Member:** "We had success with joint meetings and shared project platforms."
- **Leader:** "How can we adapt those strategies to our current situation?" (applying past successes to current challenges)

By using strategic questioning, leaders can steer the conversation toward productive solutions while engaging the team in the process, making them feel valued and heard.

Real-World Applications: Conversational Structures in Action

These conversational structures are not merely theoretical; they have been effectively applied by leaders across various contexts. For example, Ray Dalio, founder of Bridgewater Associates, uses a structured approach to dialogue within his company, promoting radical transparency and reflection through strategic questioning and reflective listening.[8] This method fosters an open environment where ideas are rigorously examined, and team members feel empowered to speak their minds.

By understanding and applying these frameworks, leaders can transform everyday interactions into powerful dialogues that drive engagement, foster collaboration, and build stronger teams. Conversations are not just about exchanging information; they are about creating connections, exploring possibilities, and guiding your team toward collective success.

183

The Neuroscience of Conversation

Leading Through Conversations: Strategic Dialogue

What's a "strategic conversation?" It's the kind of conversation that helps to shape organizational culture, drive performance, and navigate the complexities of human dynamics. As a leader, your role in these dialogues is much like that of a guide, helping to shape a shared narrative that moves the team forward. Conversations are not just exchanges of information; they are opportunities to connect, align, and inspire. In this section, we'll explore how to leverage conversations strategically, the importance of authenticity, and the ethics of dialogue in leadership.

The Power of Strategic Conversations

Conversations are a strategic tool in a leader's toolkit, influencing everything from individual motivation to organizational change. A well-timed conversation can resolve conflict, motivate a team, or clarify a strategic direction. The key is understanding the different conversational approaches available to you—coaching, facilitating, mentoring, or even just being present as a listener—and knowing when to deploy each one.

Here's an example. On a college visit during my oldest son's junior year of high school, we met with an academic advisor who embodied the art of strategic dialogue. My son was uncertain about his academic path, feeling overwhelmed by the choices ahead. Instead of directing him toward a specific decision, the advisor engaged him in a series of questions designed to narrow his focus and clarify his thoughts. One of the questions the advisor asked was this: "What could you perhaps *never* envision yourself studying in college?" My son quickly rattled off several fields of study in which he had virtually no interest. The advisor responded, "Great, that actually narrows things down quite a bit." This technique, known as appreciative advising, is a strengths-based approach that involves asking open-ended questions to guide the student toward self-discovery and empowerment, according to Bloom.

184

Biohacking Leadership

The advisor's approach was not just about finding answers; it was about creating a space where my son could explore his own ideas and make connections that felt authentic to him. This encounter was a masterclass in strategic dialogue—one where the advisor skillfully used conversation to empower a young person to find his own path. It serves as a reminder that the leader in any context, whether a corporate boardroom or an academic office, can facilitate powerful conversations that help others clarify their own intentions and actions.

Choosing the Right Conversational Approach

Just as a craftsman selects the right tool for the job, a leader must choose the appropriate conversational style for the situation. For example, when coaching, the leader might adopt a questioning approach, prompting team members to think critically about their challenges and discover their own solutions. This is particularly effective when trying to foster accountability and personal growth within your team.

In other contexts, facilitation may be the preferred approach. This involves guiding the conversation, ensuring balanced participation, and keeping the group aligned on the objective. Facilitation is especially valuable in team meetings or brainstorming sessions where the goal is to harness collective intelligence. Here, the leader is less of a direct participant and more of a conductor, orchestrating dialogue to bring out the best in everyone.

Strategic conversations also require adaptability. A leader may need to switch between styles within a single dialogue. For example, you might begin a discussion by listening to concerns (facilitation), shift to offering insights (mentoring), and then move to a coaching approach to empower your team to take action. The fluidity with which a leader can navigate these conversational styles often determines the effectiveness of the dialogue.

Authenticity and Openness

A guiding principle of impactful conversation is authenticity. Leaders who are genuine in their dialogues create trust and openness, inviting others to do the same. This concept aligns closely with the idea from Chapter 8 of "leaving a tip on the table"—sharing something of yourself to foster connection. Just as in storytelling, where vulnerability can build bridges, being open in conversations demonstrates that you are approachable, trustworthy, and invested in the dialogue.

For instance, when engaging in a difficult conversation with your team, admitting when you don't have all the answers can be a powerful moment of connection. It shows that you value honesty over pretense and are willing to navigate the uncertainty together. This was exemplified in my interaction with my son's academic advisor. The advisor didn't have a prescribed path laid out; instead, he admitted the complexity of the decision and invited my son into the process, signaling a partnership rather than a top-down directive.

Authenticity also involves being transparent about your intentions in a conversation. Instead of hiding behind vague statements, be clear about why the conversation matters and what you hope to achieve. This openness helps to align your internal intentions with your external expressions, creating a more congruent and effective interaction.

Conversational Dos and Don'ts: Navigating Ethical Boundaries

While conversations can be a powerful tool for influence, it's crucial to maintain ethical standards. Leaders must be mindful not to manipulate through conversation or use dialogue as a means to exert undue control. The ethics of conversation require a commitment to honesty, respect, and the integrity of the dialogue.

One major pitfall is conversational dominance, where the leader overwhelms the conversation, either by speaking too much or steering the dialogue to serve their agenda rather than fostering a genuine exchange. This can undermine trust and stifle the contributions of others, particularly those who may be less assertive but whose insights are equally valuable. Leaders must consciously create space for others, ensuring that conversations remain balanced and inclusive.

Conversational ethics also involve being sensitive to cultural and individual differences in communication styles. What is considered direct and transparent in one culture may be perceived as confrontational in another. Leaders should strive to understand these nuances, adapting their conversational approaches to ensure they are connecting respectfully and effectively with all team members. Here are some conversation dos and don'ts to consider.

While conversations are powerful, they also come with ethical responsibilities. Leaders must be mindful of how their words can impact others, avoiding manipulative tactics or language that undermines trust. Here are some key dos and don'ts to keep in mind when engaging in strategic conversations:

- **Do: Be Intentional:** Every conversation should have a clear purpose. Whether you are coaching a team member, mediating a conflict, or setting strategic direction, be intentional about what you want to achieve and how you want to make others feel during and after the conversation, according to Schein.[9]

- **Don't: Use Manipulation:** Strategic conversations should never cross the line into manipulation. This includes avoiding leading questions that push people toward a predetermined answer or withholding critical information to steer the outcome. Transparency and fairness are essential for maintaining integrity in dialogue.[10]

- **Do: Encourage Dialogue:** Create space for others to speak, share their perspectives, and feel heard. This is especially important in diverse teams where different viewpoints can lead to richer discussions and better decision-making. Use active listening techniques to validate contributions and show that you value input from all team members.[11]

- **Don't: Avoid Difficult Conversations:** One of the most common pitfalls for leaders is shying away from uncomfortable topics. Whether it's addressing performance issues, giving tough feedback, or confronting team conflict, avoiding these conversations can erode trust and stifle growth. Instead, approach these dialogues with empathy, clarity, and a commitment to finding constructive solutions, advises Stone.[12]

- **Do: Adapt Your Approach:** Different situations call for different conversational styles. Be adaptable and willing to adjust your tone, language, and structure to fit the context and audience. A successful leader knows how to shift from a supportive coaching style to a more directive approach when needed, maintaining flexibility while staying true to their core values.

Navigating these ethical considerations requires self-awareness and a commitment to leading with integrity. Leaders who master strategic conversations not only enhance their ability to connect and influence but also create a culture of openness, respect, and ethical communication within their teams.

Strategic dialogue is more than just talking—it's about engaging with purpose, aligning intentions with expressions, and creating shared meaning. From the personal example of my son's academic journey to the structured approaches of coaching and facilitation, this section has highlighted the many facets of conversational leadership. As you refine your ability to lead through conversations, remember that each dialogue is an opportunity to guide, connect, and inspire. In the next section, we'll delve into the challenges of conversational leadership, exploring common pitfalls and strategies for overcoming them to ensure that your dialogues remain effective, ethical, and impactful.

Choosing the Right Approach for Different Situations

Effective leaders know that every conversation serves a purpose, whether it's to motivate, clarify, resolve conflict, or build alignment. The key is to match your conversational approach to the specific context and needs of the situation. This requires a clear understanding of your objectives and a strategic mindset that guides the flow of dialogue.

For instance, when addressing a team that is struggling with low morale, a leader might choose a nurturing and motivational approach, focusing on encouragement and validation. This could involve sharing stories of past successes, highlighting team strengths, and offering reassurance about the future. Conversely, in a performance review, the conversation might need to be more direct and focused on providing constructive feedback. Here, the leader's role is to guide the individual through reflection and action planning, using targeted questions and clear, actionable language.

Let's visit again with Sarah, the startup CEO. After telling her motivational story to the entire team, Sarah needed to shift gears when having a one-on-one conversation with a key team member who was still feeling overwhelmed. Rather than using the same broad narrative, Sarah opted for a more personalized approach, asking open-ended questions to understand the individual's concerns and collaboratively exploring solutions. By adjusting her conversational style to fit the context, Sarah was able to address the specific needs of her team member, demonstrating her ability to lead through strategic dialogue.

Strategic conversations are about more than just words; they are about choosing the right method, tone, and structure to meet the moment. Leaders who master this art can navigate complex dynamics with greater agility and foster an environment where meaningful dialogue drives engagement and results.

Authenticity and Openness

As discussed in Chapter 8, the concept of "leaving a tip on the table" emphasizes the importance of authenticity and vulnerability in leadership. This principle is equally applicable to conversations. Leaders who are open, honest, and willing to share a bit of themselves in dialogue build stronger connections with their teams. Authentic conversations break down barriers and create a safe space for others to share their thoughts and feelings.

However, authenticity doesn't mean oversharing or losing professional boundaries. It's about showing up as a real person, acknowledging your own uncertainties, and being honest about the challenges you're facing. When leaders engage in conversations with a genuine openness, it fosters trust and encourages others to do the same. This approach can be particularly powerful in challenging times when teams look to their leaders for guidance and reassurance.

One compelling example of authentic and strategic conversational leadership comes from Malala Yousafzai, the young Pakistani activist and Nobel Peace Prize laureate. Known for her courage and advocacy for girls' education, Malala often engages in conversations that blend personal storytelling with strategic dialogue. Whether speaking at the United Nations or in smaller forums with young activists, Malala's conversational style is marked by sincerity, empathy, and a deep sense of purpose. She openly shares her own story of survival and resilience, not to glorify her own experiences, but to amplify the voices of millions of girls fighting for their right to education. Her conversational approach—grounded in transparency and a genuine connection with her audience—has made her a powerful force for change, uniting people across the globe in support of her cause. This authenticity not only strengthens her leadership but also inspires others to take action, demonstrating how a young leader's conversational skills can drive significant impact.[13]

Conversations as Catalysts

Conversations are where your leadership comes to life. They are the moments when values are tested, relationships are forged, and visions are shared. By mastering the art of strategic dialogue, leaders can use conversations not just as a means of communication but as powerful tools for driving engagement, fostering collaboration, and leading their teams to success. As we move forward, consider how you can apply these conversational techniques to your own leadership practice, transforming every dialogue into an opportunity to connect, inspire, and lead with purpose.

Conversational Challenges

Conversations are dynamic exchanges that can drive transformation, build trust, and foster collaboration. However, they are also fraught with challenges that can undermine their effectiveness. Just as storytelling has its pitfalls, conversations can falter due to miscommunication, cultural misunderstandings, and conversational dominance. Understanding these challenges is crucial for leaders who strive to facilitate meaningful dialogues that align with their intentions and resonate with their teams.

Miscommunication: The Silent Saboteur

Miscommunication is one of the most common challenges in leadership conversations. It often arises from assumptions, unclear language, or differing interpretations of the same message. Even the most well-intentioned conversations can go awry when what is said doesn't align with what is heard. This disconnect can erode trust, cause confusion, and lead to missed opportunities for alignment and growth.

Miscommunication is frequently rooted in cognitive biases and unspoken assumptions, which can cause leaders and team members to talk past each other without realizing it.[14] For instance, a leader might think they've clearly articulated their vision, but the team may still feel uncertain about their roles or the broader strategy. To combat this, leaders can employ active listening techniques, such as summarizing what they've heard and asking clarifying questions. This ensures mutual understanding and creates a feedback loop that catches misunderstandings before they escalate.

Cultural Misunderstandings: Navigating the Diversity of Voices

In today's globalized work environment, cultural diversity enriches teams but also presents unique conversational challenges. Differences in communication styles, language nuances, and cultural norms can lead to misunderstandings and unintended offense. For instance, a direct communication style that is typical in some Western cultures might be perceived as rude or confrontational in more collectivist societies, where indirect communication is the norm.[15]

To navigate cultural diversity, leaders must develop cultural intelligence—an awareness of and sensitivity to the communication preferences of others. Encouraging team members to share their cultural contexts and norms can foster a more inclusive environment where everyone feels respected. Leaders should also model humility and openness, demonstrating a willingness to learn from and adapt to these differences. This not only minimizes misunderstandings but also strengthens the relational fabric of the team.

Conversational Dominance: Ensuring Equity of Voice

Another significant challenge in leadership conversations is the tendency for certain voices to dominate, often due to power dynamics, personality differences, or social norms. This dominance can stifle diverse perspectives, limit creative solutions, and create an environment where team members feel undervalued. Leaders who do not actively manage conversational equity risk making decisions based on a narrow set of inputs, which can be detrimental to team morale and outcomes.

Addressing conversational dominance involves setting clear norms that value all voices. Techniques like round-robin discussions, explicitly inviting quieter members to contribute, or using structured turn-taking can create a more balanced dialogue. Leaders can also model inclusive behaviors by acknowledging contributions and redirecting attention to those who may be overshadowed. This not only enriches the conversation but also fosters a culture where every team member feels empowered to participate.

Overcoming These Challenges: Strategies for Success

You can employ various strategies to overcome these common conversational challenges and create a more effective dialogue within your teams:

- **Mitigating Miscommunication:** Use reflective listening, paraphrasing, and feedback loops to confirm understanding. By restating key points and encouraging team members to do the same, leaders can bridge the gap between intention and interpretation.

- **Navigating Cultural Misunderstandings:** Cultivate cultural awareness by encouraging open discussions about communication preferences and cultural norms. Leaders should approach conversations with curiosity and a willingness to adapt, demonstrating respect for diverse perspectives.

- **Addressing Conversational Dominance:** Implement conversational structures that ensure equitable participation. Techniques like turn-taking, explicit invitations to speak, and acknowledgment of quieter voices help balance the conversation, making it more inclusive and productive.

Navigating the challenges of leadership conversations requires intentionality, awareness, and a commitment to inclusivity. By addressing these common pitfalls, leaders can foster dialogue that not only aligns with their intentions but also engages and empowers their teams. As we move forward, we will explore how mastering these conversational skills can impact team dynamics and drive meaningful change. Let's turn our focus to how conversations influence team cohesion, resilience, and motivation, setting the stage for deeper connections and shared success.

The Impact of Conversations on Teams

Conversations directly influence cohesion, motivation, and resilience. Effective conversations can transform a group of individuals into a united team with shared goals and a strong sense of purpose. Leaders who excel at fostering meaningful dialogue not only enhance communication but also create an environment characterized by trust, collaboration, and innovation.

Enhancing Team Cohesion: Building Stronger Bonds Through Dialogue

Effective conversations play a critical role in building team cohesion. When you facilitate open and honest communication, you create a space where team members feel safe to share their ideas, concerns, and feedback. This openness helps break down barriers, fostering a sense of belonging and shared identity. Teams that regularly engage in meaningful conversations are more likely to work cohesively because they better understand each other's strengths, weaknesses, and perspectives.

Teams with high levels of cohesion perform better, are more innovative, and demonstrate greater resilience in the face of challenges.[16] You can enhance cohesion by encouraging team members to voice their opinions and actively listen to one another. When this occurs, you will be creating a culture where every voice matters. This not only strengthens relationships but also ensures that the team functions as a unified whole, capable of overcoming obstacles together.

Boosting Motivation: Conversations That Inspire and Engage

Motivating a team goes beyond setting targets and offering incentives; it involves engaging team members on an emotional level. Conversations that connect individual roles to the broader mission of the organization can ignite a sense of purpose, driving motivation from within. Leaders who consistently communicate a compelling vision through their conversations inspire their teams to go above and beyond, aligning their daily tasks with the larger goals of the organization.

One powerful example of this is Emmanuel Macron, President of France, who often uses conversation as a tool to motivate and mobilize. During his presidential campaign and in office, Macron frequently engaged in town hall-style meetings and direct dialogues with citizens, using these conversations to connect, address concerns, and inspire collective action. His conversational approach helped bridge the gap between leadership and the public, fostering a sense of shared purpose and motivating action during times of national challenge.[17]

Fostering Resilience: Conversations as a Tool for Overcoming Adversity

Resilience is critical for teams navigating complex and ever-changing environments. Leaders who prioritize open dialogue help their teams develop the resilience needed to weather setbacks and adapt to new circumstances. Conversations that address challenges transparently and focus on problem-solving rather than blame encourage a culture of learning and continuous improvement. These dialogues empower teams to view failures as opportunities for growth, rather than insurmountable obstacles.

A compelling example of conversational leadership comes from Sazi Bongwe, a high school student in Johannesburg who co-created "Ukuzibuza," an online platform for youth to discuss social issues like race, gender, and education. Sazi used conversations to engage peers in meaningful dialogue, encouraging them to express their perspectives and build confidence in their voices. His leadership through conversation not only fostered a supportive community but also demonstrated how young leaders can drive social change through strategic, empathetic dialogue.[18]

Driving Change and Building Trust Through Dialogue

Conversations are instrumental in driving change and building trust within teams. Leaders who communicate transparently about the reasons behind strategic shifts or organizational changes help demystify the decision-making process, reducing uncertainty and fear. By involving team members in conversations about change, leaders foster a sense of ownership and commitment, making it more likely that their teams will support new initiatives.

Effective conversations also build trust, which is the foundation of any high-performing team. Leaders who engage in consistent, honest, and empathetic dialogue create a culture where trust flourishes. This trust, in turn, encourages team members to take risks, voice their opinions, and collaborate more effectively, leading to better outcomes.

The Power of Conversations in Action

From motivating teams to navigating crises, the impact of conversations in leadership cannot be overstated. Leaders who master the art of strategic dialogue can elevate their teams, fostering a culture of trust, resilience, and shared purpose. As we conclude this chapter, we'll reflect on the broader implications of the biomechanics of conversation, emphasizing how these skills can transform not just individual interactions, but entire organizational dynamics.

Becoming a Conversation Biohacker

In the previous chapter you were challenged to become a storytelling biohacker. Similarly, to leverage the power of conversation in your leadership practice you will also need to become a conversation biohacker. Mastering the science of conversation will mean continuously experimenting with your dialogues, observing their impact, and refining your approach based on what you learn. Just as a scientist tests hypotheses, you can test conversational techniques to see how they foster connections, influence decision-making, and enhance team dynamics.

- **Experiment, Observe, and Adapt:**
  - Every conversation you engage in is an experiment in connection, influence, and leadership. Test different conversational structures, questioning techniques, and active listening strategies to see what best resonates with your audience. Reflect on the dynamics: Did your conversation foster engagement? Did it clarify complex issues or help navigate a challenging decision? Treat these outcomes as valuable data, approaching them with a sense of curiosity rather than judgment.
  - Once a conversation is underway, be keenly observant of its flow and impact. Watch for verbal and nonverbal cues—tone, body language, pauses, and eye contact—that indicate how the dialogue is being received. Are team members leaning in,

showing signs of connection, or are they withdrawing or disengaged? These subtle cues provide crucial feedback, guiding you toward more effective conversational techniques. Reflect on when your dialogue energized the room and when it didn't, using these insights to refine your approach.

o Adaptation is key. As a conversation scientist, you must be flexible, adjusting your approach based on real-time feedback. This might mean changing your line of questioning, rephrasing to ensure clarity, or shifting from a directive style to a more collaborative tone. The goal isn't to conduct the perfect conversation but to engage in one that best facilitates understanding, connection, and action at any given moment.

- **Align Intent with Execution:**
  o Effective conversations require alignment between your internal intentions and your external delivery. This is where techniques like "physicality of intent" and "verbalizing intentions" come into play. Before entering a conversation, ask yourself: What am I trying to achieve? Am I aiming to resolve, motivate, challenge, or connect? The clarity of your intent will shape the structure and flow of the dialogue, aligning your internal mindset with your external communication.

  o Beyond verbal content, pay attention to your nonverbal cues—your posture, gestures, tone, and overall physical presence. Are you open and engaged, or are you sending unintended signals of disinterest or impatience? Physicalizing your intent ensures that your body language, voice, and facial expressions reinforce your message, creating a cohesive and impactful conversation. This alignment makes your dialogue feel authentic and intentional, enhancing the emotional and cognitive impact on your audience.

- **Foster a Culture of Conversation and Continuous Learning:**
  o Becoming a conversation scientist also means cultivating a culture of open, meaningful dialogue within your team. Encourage team members to engage in conversations that

197

The Neuroscience of Conversation

matter—whether they're tackling complex challenges, celebrating successes, or simply sharing insights. This collective commitment to dialogue builds a shared narrative, strengthens team cohesion, and fosters a culture where every voice is valued.

o Commit to continuous learning and refinement of your conversational skills. Stay curious about new communication techniques, evolving cultural contexts, and emerging research on dialogue dynamics. By seeking feedback, practicing new approaches, and staying engaged with the latest insights, you ensure that your conversational skills remain sharp, relevant, and effective. This mindset of continuous improvement not only helps you grow as a leader but also keeps your conversations dynamic and impactful.

The Conversation Biohacker in Action

By embracing the mindset of a conversation biohacker, you evolve beyond merely participating in conversations to strategically guiding them. It's about using dialogue as a tool to connect, motivate, and lead with intention. As you continue to develop these skills, consider how they integrate with storytelling, creating a powerful synergy between narrative and dialogue that can drive team cohesion, innovation, and shared success. Conversations, like stories, are collaborative acts that shape the collective experience, and mastering both will elevate your leadership presence to new heights.

Chapter 10

The Neuroscience of Play

By Matthew D. Jones

You are 10 years old and it is a Friday night on the cul-de-sac. School is out for the week, homework is put off for a while, and it's time to go outside and play. You grab the red rubber ball from the garage and head out into your driveway. You inspect the safe enclosure of homes around you. Who will come to play? You dribble the rubber ball along the pavement as you slowly walk to the edge of your driveway. The sun is going down, but there is plenty of light. It's perfect for a game of kickball.

After just 30 seconds of dribbling, two kids from next door—six and nine years old—come racing. They had heard the rubber slapping the concrete and came as fast as they could. "How about you guys start setting up the bases," you tell them, "And I'll go see who can play." They sprint away with enthusiasm for a task you know they can do well.

Everything you're wearing signals that it's gametime: worn baseball cap, grass-stained jeans, and your favorite weekend T-shirt. But nothing shouts "Let's play ball" more than your classic, winning tennis shoes. You're ready to sprint, slide, and kick with the best of them. And as you stand at each door and your neighbor friends answer, within milliseconds of seeing you they get the message. Some of them barely have their shoelaces tied before they're off the porch to join the recruits.

Now that you have your players, here comes the challenging part: Who plays on what team? It has to be right, or it's mutiny and your Friday night is in the toilet. You analyze the neighbor kids.

Who's fast? Who can kick? Who can catch? Who just makes it fun? Who keeps score? Who do you know tries to bend the rules? And on and on. The 12-year-old from a few houses down is someone you know can handle this task. You select him as a team captain to help in the choosing. Then, after a few minutes of dividing teams, setting rules and boundaries, and choosing who kicks first, the game is on. While you'll play for hours that feel like minutes, you will remember it forever.

This snapshot from a quintessential childhood is a metaphor. And, as you've read the preceding chapters, you can begin to see the powerful biodynamics of leadership already in force in a small neighborhood game of kickball. Play is not just a good place for metaphors; it is a facilitator, a catalyst, for the some of the best outcomes in the human experience.

Play has many definitions. It is also one of those things in life that defies being bottled into words. Academics rarely agree and so pinpointing any one definition as "the one" is not only futile but potentially contentious. However, Van Vleet and Feeney's definition of play is consistently used as a basis for discussing play in adulthood: "an activity that is carried out for the purpose of amusement and fun, that is approached with an enthusiastic and in-the-moment attitude, and that is highly-interactive."[1] Play is fun on purpose. We are enthusiastic about it and, most key of all, it is highly engaging.

This is critical in a world where engagement at work (and in life) seems to be at an all new low. We live in an age of "quiet quitting" and disengagement.[2] People are leaving work in unprecedented rates for reasons baffling human resource departments around the world. "I just want to find something more fulfilling," the employees say. Therefore, if play is something people choose to do of their own free will and is highly engaging, we need to study it rigorously. We need to pay attention to it to see if we can bring a sense of play into our work and our leadership to increase our own fulfillment and engagement.

And there is a case to be made that play is so central to human behavior and human development that to leave it out of a discussion on leadership is not only foolish, but negligent. To really make that case, however, we must start in the brain.

The Neurobiology of Play

The human brain is the most complex adaptive system known to humankind. The double-fist-sized organ of grey matter sitting in each of our heads contains a vast network of circuits, connecting functions and thoughts. Neuroscientists have identified patterns in this circuitry, enough to label whole systems with core responsibilities. Neuroscientist Jaak Panksepp identified seven such core circuits and called them *Affective Systems*, using full caps to designate them: SEEKING, RAGE, LUST, FEAR, PANIC/GRIEF, CARE, and PLAY.[3]

The SEEKING circuit is the primary system and helps run the others. LUST comes into view at the onset of puberty. Interesting, however, is the role of the PLAY circuit, which has been observed in the brains of an array of mammals, thus leading to the idea that it exists in all mammalian species, including us. Panksepp also identified this system as perhaps the brain's major sources of joy.[4] Think of it: The brain's home for joy is in play.

Within your brain, sprawling across your temporal lobe, lies the autonomic nervous system (ANS). It is responsible for the autonomic functions of heartrate, breathing, and so forth. It responds to varying degrees of arousal. In a moderate state of arousal, you're in the "fight or flight" state, looking to defend or disappear. Living in this way, you're anxious at work, always seeking to "do this" and "do that." At night, you can't get your brain to "shut off," making falling asleep difficult. In a high state of arousal, you're in the "freeze" state. When you've reached this place, it is because either the stressor was terrible (i.e., severe car accident or major work trauma) or you have had chronic stress, or both. Out of a sense of preservation, your brain begins decelerating your system (i.e., slowing heart rate, triggering brain fog, etc.) and desensitizing you from your environment (e.g., you begin to feel numb to what's around you).

But the lowest state of arousal is your homeostasis. You feel good here. Operations are generally at optimum functionality. Your connection to self and others is extremely high because you feel grounded—to yourself and your environment. From an evolutionary

201

The Neuroscience of Play

standpoint, this is your brain sending the signals that you're safe. And by having our states of arousal in check—meaning that we're not looking to flee, fight, or freeze—the best science in neurobiology says that we're ready to play.

Think of bear cubs. While mama bear is hunting for fish in the nearby river, the cubs are tussling and playing in the grass nearby. The place is safe, so why not do some roughhousing? But when an intruding male bear approaches, mama bear sends the signal for the cubs to stop playing and get up in the tree (flight). When the male bear wanders off and the all-clear is given, bear cub brains get the cue that it is time to go back to "safe" mode, meaning "Let's play!" Now, while we like to think humans are more sophisticated than bear cubs, our brains share a similar objective: Keep my body alive! So, like the other mammals on this planet, we live our lives riding the roller coaster of arousal states, being in the fight-or-flight or freeze or safe zones throughout every day. And yet we forget that play is the ultimate expression of the stress response in check.

Play is so critical to brain development that without it we may incur cognitive and social deficiencies that are hard to overcome. For several years and over multiple studies, scientists took recently weaned rats (somewhere between 22 and 40 days old) and put them into isolation. These rats would remain alone for several days, even weeks, depending on the study. Then the young rats were reintroduced to non-isolated peers. This resocialization occurred over a month, or sometimes just 14 days, while for others it was only for an hour a day spread over weeks. After considerable observation, these rats were seen to experience an array of cognitive, social, and even emotional side effects from their prolonged absence from social play. Some notable consequences included an inability to cope with aggression from others, slower learning capabilities, increases in depression, learned helplessness during physical challenges, and—most startling of all—they struggled to differentiate between friend and foe.

Play-deprived animals can eventually figure out how to hunt or fight. But research also reveals they cannot build strong social relationships. In Dr. Stuart Brown's landmark book on play in human development, he argues that such is true of humans too. Without play, we struggle to connect with others effectively.[5]

202

Biohacking Leadership

And therein lies the case for play as a key component of leadership biodynamics. Play—and our need for it—is deeply wired in our brains. We instinctively know play as a primal way of determining a safe environment from a hostile one, for learning and growing, of connecting and bonding. As a leader interested in biohacking their life, learning how to use play to interact with others cannot be overstated.

The Motivations to Play

IKEA and LEGO® have researched for years the role of play in human relationships, development, and society. In IKEA's play report in 2017,[6] they surveyed over 300 individuals from the United States, China, and Germany. They documented five key motivations for play:

1. To repair
2. To connect
3. To escape
4. To explore
5. To express

This chapter is not intended to give a full treatment on these concepts. However, the motivations to connect, express, and explore align perfectly with the major principles of this book: warmth, competence, and gravitas. Therefore, the rest of this chapter strives to demonstrate the powerful connection between the biodynamics of leadership and the motivations we have to play. I will provide specific examples for each to give the most eager biohacker key takeaways to put to work immediately.

Warmth: Play as Connection

The origins of play are rooted in connection. Beginning in the cerebellum and then through to the frontal lobe, infant brains process information at an astonishing pace. "Mirror neurons," which develop in the inferior frontal cortex and inferior parietal lobule, help infants imitate mom's smile or dad's surprised expression. But mirror neurons have dual purpose. Not only do they activate when we perform an action but also when we see that same action performed by others. It's a neurological dance of interpreting and understanding others' actions, intentions, and emotions with our own.

As our brains continue to develop, we pick up on cues for play. A smile, a laugh, animated expressions, or exaggerated sounds tell us it is time for fun. The mirror neuron system helps us imitate the play cues we see in others to engage and communicate. A baby will laugh, then pause for more of that hilarious stimulus. Then, when overstimulated, they turn their head for a break. Such little acts build the foundation for understanding other social signals that guide our relationships throughout life.

While all social cues have meaning, cues for play indicate several things that we will consider here. Play cues send these signals to our brain:

1. The environment is safe.
2. The people around us are physically and psychologically safe to be with.
3. It's time to engage with others.

Environmental play cues are easily conveyed on a school playground—bright colors, dynamic shapes, and varied levels invite movement, exploration, and connection. However, these same principles of design can transform spaces for adults. Steve Jobs applied environmental play cues when he designed the Steve Jobs Building on the Pixar campus. Its two wings are connected by a central atrium that serves as the heart of the building. With the only bathrooms and the food court located there, the atrium ensures that everyone passes through, creating opportunities for spontaneous interaction. Like a playground, it's designed to spark curiosity, movement, and connection, making playfulness part of everyday work. What does your work environment suggest about your willingness to connect?

204

Biohacking Leadership

People themselves also send signals for connection. All the body language cues detailed in the chapter on warmth can also be seen as signals for play. Humor, smiles, open posture, and putting yourself at eye level with your interlocular demonstrate warmth and a willingness to engage with others. But play also has a unique neurobiological effect: it equalizes power. Animals show submission before play, and a round of golf with a potential client is really no different. Through play on the golf course, we become more social, open, and ready to engage—even making negotiations flow more smoothly.

One very small way to hack into this idea of equalizing power structures is how you dress. As in all situations, a particular attire sends certain signals to others. Therefore, when appropriate, dress a bit more casually and with more varieties in color. While jeans are incongruous for all occasions, find other ways to break down the power dynamics with your attire and level the playing field. Your approachability communicated through clothes will trigger the primal neurobiology in others that you want to connect and, more importantly, that the connection is both of warmth and safety.

Finally, play cues inform and may even determine our behavior. Research at Harvard has shown that having toys in the boardroom encourages more prosocial and ethical behavior.[7] Play signals in childhood apparently still influence us. But toys as decor is a small thing. What if you played with them? LEGO® SERIOUS PLAY® (LSP), developed in the 1990s by academics and the LEGO® Group, uses LEGO® bricks to visualize ideas, tell stories, and build strategies. Its success has expanded beyond LEGO® to organizations like NASA, the US Air Force, Google, and more. LSP is so globally effective because it's not just about having bricks in the office—it's about using them to engage teams, solve problems, and strategize, all while sending an unmistakable cue: it's time to play.

Here are the key takeaways from this:

- **Create Playful Spaces:** Adapt physical (or virtual) space, to help your team connect more playfully and more genuinely. Avoid right angles and bring in some color.

205

The Neuroscience of Play

- **Send Personal Cues:** Smile, dress casually when appropriate, use humor. Find ways to break the barriers of power by leveling the playing field.

- **Leverage Objects:** Toys in meeting rooms or the use of LEGO® SERIOUS PLAY® methods are a few ways to fuel and foster engagement and connection through nostalgic play cues.

Competence: Play as Expression

Think of a time when you became so truly engrossed in an activity that you lost track of time. Your focus was like a laser beam. Everything faded into the background. You felt energized and yet, at the same time, almost outside of yourself. Psychologist Mihaly Csikszentmihalyi calls this state *flow,* and it is found in play.[8] While flow is universal, we all find it in different places, doing different things. Therefore, flow is a form of personal expression. By harnessing the power of flow at work, you enable your team to express themselves in playful ways.

Research indicates that there are four essential ingredients to flow:

1. Control
2. Goals
3. Feedback
4. Balance between challenge and skill

To find flow, a person must feel in control of their actions and the task before them. Clear, achievable goals—what we often call "small wins"—provide direction, while continuous, unambiguous feedback keeps progress on track. When the challenge perfectly matches their skill, time seems to disappear, and they become fully absorbed in the task. Together, these ingredients create a system that not only motivates but captivates, turning work into an engaging, almost effortless pursuit.

Toyota's system of continuous improvement under Taiichi Ohno exemplifies these four pillars of flow. Workers were given control through the Andon cord, empowering them to halt production and address issues directly. Initiatives like reducing waste (Muda), improving setup times, and organizing workstations provided clear, actionable goals. A systemized approach to error reporting ensured consistent feedback, driving continuous improvement (kaizen). By challenging employees to innovate while respecting their expertise, Toyota achieved a balance between challenge and skill, creating an environment where flow could thrive on the production line.

Playful work design is the idea of turning work tasks into opportunities for fun or, in this case, flow. Playful work design has shown to increase stress resilience and task productivity even amidst times of crisis. While there is a great deal of research on the topic, the focus here is to help you think of your work in the context of flow. To start, focus on yourself: What elements around your job can you control? Make small adjustments to those elements that will bring about the other three ingredients. For example, what proximal goals can you set for yourself? How will you know you've reached them? What can you do to make a mundane task more challenging and interesting for yourself? Answering these questions will lead you to being more playful and productive.

The next step is to help your team do the same for themselves. Helping them find flow through playful work design is an enormous gift of trust. It also sends the message that you want to celebrate playful expressions of self. Because the safe zone is the play zone, encouraging playful work design means work is a place where it is safe to be yourself.

Another way to honor playful expressions is by celebrating the flow experiences of others that occur outside of work. Doing so may increase engagement in your team too. For example, do you have an employee who loves to smoke meat as a hobby? Let them share their skills and cooking at a work event. Have artistic team members? Set up a display case in a prominent area of the office to show off their work. You can give the exhibit a fun name like "Our Side-Gig Hall of Fame" or other wordplay. Digital celebrations for hybrid teams matter (and work) too.

Flow is where work and play converge, offering a path to deeper engagement and creativity. By fostering control, setting clear goals, providing feedback, and balancing challenge with skill, you create an environment where productivity feels effortless. Supporting playful work design and celebrating your team's unique passions builds trust and connection, turning the workplace into a safe haven for self-expression. When work becomes play, it's no longer just about getting the job done—it's about thriving together.

Here are the key takeaways from this:

- **Recognize Flow in Yourself and Others:** Paying attention to what you and others find energizing can help you find better job and task alignment.

- **Create Flow Systems:** Using the four pillars of flow, create opportunities for people to take playful ownership of their work.

- **Celebrate Personal Flow:** Discover how others find flow (play) in and out of work and find playful ways to honor and celebrate what makes them unique.

Gravitas: Play as Exploration

Play as exploration is the most primal form of problem-solving. Intelligent mammals instinctively poke, prod, and experiment with their surroundings to understand new things. Humans do that too. As infants, we put objects in our mouths, bang them on the floor, or try to put every shape in a hole till we find the one that fits. Through curiosity and experimentation as we grow, explorative play teaches us how to solve problems.

Mr. Moss, my high school drama teacher, fostered such explorative play in his leadership. He never said no to our ideas. When we'd ask, "Can we try [x]?" in a scene, his answer was always "Let's try it." We'd perform our experiment, brimming with excitement. He would pause us with a simple but profound question: "What was the objective of the scene?" It wasn't about impressing him but about whether our choices served the story. Together, we'd evaluate: "Did it work?" If it did, we kept it. If not, he'd smile and say, "Let's try something different." In Mr. Moss's classroom, failure didn't exist—only learning tethered to key objectives. He created a space where discovery was celebrated.

If there is a sad part to this story, it is knowing that we don't always work this way. Think of Little League games where parents and coaches overreact to failures. Picture new hires who strive to learn the ropes and receive outsized critical feedback. Imagine students harshly penalized in grades because they tried something new on an assignment. What should be moments of explorative play and learning become punitive and painful. And that has real effects on our brain.

Reward and punishment are a behaviorist's bread and butter for learning. To achieve hoped-for results, we curb poor behavior by punishing it and improve the desired behavior through reward. However, looking at the premotor cortex in the frontal lobe through fMRI scans during skill training shows a much more complex story. Excessive use of punishment hinders the brain's ability to integrate motor and sensory information. And adolescents who experienced harsh parenting (i.e., parents repeatedly getting angry, shaking, or yelling) as children had smaller brain structures in the prefrontal cortex and amygdala than their peers. Overreactions to human foibles, especially in spaces of learning, decrease our capacity for growth. And in a world that demands innovation—a form of explorative learning and play—how we manage failure is mission critical.

Amy Edmondson has devoted her life to studying how leaders and teams approach failure. She found that failure runs along a spectrum ranging from praiseworthy to blameworthy.[9] Most leaders, she says, misdiagnose failures as blameworthy when in fact, most of the mistakes experienced at work are worth celebrating. Simply put, most leaders act like out-of-control soccer parents when we should be acting like Mr. Moss. So how did he do it?

First, Mr. Moss had clearly communicated objectives that were known and shared by the team. We all agreed on our end goal. We knew where we were going, but how to get there was the experiment.

209

The Neuroscience of Play

Second, therefore, he trusted us. He trusted those whom he had "hired" through audition and training to work toward those objectives. Creativity and play within those guidelines was expected and encouraged.

In the end, he did not make himself the source for finding answers. Rather, he preferred to be the guide on the side that asked the key questions, like "Did your experiment achieve the objective?" He trained us to think about fulfilling objectives as the great evaluator of our work. We then became the best judges of our own work, not him.

When we stand at the edge of what separates us from the known and the unknown, all attempts at crossing that divide are of equal value. We can all quote back Edison's famous words regarding his attempts at the lightbulb: "I have not failed. I've just found 10,000 ways that won't work." Edison was a man who knew how to use explorative play to solve challenging problems. I think he would have loved Mr. Moss's class.

Here are the key takeaways from this:

- **Reframe Failures:** Use them as learning opportunities. Remember, most mistakes at work are praiseworthy.

- **Clearly Define Objectives:** Once in place, trust your team to find creative ways to accomplish them.

- **Model Resilience:** You can do this by celebrating effort over outcomes.

Conclusion

Let's go back to the kickball game where we started to see how warmth, competence, and gravitas are found in that snapshot of play. We began with play cues: attire fit for kickball and the sound of rubber bouncing on the pavement. You demonstrated your own competence as a leader and your trust in others by delegating responsibilities and initiating the game. Establishing rules and objectives set the stage for explorative play. While evolutionary and cognitive neuroscientists struggle to agree on many things around play, it is clear that the lessons we learn in childhood really do prepare us for the world ahead.

We play throughout our lives to connect with others. We have Wednesday night bowling night with our friends, we wine and dine potential clients or business partners at the golf course, and we set up board games and puzzles during the holidays with family. We seek to cultivate a life partner through such means as going to the theater, the symphony, a theme park, or a studio for hand-painting ceramic art. It means the world to our kids when we support them in their play spaces by going to a sports game, learning to braid a doll's hair, sitting down with a controller in front of a screen alongside them, or ordering plastic food from their makeshift restaurant. At any age and in every culture, we play together so we can be together.

Play is a form of expression that is tied deeply to our sense of self. "I'm a gamer" or "I'm an athlete" or "I'm an artist." Losing a job or even saying goodbye to a long-term project can cause an identity crisis. But leaving play behind creates the biggest loss of identity of all because we are neglecting a major part of what makes us human.

Play is intended to help us explore uncharted horizons, test out new ideas, and push past the barriers of what is known. Therefore, fostering play amidst exploration requires wise and gentle hands. While we don't want to lose the farm, we certainly can do more to help praise the experiments our brilliant team members perform every day. We tend to negatively overreact when we just need to smile and say, "Great! Let's try again."

Ultimately, play is deep in our brains—from neural circuitry to stress responses. Play is the facilitator of our learning, communication, and creativity. It is our tutor for learning the rules of the road in our relationships with others. It is one of the greatest physiological metrics for us to know we are safe and sound and ready to grow. And yet it feels as though no one takes play seriously.

Isn't it a shame that in our efforts to be "mature" or "adult" we neglect a part of us that is as primal as looking for food? Isn't it ironic that we have relegated play—the very means by which we learn to adapt and bond in this world—to a place of such disregard that the United Nations has to call for an International Day of Play just to spread awareness of its importance? And yet most of us spend our entire lives working to make enough money to afford our play. Many of us pine for a job that feels more like fun than work (i.e., "I want to do something I love, that is fun, and for the joy I get out of it"). We love play. We need play. And yet we treat it like an embarrassing photo from junior high.

It has been my goal in this chapter to make the case that play is not only a big part of our lives, but that it is a necessary neurobiological and interpersonal component. Steven Johnson, the great writer on innovation, wrote in his ode to play, "Because play is often about breaking rules and experimenting with new conventions, it turns out to be the seedbed for many innovations that ultimately develop into much sturdier and more significant forms. ...You will find the future wherever people are having the most fun."[10] Therefore, the future of leadership is found not by looking ahead, but by looking inward into the biodynamics of play. Yes, you may feel like you've forgotten all about it. Or you may feel like play is just not for you. But the script is written in your neurons.

So let's reclaim play—not as a frivolous escape, but as a vital force for leadership, innovation, and human connection. Embrace its cues, its lessons, and its power to unite us. Begin by creating spaces where play can thrive—in your work, your relationships, and your own life. Encourage experimentation, celebrate curiosity, and lead with the joy of discovery. The future belongs to those who dare to play boldly. Now is the time to rediscover what play can unlock in you and those you lead.

Conclusion

Leadership as a Lifelong Journey

Leadership is not a static trait but a dynamic interplay of behaviors, decisions, and relationships that evolve over time. As we've explored in this book, the three channels of warmth, competence, and gravitas form the foundation of what I call Leadership Biodynamics—a practical, evidence-based approach to optimizing your leadership influence.

But this is just the beginning. Understanding and applying these principles is not a one-time effort but a continuous process of reflection, learning, and adjustment. Leadership is a journey, and like any journey, it's shaped by the paths you choose to take and the tools you bring along the way.

Taking the Next Step: Your Leadership Biodynamics Profile

To fully unlock the potential of this framework, self-awareness is key. The *Leadership BioPresence Profile* is a personalized assessment tool designed to help you understand how you currently show up across the three biodynamic channels and 18 behavioral biomarkers. This profile will provide insights into your strengths, opportunities for growth, and specific actions to enhance your leadership effectiveness.

I invite you to take the next step by visiting www.biohacking leadership.com/profile. Here, you'll find everything you need to complete the Leadership BioPresence Profile assessment. By investing in this process, you'll gain a deeper understanding of how to align your behaviors with the needs of your teams and organizations, ensuring that your leadership is both impactful and sustainable.

Leadership That Lasts

As you move forward, remember that leadership is about more than what you achieve; it's about the legacy you create. Leaders with warmth foster trust and connection, leaders with competence deliver meaningful outcomes, and leaders with gravitas inspire collaboration and resilience. By mastering these channels, you become not just a leader for today but a leader for the future—one who empowers others to thrive and leaves an enduring impact.

Thank you for embarking on this journey with me. I look forward to seeing how you apply the principles of Biohacking Leadership to transform your teams, your organizations, and perhaps even your own life.

Are you ready for your next steps in biohacking your leadership?

Notes

Chapter 2

1. Hellhammer, D. H., Wüst, S., & Kudielka, B. M. (2009). Salivary cortisol as a biomarker in stress research. *Psychoneuroendocrinology*, 34(2), 163–171.
2. Thayer, J. F., Åhs, F., Fredrikson, M., Sollers III, J. J., & Wager, T. D. (2012). A meta-analysis of heart rate variability and neuroimaging studies: Implications for heart rate variability as a marker of stress and health. *Neuroscience & Biobehavioral Reviews*, 36(2), 747–756.
3. McCraty, R., & Shaffer, F. (2015). Heart rate variability: New perspectives on physiological mechanisms, assessment of self-regulatory capacity, and health risk. *Global Advances in Health and Medicine*, 4(1), 46–61.
4. Grossman, P., & Taylor, E. W. (2007). Toward understanding respiratory sinus arrhythmia: Relations to cardiac vagal tone, evolution, and biobehavioral functions. *Biological Psychology*, 74(2), 263–285.
5. Jerath, R., Edry, J. W., Barnes, V. A., & Jerath, V. (2006). Physiology of long pranayamic breathing: Neural respiratory elements may provide a mechanism that explains how slow deep breathing shifts the autonomic nervous system. *Medical Hypotheses*, 67(3), 566–571.
6. Rizzolatti, G., & Craighero, L. (2004). The mirror-neuron system. *Annual Review of Neuroscience*, 27(1), 169–192.
7. Hölzel, B. K., Lazar, S. W., Gard, T., Schuman-Olivier, Z., Vago, D. R., & Ott, U. (2011). How does mindfulness meditation work? Proposing mechanisms of action from a conceptual and neural perspective. *Perspectives on Psychological Science*, 6(6), 537–559.
8. Rogers, F. (2019). *Life's Journeys According to Mister Rogers: Things to Remember Along the Way*. Hachette Books.

Chapter 3

1. Meyerhold, V. (1969). *Meyerhold on Theatre* (E. Braun, Ed. & Trans.). Hill and Wang.
2. Robinson, K. (2011). *Out of Our Minds: Learning to Be Creative*. Capstone.
3. Morrison, E., Hutcheson, S., Nilsen, E., Fadden, J., & Franklin, N. (2019). *Strategic Doing: Ten Skills for Agile Leadership*. Wiley.
4. Willis, J., & Todorov, A. (2006). First impressions: Making up your mind after a 100-ms exposure to a face. *Psychological Science, 17*(7), 592–598.
5. Antonakis, J., & House, R. J. (2014). Instrumental leadership: Measurement and extension of transformational-transactional leadership theory. *Leadership Quarterly, 25*(4), 746–771.
6. Kaiser, R. B., Hogan, R., & Craig, S. B. (2008). Leadership and the fate of organizations. *American Psychologist, 63*(2), 96–110.
7. Knapp, M. L., Hall, J. A., & Horgan, T. G. (2014). *Nonverbal Communication in Human Interaction*. Cengage Learning.
8. Dirks, K. T., & Ferrin, D. L. (2002). Trust in leadership: Meta-analytic findings and implications for research and practice. *Journal of Applied Psychology, 87*(4), 611–628.
9. Lakoff, G., & Johnson, M. (1999). *Philosophy in the Flesh: The Embodied Mind and Its Challenge to Western Thought*. Basic Books.
10. Riskind, J. H., & Gotay, C. C. (1982). Physical posture: Could it have regulatory or feedback effects on motivation and emotion? *Motivation and Emotion, 6*(3), 273–298.
11. Wilson, M. (2002). Six views of embodied cognition. *Psychonomic Bulletin & Review, 9*(4), 625–636.
12. Carney, D. R., Cuddy, A. J. C., & Yap, A. J. (2010). Power posing: Brief nonverbal displays affect neuroendocrine levels and risk tolerance. *Psychological Science, 21*(10), 1363–1368.
13. Goldin-Meadow, S., & Beilock, S. L. (2010). Action's influence on thought: The case of gesture. *Perspectives on Psychological Science, 5*(6), 664–674.

14. Strack, F., Martin, L. L., & Stepper, S. (1988). Inhibiting and facilitating conditions of the human smile: A nonobtrusive test of the facial feedback hypothesis. *Journal of Personality and Social Psychology, 54*(5), 768–777.
15. Barsalou, L. W. (2008). Grounded cognition. *Annual Review of Psychology, 59*, 617–645.
16. Niedenthal, P. M., Barsalou, L. W., Winkielman, P., Krauth-Gruber, S., & Ric, F. (2005). Embodiment in attitudes, social perception, and emotion. *Personality and Social Psychology Review, 9*(3), 184–211.
17. Ambady, N., & Rosenthal, R. (1992). Thin slices of expressive behavior as predictors of interpersonal consequences: A meta-analysis. *Psychological Bulletin, 111*(2), 256–274.

Chapter 4

1. Weber, M. (1947). *The Theory of Social and Economic Organization*. Free Press.
2. Burns, J. M. (1978). *Leadership*. Harper & Row.
3. Bass, B. M. (1985). *Leadership and Performance beyond Expectations*. Free Press.
4. Judge, T. A., & Cable, D. M. Cable, D. M. (2004). The effect of physical height on workplace success and income: Preliminary test of a theoretical model. *Journal of Applied Psychology, 89*(3), 428–441.
5. Eagly, A. H., & Carli, L. L. (2007). *Through the Labyrinth: The Truth about How Women Become Leaders*. Harvard Business School Press.
6. Nembhard, I. M., & Edmondson, A. C. (2006). Making it safe: The effects of leader inclusiveness and professional status on psychological safety and improvement efforts in health care teams. *Journal of Organizational Behavior, 27*(7), 941–966.
7. Ibarra, H., & Scoular, A. (2019). The leader as coach. *Harvard Business Review, 97*(6), 110-119.
8. Kaiser, R. B., LeBreton, J. M., & Hogan, J. (2015). The dark side of personality at work. *Journal of Applied Psychology, 100*(6), 1919–1938.

9. Edmondson, A. C. (1999). Psychological safety and learning behavior in work teams. *Administrative Science Quarterly*, 44(2), 350–383.

10. Bass, B. M., & Avolio, B. J. (1994). *Improving Organizational Effectiveness through Transformational Leadership*. Sage.

11. Thaler, R. H., & Sunstein, C. R. (2008). *Nudge: Improving Decisions about Health, Wealth, and Happiness*. Yale University Press.

12. Uhl-Bien, M., Marion, R., & McKelvey, B. (2007). Complexity leadership theory: Shifting leadership from the industrial age to the knowledge era. *The Leadership Quarterly*, 18(4), 298–318.

13. Edmondson, A. C. (1999). Psychological safety and learning behavior in work teams. Administrative Science Quarterly, 44(2), 350–383.

Chapter 5

1. Goodwin, D. K. (2005). *Team of Rivals: The Political Genius of Abraham Lincoln*. Simon & Schuster.

2. Hodson, G., Turner, R. N., & Choma, B. L. (2016). Individual differences in intergroup contact propensity and prejudice reduction. In Loris Vezzali and Sofia Stathi (eds.), *Intergroup Contact Theory*, Routledge, 16–38.

3. Cable, D. (2018). *Alive at Work: The Neuroscience of Helping Your People Love What They Do*. Harvard Business Review Press.

4. Boyatzis, R. E., McKee, A., & Johnston, F. (2008). *Becoming a Resonant Leader: Develop Your Emotional Intelligence, Renew Your Relationships, Sustain Your Effectiveness*. Harvard Business Review Press.

5. Zenger, J. H., & Folkman, J. (2016). *The Extraordinary Leader Turning Good Managers into Great Leaders*. McGraw-Hill Education.

6. King, M. (2018). *The Good Neighbor: The Life and Work of Fred Rogers*. Abrams.

7. Cameron, K. S. (2012). *Positive Leadership: Strategies for Extraordinary Performance*. Berrett-Koehler Publishers.

8. Sironi, E. (2019). Job satisfaction as a determinant of employees' optimal well-being in an instrumental variable approach. *Quality & Quantity*, 53(4), 1721–1742.

9. Edmondson, A. C. (2019). *The Fearless Organization: Creating Psychological Safety in the Workplace for Learning, Innovation, and Growth.* Wiley.

10. Lee, H. (1960). *To Kill a Mockingbird.* J.B. Lippincott & Co.

11. Gino, F. (2019). *Rebel Talent: Why It Pays to Break the Rules at Work and in Life.* Dey Street Books.

12. Feiler, A. (2021). *A Better Life for Their Children: Julius Rosenwald, Booker T. Washington, and the 4,978 Schools that Changed America.* University of Georgia Press.

13. Goleman, D. (1995). *Emotional Intelligence: Why It Can Matter More Than IQ.* Bantam Books.

14. Smith, R. (1996). *The Making of It's a Wonderful Life.* St. Martin's Press.

15. Chapman, G., & White, P. (2019). *The 5 Languages of Appreciation in the Workplace: Empowering Organizations by Encouraging People.* Northfield Publishing.

16. Gill, G. (2004). *Nightingales: The Extraordinary Upbringing and Curious Life of Miss Florence Nightingale.* Ballantine Books.

Chapter 6

1. Thoma, L., Auer, A., & Fiedler, K. (2020). Impulsiveness, stress, and decision-making: A modern take on emotional regulation. *Journal of Behavioral Decision Making, 33(3),* 201–215.

2. Lipshitz, R., & Strauss, O. (1997). Coping with uncertainty: A naturalistic decision-making analysis. *Organizational Behavior and Human Decision Processes, 69(2),* 149–163.

3. Bono, J. E., & Judge, T. A. (2003). Self-concordance at work: Toward understanding the motivational effects of transformational leaders. *Academy of Management Journal, 46(5),* 554–571.

4. Schwantes, M. (2021, November 6). Warren Buffett says you can ruin your life in 5 minutes by making 1 critical mistake. *Inc.*

5. Gino, F. (2020). *Rebel Talent: Why It Pays to Break the Rules at Work and in Life.* Dey Street Books.

6. McChesney, C., Covey, S. R., & Huling, S. J. (2012). *The 4 Disciplines of Execution: Achieving Your Wildly Important Goals*. Free Press.
7. Gino, *Rebel Talent*.
8. Rice, C. (2011). *No Higher Honor: A Memoir of My Years in Washington*. Crown Publishers.
9. Gino, *Rebel Talent*.
10. Gino, *Rebel Talent*.
11. Gino, *Rebel Talent*.
12. Newport, C. (2016). *Deep Work: Rules for Focused Success in a Distracted World*. Grand Central Publishing.
13. Baumeister, R. F., Vohs, K. D., & Tice, D. M. (2018). The strength model of self-control: Recent developments and future directions. *Current Directions in Psychological Science, 27*(2), 109–118.
14. Tang, Y. Y., Holzel, B. K., & Posner, M. I. (2016). The neuroscience of mindfulness meditation. *Nature Reviews Neuroscience, 16*(4), 213–225.
15. Kahneman, D. (2018). *Thinking, Fast and Slow*. Farrar, Straus and Giroux.
16. Zhou, J., & George, J. M. (2018). Awakening creativity: The role of leader emotional intelligence. *Leadership Quarterly, 29*(3), 344–357.
17. Baumeister, R. F., Vohs, K. D., & Tice, D. M. (2018). The strength model of self-control: Recent developments and future directions. *Current Directions in Psychological Science, 27*(2), 109–118.
18. Kornblum, A. (2013). *Angela Merkel: Europe's Most Influential Leader*. ABC-CLIO.
19. Krings, F., Bangerter, A., Gomez, P., & Grob, A. (2020). Why people are late: Exploring the dimensions and underlying causes of punctuality problems. *Journal of Personality and Social Psychology, 119*(1), 56–73.
20. Aeon, B., & Aguinis, H. (2020). It's about time: New perspectives and insights on time management. *Academy of Management Perspectives, 34*(3), 300–318.
21. Aeon, & Aguinis, It's about Time.
22. Vincent, A. (2020, January 6). *The last nice guy left in Hollywood: Just how good is Tom Hanks, really? The Telegraph*.

23. Gawande, A. (2010). *The Checklist Manifesto: How to Get Things Right*. Metropolitan Books.

24. Sutton, R. I. (2019). *The No Asshole Rule: Building a Civilized Workplace and Surviving One that Isn't*. Business Plus.

25. Lipshitz, R., Klein, G., Orasanu, J., & Salas, E. (2018). Taking stock of naturalistic decision making. *Journal of Behavioral Decision Making, 25*(4), 432–453.

26. Gino, *Rebel Talent*.

27. Sutton, *The No Asshole Rule*.

28. Alter, J. (2020). *His Very Best: Jimmy Carter a Life*. Simon & Schuster.

29. Denton, K., & Wilkinson, A. (2019). The impact of organization on team performance: A critical review. *Journal of Organizational Behavior, 41*(2), 210–225.

30. Aeon & Aguinis, It's about time.

31. Hibbert, P., & Duncan, R. (2020). Organizational goals: How planning and structure drive long-term success. *Management Journal, 57*(1), 45–61.

32. Kondo, M. (2014). *The Life-Changing Magic of Tidying Up: The Japanese Art of Decluttering and Organizing*. Ten Speed Press.

Chapter 7

1. Nadella, S. (2017). *Hit Refresh: The Quest to Rediscover Microsoft's Soul and Imagine a Better Future for Everyone*. HarperBusiness.

2. Barra, M. (n.d.). *Fom co-op student to CEO*. LinkedIn. Accessed January 28, 2025, from https://www.linkedin.com/pulse/from-co-op-student-ceo-mary-barra/

3. Burns, U. (2018). *Where You Are Is Not Who You Are: A Memoir*. HarperCollins.

4. Barsade, S. G., & Gibson, D. E. (2007). Why does affect matter in organizations? *Academy of Management Perspectives, 21*(1), 36–59.

5. Hülsheger, U. R., Alberts, H. J., Feinholdt, A., & Lang, J. W. (2013). Benefits of mindfulness at work: The role of mindfulness in emotion regulation, emotional exhaustion, and job satisfaction. *Journal of Applied Psychology, 98*(2), 310–325.

6. Kraus, M. W. (2017). Voice-only communication enhances empathic accuracy. *American Psychologist*, 72(7), 644–654.
7. Sampson, A. (2018). *Mandela: The Authorized Biography*. HarperCollins.
8. King, M. (2018). *The Good Neighbor: The Life and Work of Fred Rogers*. Abrams Press.

Chapter 8

1. Zak, P. J. (2014). Why your brain loves good storytelling. *Harvard Business Review*.
2. Hasson, U., Ghazanfar, A. A., Galantucci, B., Garrod, S., & Keysers, C. (2012). Brain-to-brain coupling: A mechanism for creating and sharing a social world. *Trends in Cognitive Sciences*, 16(2), 114–121.
3. Jobs, S. (2005, June 12). 'You've got to find what you love', Jobs says [Commencement address]. Stanford Report.
4. Zak, Why your brain loves good storytelling.
5. Green, M. C., & Brock, T. C. (2000). The role of transportation in the persuasiveness of public narratives. *Journal of Personality and Social Psychology*, 79(5), 701–721.
6. Morgan, N. (2015). *Power Cues: The Subtle Science of Leading Groups, Persuading Others, and Maximizing Your Personal Impact*. Harvard Business Review Press.
7. Cialdini, R. B. (2016). *Pre-Suasion: A Revolutionary Way to Influence and Persuade*. Simon & Schuster.
8. Green & Brock, The role of transportation.
9. Gill, R. (2015). Why the PR Strategy that Worked for Apple Won't Work for You. *Harvard Business Review*.
10. Meyerhold, V. (1969). *Meyerhold on Theatre*. (E. Braun, Ed. & Trans.). Hill and Wang.
11. Gillett, J. (2014). *Acting on the Stage: Techniques for the Modern Actor*. Methuen Drama.
12. Oreg, S., & Berson, Y. (2019). Leadership and employees' reactions to change: The role of leaders' personal attributes and organizational context. *Personnel Psychology*, 72(4), 695–726.

13. Fischer, T., Dietz, J., & Antonakis, J. (2017). Leadership process models: A review and synthesis. *Journal of Management*, 43(6), 1726–1750.

14. Campbell, J. (2008). *The Hero with a Thousand Faces*. New World Library.

15. Greenleaf, R. K. (2002). *Servant Leadership: A Journey into the Nature of Legitimate Power and Greatness*. Paulist Press.

16. Vonnegut, K. (1999). *Bagombo Snuff Box: Uncollected Short Fiction*. G. P. Putnam's Sons.

17. Heath, C., & Heath, D. (2007). *Made to Stick: Why Some Ideas Survive and Others Die*. Random House.

18. Olson, R. (2015). *Houston, We Have a Narrative: Why Science Needs Story*. University of Chicago Press.

19. Heath & Heath, *Made to Stick*.

20. Denning, S. (2020). *The Leader's Guide to Storytelling: Mastering the Art and Discipline of Business Narrative*. Wiley.

21. Oreg & Berson, Leadership and employees' reactions to change.

22. Crystal, B. (2013). *Still Foolin''Em: Where I've Been, Where I'm Going, and Where the Hell Are My Keys?* Henry Holt and Co.

23. Brown, B. (2018). *Dare to Lead: Brave Work. Tough Conversations Whole Hearts*. Random House.

24. Avolio, B. J. (1999). *Full Leadership Development: Building the Vital Forces in Organizations*. SAGE Publications.

25. Cialdini, R. B. (2016). *Pre-Suasion: A Revolutionary Way to Influence and Persuade*. Simon & Schuster.

26. Brown, *Dare to Lead*.

27. Guber, P. (2011). *Tell to Win: Connect, Persuade, and Triumph with the Hidden Power of Story*. Crown Business.

28. Heath & Heath, *Made to Stick*.

29. Avolio, *Full Leadership Development*.

30. Times of India. (2024, January 7). *Ratan Tata's Vision: Nano and the Concept of the People's Car*. Times of India.

31. Okonjo-Iweala, N. (2018). *Fighting Corruption is Dangerous: The Story Behind the Headlines*. MIT Press.

32. Ghosn, C., & Riès, P. (2005). *Shift: Inside Nissan's Historic Revival*. Currency/Doubleday.

33. Lee, K. Y. (2000). *From Third World to First: The Singapore Story: 1965–2000*. HarperCollins.

34. Johnson Sirleaf, E. (2009). *This Child will be Great: Memoir of a Remarkable Life by Africa's First Woman President*. HarperCollins.

Chapter 9

1. Iacoboni, M. (2008). *Mirroring People: The New Science of How We Connect with Others*. Farrar, Straus and Giroux.

2. Rogers, C. R., & Farson, R. E. (2015). *Active Listening*. University of Chicago Press.

3. Catron, M. L. (2015, January 9). To fall in love with anyone, do this. New York Times.

4. Woolley, A. W., et al. (2010). Evidence for a collective intelligence factor in the performance of human groups. *Science,* 330(6004), 686–688.

5. Paul, R., & Elder, L. (2019). *The Thinker's Guide to Socratic Questioning*. Foundation for Critical Thinking.

6. Tschannen-Moran, B., & Tschannen-Moran, M. (2018). *Coaching Conversations: Transforming Your School One Conversation at a Time*. Corwin Press.

7. Rogers & Farson, *Active Listening*.

8. Dalio, R. (2017). *Principles: Life and Work*. Simon & Schuster.

9. Schein, E. H. (2016). *Humble Inquiry: The Gentle Art of Asking Instead of Telling*. Berrett-Koehler Publishers.

10. Groysberg, B., & Slind, M. (2012, June). Leadership Is a Conversation. *Harvard Business Review*.

11. Covey, S. R. (2013). *The 7 Habits of Highly Effective People*. Simon & Schuster.

12. Stone, D., Patton, B., & Heen, S. (2010). *Difficult Conversations: How to Discuss What Matters Most*. Penguin Books.

13. Yousafzai, M. (2018). *We Are Displaced: My Journey and Stories from Refugee Girls Around the World*. Little, Brown Books for Young Readers.

14. Rogers & Farson, *Active Listening*.

15. Ting-Toomey, S. (1999). *Communicating Across Cultures*. Guilford Press.

16. Salas, E., et al. (2015). Team dynamics and effectiveness: Key insights for building stronger teams. *Journal of Organizational Behavior*, 36(4).

17. Kauffmann, S. (2018). *Macron's Public Conversations: Building a Narrative for France*. Le Monde.

18. Bongwe, S. (2021). Interview on creating platforms for youth dialogue. News24.

Chapter 10

1. Van Vleet, M., & Feeney, B. C. (2015). Play behavior and playfulness in adulthood. *Social and Personality Psychology Compass*, 9(11), 630–643.

2. Harter, J. (2024). U.S. engagement hits 11-year low. Gallup.

3. Panksepp, J. (1998). *Affective Neuroscience: The Foundations of Human and Animal Emotions*. Oxford University Press.

4. Kestly, T. A. (2014). *The Interpersonal Neurobiology of Play: Brain-building Interventions for Emotional Well-being*. Norton.

5. Brown, S., & Vaughan, C. (2009). *Play: How It Shapes the Brain, Opens the Imagination, and Invigorates the Soul*. Penguin.

6. IKEA. (2017). (rep.). *Play Report 2017: A spark of play every day* (vol. 3, pp. 1–41). IKEA.

7. Kouchaki, M., Smith, I. H., & Smith, J. R. (2011, September). Adults behave better when teddy bears are in the room. *Harvard Business Review*.

8. Csikszentmihalyi, M. (1997). *Finding Flow: The Psychology of Engagement with Everyday Life*. Basic Books.

9. Edmondson, A.C. (2023). *Right Kind of Wrong: The Science of Failing Well*. Atria Books.

10. Johnson, S. (2016). *Wonderland: How Play Made the Modern World*. Riverhead Books.

Bibliography

Chapter 1

Argyris, C. (1991). *Teaching Smart People How to Learn*. Harvard Business Review Press.

Baker, B. J., & Hill, E. P. (2003). Beaver *(Castor canadensis)*. In G. A. Feldhamer, B. C. Thompson, and J. A. Chapman *Wild Mammals of North America: Biology, Management, and Conservation* (pp. 288–310). Johns Hopkins University Press.

Cohen, S. G., & Bailey, D. E. (1997). What makes teams work: Group effectiveness research from the shop floor to the executive suite. *Journal of Management*, 23(3), 239–290.

Creel, S., & Christianson, D. (2008). Relationships between direct predation and risk effects: Interactions between wolves and elk. *Ecology*, 89(2), 452–464.

Cummings, T. G., & Worley, C. G. (2014). *Organization Development and Change* (10th ed.). Cengage Learning.

Elkin, G., & Swain, J. (2016). Promoting diversity: A review of the evidence. *International Journal of Educational Management*, 30(1), 2–16.

Gese, E. M., & Mech, L. D. (1991). Social and nutritional influences on gray wolf (Canis lupus) pack behavior. *Canadian Journal of Zoology*, 69(3), 755–762.

Graham, N. A. J., Nash, K. L., & Waples, R. (2007). Impacts of sea stars on the community structure of a temperate rocky intertidal zone. *Marine Ecology Progress Series*, 335, 113–120.

Hackman, J. R., & Oldham, G. R. (1976). Motivation through the design of work: Test of a theory. *Organizational Behavior and Human Performance*, 16(2), 250–279.

Jangsang, K., Park, J. S., & Choi, Y. K. (2021). Predator-prey interactions and habitat use of sea stars and their prey. *Marine Biology*, 168(3), 1–10.

Keller, J. M., Morrow, J. L., & Becker, W. J. (2018). The resilience of organizations: Adaptation and growth in a complex environment. *Journal of Organizational Behavior*, 39(3), 315–330.

Kotter, J. P. (1996). *Leading Change*. Harvard Business Review Press.

Kramer, M. A., Dunbar, M. R., & Griffiths, C. (2007). Beaver habitat use and the significance of dam structure in wetlands. *Wetlands Ecology and Management*, 15(2), 169–179.

Lett, N. R., & Bock, D. (2010). The role of sea stars in maintaining biodiversity in intertidal ecosystems. *Ecological Applications*, 20(4), 1052–1061.

MacNulty, D. R., Smith, D. W., & Mech, L. D. (2009). A proposed method for identifying the significance of social structure in wolf packs. *Journal of Wildlife Management*, 73(2), 225–232.

Mech, L. D. (1970). The Wolf: The ecology and behavior of an endangered species. *American Scientist*, 58(6), 620–635.

Mech, L. D., & Boitani, L. (2003). *Wolves: Behavior, Ecology, and Conservation*. University of Chicago Press.

Mladenov, P. V., Purcell, S. W., & Meyer, K. E. (1995). Regeneration in sea stars: The importance of behavioral plasticity. *Marine Ecology Progress Series*, 120, 217–225.

Naiman, R. J., Decamps, H., & Pastor, J. (1988). The potential for biodiversity in the boreal forest. *BioScience*, 38(6), 379–386.

Nolet, B. A., & Rosell, F. (1998). A review of the ecological effects of beavers on wetlands. *Ecological Applications*, 8(4), 837–845.

Paine, R. T. (1966). Food web complexity and species diversity. *American Naturalist*, 100(910), 65–75.

Parker, K. L., Gauthier, D., & Hovey, F. W. (2008). The importance of strategic intervention in organizational behavior. *International Journal of Organizational Analysis*, 16(3), 241–265.

Rosell, F., Bozser, O., Collen, P., & Parker, H. (2005). Ecological impact of beavers Castor fiber and Castor canadensis and their ability to modify ecosystems. *Ecohydrology*, 1(2), 233–241.

Tharp, B. R. (2009). Leadership and resource management: A case for adapting strategies in dynamic environments. *Journal of Leadership Studies*, 3(3), 46–60.

Wang, Y., Zhang, Z., & Wu, X. (2005). Behavior and ecology of wolves: A review of the literature. *Wildlife Biology*, 11(2), 107–116.

Chapter 2

Clark, L., & Strauss, J. (2019). The neuroscience of decision-making: How our brains shape leadership choices. *Leadership Science Journal*, 25(4), 220–235.

Ekman, P. (2003). *Emotions Revealed: Recognizing Faces and Feelings to Improve Communication and Emotional Life*. Henry Holt and Co.

Fredrickson, B. L. (2001). The role of positive emotions in positive psychology: The broaden-and-build theory of positive emotions. *American Psychologist*, 56(3), 218–226.

Goman, C. K. (2008). *The Nonverbal Advantage: Secrets and Science of Body Language at Work*. Berrett-Koehler Publishers.

Grossman, P., & Taylor, E. W. (2007). Toward understanding respiratory Sinus Arrhythmia: Relations to cardiac vagal tone, evolution, and biobehavioral functions. *Biological Psychology*, 74(2), 263–285.

Hatfield, E., Cacioppo, J. T., & Rapson, R. L. (1993). Emotional contagion. *Current Directions in Psychological Science*, 2(3), 96–100.

Hellhammer, D. H., Wüst, S., & Kudielka, B. M. (2009). Salivary cortisol as a biomarker in stress research. *Psychoneuroendocrinology*, 34(2), 163–171.

Hölzel, B. K., Lazar, S. W., Gard, T., Schuman-Olivier, Z., Vago, D. R., & Ott, U. (2011). How does mindfulness meditation work? Proposing mechanisms of action from a conceptual and neural perspective. *Perspectives on Psychological Science*, 6(6), 537–559.

Jerath, R., Edry, J. W., Barnes, V. A., & Jerath, V. (2006). Physiology of long pranayamic breathing: Neural respiratory elements may provide a mechanism that explains how slow deep breathing shifts the autonomic nervous system. *Medical Hypotheses*, 67(3), 566–571.

Juslin, P. N., & Scherer, K. R. (2005). Vocal expression of affect. In J. A. Harrigan, R. Rosenthal, & K. R. Scherer *The New Handbook of Methods in Nonverbal Behavior Research* (pp. 65–135). Oxford University Press.

Kleinke, C. L. (1986). Gaze and eye contact: A research review. *Psychological Bulletin*, 100(1), 78–100.

McCraty, R., & Shaffer, F. (2015). Heart rate variability: New perspectives on physiological mechanisms, assessment of self-regulatory capacity, and health risk. *Global Advances in Health and Medicine*, 4(1), 46–61.

Matsumoto, D. (2006). *Culture and Nonverbal Behavior*. Cambridge University Press.

Rizzolatti, G., & Craighero, L. (2004). The mirror-neuron system. *Annual Review of Neuroscience*, 27(1), 169–192.

Zak, P. J. (2011). The physiology of moral sentiments. *Journal of Economic Behavior & Organization*, 77(1), 53–65.

Chapter 3

Avolio, B. J., & Gardner, W. L. (2005). Authentic leadership development: Getting to the root of positive forms of leadership. *Leadership Quarterly*, 16(3), 315–338.

Barsalou, L. W. (2008). Grounded cognition. *Annual Review of Psychology*, 59, 617–645.

Carney, D. R., Cuddy, A. J. C., & Yap, A. J. (2010). Power posing: Brief nonverbal displays affect neuroendocrine levels and risk tolerance. *Psychological Science*, 21(10), 1363–1368.

Coyle, D. (2018). *The Culture Code: The Secrets of Highly Successful Groups*. Bantam Books.

Dirks, K. T., & Ferrin, D. L. (2002). Trust in leadership: Meta-analytic findings and implications for research and practice. *Journal of Applied Psychology*, 87(4), 611–628.

Forthomme, B., Croisier, J. L., Ciccarone, G., Crielaard, J. M., & Cloes, M. (2005). Factors correlated with volleyball spike velocity. *American Journal of Sports Medicine, 33*(10), 1513–1519.

Fox Cabane, O. (2012). *The Charisma Myth: How Anyone Can Master the Art and Science of Personal Magnetism.* Portfolio/Penguin.

Gentry, W. A., Weber, T. J., & Sadri, G. (2012). *Empathy in the Workplace: A Tool for Effective Leadership.* Society for Human Resource Management.

Goldin-Meadow, S., & Beilock, S. L. (2010). Action's influence on thought: The case of gesture. *Perspectives on Psychological Science, 5*(6), 664–674.

Goleman, D., Boyatzis, R., & McKee, A. (2013). *Primal Leadership: Unleashing the Power of Emotional Intelligence.* Harvard Business Review Press.

Goman, C. K. (2011). *The Silent Language of Leaders: How Body Language Can Help—or Hurt—how You Lead.* Jossey-Bass.

Gronau, Q. F., van Erp, S., Heck, D. W., Cesario, J., Jonas, K. J., & Wagenmakers, E.-J. (2017). A Bayesian model-averaged meta-analysis of the power pose effect with informed and default priors: The case of felt power. *Comprehensive Results in Social Psychology, 2*(1), 123–138.

Heifetz, R., Grashow, A., & Linsky, M. (2009). *The Practice of Adaptive Leadership: Tools and Tactics for Changing Your Organization and the World.* Harvard Business Review Press.

Johnson, C. E. (2016). *Meeting the Ethical Challenges of Leadership: Casting Light or Shadow.* SAGE.

Kaiser, R. B., Hogan, R., & Craig, S. B. (2008). Leadership and the fate of organizations. *American Psychologist, 63*(2), 96–110.

Knapp, M. L., Hall, J. A., & Horgan, T. G. (2014). *Nonverbal Communication in Human Interaction.* Cengage Learning.

Lakoff, G., & Johnson, M. (1999). *Philosophy in the Flesh: The Embodied Mind and its Challenge to Western Thought.* Basic Books.

Leach, R. (2012). *Meyerhold and Biomechanics.* Routledge.

Mehrabian, A. (2017). *Nonverbal Communication.* Routledge.

Niedenthal, P. M., Barsalou, L. W., Winkielman, P., Krauth-Gruber, S., & Ric, F. (2005). Embodiment in attitudes, social perception, and emotion. *Personality and Social Psychology Review, 9*(3), 184–211.

Oppezzo, M., & Schwartz, D. L. (2014). Give your ideas some legs: The positive effect of walking on creative thinking. *Journal of Experimental Psychology: Learning, Memory, and Cognition, 40*(4), 1142–1152.

Pease, A., & Pease, B. (2016). *The Definitive Book of Body Language*. Bantam Books.

Peters, T. (2005). *Re-imagine! Business Excellence in a Disruptive Age*. Dorling Kindersley.

Reynolds, A., & Lewis, D. (2018). The two traits of the best problem-solving teams. *Harvard Business Review*.

Riggio, R. E. (2014). Leadership development: The current state and future expectations. *Consulting Psychology Journal: Practice and Research, 66*(1), 3–10.

Riskind, J. H., & Gotay, C. C. (1982). Physical posture: Could it have regulatory or feedback effects on motivation and emotion? *Motivation and Emotion, 6*(3), 273–298.

Robinson, K. (2011). *Out of Our Minds: Learning to be Creative*. Capstone.

Simons, T. (2002). Behavioral integrity: The perceived alignment between managers' words and deeds as a research focus. *Organization Science, 13*(1), 18–35.

Strack, F., Martin, L. L., & Stepper, S. (1988). Inhibiting and facilitating conditions of the human smile: A nonobtrusive test of the facial feedback hypothesis. *Journal of Personality and Social Psychology, 54*(5), 768–777.

Van Kleef, G. A., De Dreu, C. K. W., & Manstead, A. S. R. (2015). The interpersonal effects of emotions in negotiations: A motivated information processing approach. *Journal of Personality and Social Psychology, 87*(4), 510–528.

Willis, J., & Todorov, A. (2006). First impressions: Making up your mind after a 100-ms exposure to a face. *Psychological Science, 17*(7), 592–598.

Wilson, M. (2002). Six views of embodied cognition. *Psychonomic Bulletin & Review, 9*(4), 625–636.

Chapter 4

Barsalou, L. W. (2008). Grounded cognition. *Annual Review of Psychology, 59*(1), 617–645.

Bass, B. M. (1985). *Leadership and Performance Beyond Expectations*. Free Press.

Bass, B. M., & Avolio, B. J. (1994). *Improving Organizational Effectiveness Through Transformational Leadership*. Sage.

Baumeister, R. F., & Tierney, J. (2011). *Willpower: Rediscovering the Greatest Human Strength*. Penguin.

Bazerman, M. H., & Tenbrunsel, A. E. (2011). *Blind Spots: Why We Fail to do What's Right and What to do About It*. Princeton University Press.

Burns, J. M. (1978). *Leadership*. Harper & Row.

Conger, J. A. (1990). The dark side of leadership. *Organizational Dynamics, 19*(2), 44–55.

Covey, S. R. (1989). *The 7 Habits of Highly Effective People: Powerful Lessons in Personal Change*. Free Press.

Cuddy, A. J., Kohut, M., & Neffinger, J. (2013). Connect, then lead. *Harvard Business Review, 91*(7–8), 54–61.

Eagly, A. H., & Carli, L. L. (2007). *Through the Labyrinth: The Truth About How Women Become Leaders*. Harvard Business School Press.

Edmondson, A. C. (1999). Psychological safety and learning behavior in work teams. *Administrative Science Quarterly, 44*(2), 350–383.

Ericsson, K. A., Krampe, R. T., & Tesch-Römer, C. (1993). The role of deliberate practice in the acquisition of expert performance. *Psychological Review, 100*(3), 363–406.

Ericsson, K. A., Prietula, M. J., & Cokely, E. T. (2007). The making of an expert. *Harvard Business Review, 85*(7/8), 114–121.

Goffee, R., & Jones, G. (2006). *Why Should Anyone be Led by You? What It Takes to be an Authentic Leader*. Harvard Business School Press.

Goleman, D. (1995). *Emotional Intelligence: Why It Can Matter More Than IQ*. Bantam Books.

Goleman, D. (2011). *Leadership: The Power of Emotional Intelligence*. More Than Sound.

Goleman, D., Boyatzis, R., & McKee, A. (2002). *Primal Leadership: Realizing the Power of Emotional Intelligence*. Harvard Business School Press.

Grant, A. M. (2013). *Give and Take: A Revolutionary Approach to Success*. Viking.

Greenleaf, R. K. (1977). *Servant Leadership: A Journey into the Nature of Legitimate Power and Greatness*. Paulist Press.

Gupta, A. (2016). The role of punctuality in organizational effectiveness. *Journal of Business Ethics, 140*(2), 365–373.

Hewitt, S. A. (2014). *Executive Presence: The Missing Link Between Merit and Success*. HarperCollins.

Hill, L. A., & Lineback, K. (2011). *Being the Boss: The 3 Imperatives for Becoming a Great Leader*. Harvard Business Review Press.

Hofstede, G. (1980). *Culture's Consequences: International Differences in Work-Related Values*. Sage.

Iacoboni, M. (2009). *Mirroring People: The New Science of How We Connect with Others*. Picador.

Ibarra, H., Ely, R. J., & Kolb, D. M. (2013). Women rising: The unseen barriers. *Harvard Business Review, 91*(9), 60–66.

Ibarra, H., & Scoular, A. (2019). The leader as coach. *Harvard Business Review, 97*(6), 110–119.

Judge, T. A., Cable, D. M., & Boudreau, J. W. (2004). The effect of physical attractiveness on hiring decisions. *Journal of Applied Psychology, 89*(4), 796–804.

Kahneman, D. (2011). *Thinking, Fast and Slow*. Farrar, Straus and Giroux.

Karasek, R. A., & Theorell, T. (1990). *Healthy Work: Stress, Productivity, and the Reconstruction of Working Life*. Basic Books.

Kaiser, R. B., LeBreton, J. M., & Hogan, J. (2015). The dark side of personality at work. *Journal of Applied Psychology, 100*(6), 1919–1938.

Mehrabian, A. (1981). *Silent Messages: Implicit Communication of Emotions and Attitudes*. Wadsworth Publishing.

Morgan, N. (2001). How to become an authentic speaker. *Harvard Business Review, 79*(12), 92–97.

Nembhard, I. M., & Edmondson, A. C. (2006). Making it safe: The effects of leader inclusiveness and professional status on psychological safety and improvement efforts in health care teams. *Journal of Organizational Behavior, 27*(7), 941–966.

Pearce, C. L., & Conger, J. A. (2003). *Shared Leadership: Reframing the Hows and Whys of Leadership*. Sage.

Roche, M., Haar, J. M., & Luthans, F. (2014). The role of mindfulness and psychological capital on the well-being of leaders. *Journal of Occupational Health Psychology,* 19(4), 476–489.

Rudman, L. A., & Glick, P. (2001). Prescriptive gender stereotypes and backlash toward agentic women. *Journal of Social Issues,* 57(4), 743–762.

Tannen, D. (1990). *You Just Don't Understand: Women and Men in Conversation.* Ballantine Books.

Thaler, R. H., & Sunstein, C. R. (2008). *Nudge: Improving Decisions About Health, Wealth, and Happiness.* Yale University Press.

Tjosvold, D. (2008). The conflict-positive organization: It depends upon us. *Journal of Organizational Behavior,* 29(1), 19–28.

Uhl-Bien, M., Marion, R., & McKelvey, B. (2007). Complexity leadership theory: Shifting leadership from the industrial age to the knowledge era. *Leadership Quarterly,* 18(4), 298–318.

Weber, M. (1947). *The Theory of Social and Economic Organization.* Free Press.

Chapter 5

Brown, B. (2018). *Dare to Lead: Brave Work. Tough Conversations. Whole Hearts.* Random House.

Cable, D. (2018). *Alive at Work: The Neuroscience of Helping Your People Love What They Do.* Harvard Business Review Press.

Cameron, K. S. (2012). *Positive Leadership: Strategies for Extraordinary Performance.* Berrett-Koehler Publishers.

Carlin, J. (2008). *Playing the Enemy: Nelson Mandela and the Game that Made a Nation.* Penguin Press.

Chapman, G., & White, P. (2019). *The 5 Languages of Appreciation in the Workplace: Empowering Organizations by Encouraging People.* Northfield Publishing.

Covey, S. R. (1989). *The 7 Habits of Highly Effective People: Powerful Lessons in Personal Change.* Free Press.

Coyle, D. (2018). *The Culture Code: The Secrets of Highly Successful Groups.* Bantam Books.

Edmondson, A. C. (2019). *The Fearless Organization: Creating Psychological Safety in the Workplace for Learning, Innovation, and Growth.* Wiley.

Feiler, A. (2021). *A Better Life for Their Children: Julius Rosenwald, Booker T. Washington, and the 4,978 Schools that Changed America.* University of Georgia Press.

Gino, F. (2019). *Rebel Talent: Why It Pays to Break the Rules at Work and in Life.* Dey Street Books.

Goleman, D. (1995). *Emotional Intelligence: Why It Can Matter More Than IQ.* Bantam Books.

Hodson, G., Turner, R. N., & Choma, B. L. (2016). Individual differences in intergroup contact propensity and prejudice reduction. *Intergroup Contact Theory,* 16–38.

Hodson, G., Turner, R. N., & Choma, B. L. (2016). Understanding the roots of empathy and prejudice: The role of implicit and explicit intergroup attitudes and empathy. *Journal of Experimental Social Psychology, 63,* 1–11.

King, M. (2018). *The Good Neighbor: The Life and Work of Fred Rogers.* Abrams.

Kouzes, J. M., & Posner, B. Z. (2017). *The Leadership Challenge: How to Make Extraordinary Things Happen in Organizations.* Wiley.

Lee, H. (1960). *To Kill a Mockingbird.* J.B. Lippincott & Co.

Reynolds, A., & Lewis, D. (2018). The two traits of the best problem-solving teams. *Harvard Business Review.*

Smith, R. (1996). *The Making of It's a Wonderful Life.* St. Martin's Press.

Yip, J., & Fisher, D. M. (2022). The power of listening: How leaders who listen create more effective teams. Harvard Business Review.

Zenger, J. H., & Folkman, J. (2016). *The Extraordinary Leader: Turning Good Managers into Great Leaders.* McGraw-Hill Education.

Chapter 6

Aeon, B., & Aguinis, H. (2020). It's about time: New perspectives and insights on time management. *Academy of Management Perspectives,* 34(3), 300–318.

Alter, J. (2020). *His Very Best: Jimmy Carter, A Life*. Simon & Schuster.

Baumeister, R. F., Vohs, K. D., & Tice, D. M. (2018). The strength model of self-control: Recent developments and future directions. *Current Directions in Psychological Science, 27*(2), 109–118.

Carmon, I., & Knizhnik, S. (2015). *Notorious RBG: The Life and Times of Ruth Bader Ginsburg*. Dey Street Books.

Connors, R. J., & Buffett, W. (2010). *Warren Buffett on Business: Principles from the Sage of Omaha*. Wiley.

Denton, K., & Wilkinson, A. (2019). The impact of organization on team performance: A critical review. *Journal of Organizational Behavior, 41*(2), 210–225.

Gigerenzer, G. (2017). *Gut Feelings: The Intelligence of the Unconscious*. Penguin Books.

Gino, F. (2019). The discipline of managing your time. *Harvard Business Review*. https://hbr.org/2019/01/the-discipline-of-managing-your-time

Gino, F. (2020). *Rebel Talent: Why It Pays to Break the Rules at Work and in Life*. Dey Street Books.

Hackman, J. R., & Oldham, G. R. (2019). Motivation through the design of work: Test of a theory. *Organizational Behavior and Human Performance, 45*(3), 250–279.

Hibbert, P., & Duncan, R. (2020). Organizational goals: How planning and structure drive long-term success. *Management Journal, 57*(1), 45–61.

Judge, T. A., & Bono, J. E. (2007). Relationship of core self-evaluations traits—self-esteem, generalized self-efficacy, locus of control, and emotional stability—with job satisfaction and job performance: A meta-analysis. *Journal of Applied Psychology, 92*(2), 438–451.

Kahneman, D. (2018). *Thinking, Fast and Slow*. Farrar, Straus and Giroux.

Krings, F., Bangerter, A., Gomez, P., & Grob, A. (2020). Why people are late: exploring the dimensions and underlying causes of punctuality problems. *Journal of Personality and Social Psychology, 119*(1), 56–73.

Kondo, M. (2014). *The Life-Changing Magic of Tidying Up: The Japanese Art of Decluttering and Organizing*. Ten Speed Press.

Kornblum, A. (2013). *Angela Merkel: Europe's Most Influential Leader*. ABC-CLIO.

Lipshitz, R., Klein, G., Orasanu, J., & Salas, E. (2018). Taking stock of naturalistic decision making. *Journal of Behavioral Decision Making,* 25(4), 432–453.

McChesney, C., Covey, S. R., & Huling, S. J. (2012). *The 4 Disciplines of Execution: Achieving Your Wildly Important Goals.* Free Press.

Newport, C. (2016). *Deep Work: Rules for Focused Success in a Distracted World.* Grand Central Publishing.

Sutton, R. I. (2019). *The No Asshole Rule: Building a Civilized Workplace and Surviving One That Isn't.* Business Plus.

Tang, Y. Y., Holzel, B. K., & Posner, M. I. (2016). The neuroscience of mindfulness meditation. *Nature Reviews Neuroscience,* 16(4), 213–225.

Thoma, L., Auer, A., & Fiedler, K. (2020). Impulsiveness, stress, and decision-making: A modern take on emotional regulation. *Journal of Behavioral Decision Making,* 33(3), 201–215.

Trello. (2021). The ultimate guide to personal productivity methods. https://blog.trello.com/the-ultimate-guide-to-personal-productivity

Zhou, J., & George, J. M. (2018). Awakening creativity: The role of leader emotional intelligence. *Leadership Quarterly,* 29(3), 344–357.

Chapter 7

Barker, J. R., & Gower, K. (2019). Adaptive leadership and communication: Lessons from healthcare. *Journal of Healthcare Leadership,* 11, 1–15.

Barsade, S. G., & Gibson, D. E. (2007). Why does affect matter in organizations? *Academy of Management Perspectives,* 21(1), 36–59.

Bass, B. M. (1990). *Bass & Stogdill's Handbook of Leadership: Theory, Research, and Managerial Applications.* Free Press.

Bauman, C. W., & Skitka, L. J. (2020). Corporate social responsibility as a source of employee satisfaction. *Journal of Business Ethics,* 163(2), 211–230.

Berson, Y., & Stieglitz, N. (2019). The strategic value of leaders' emotional displays: A communication perspective. *Leadership Quarterly,* 30(1), 18–32.

Burns, U. (2018). *Where You Are Is Not Who You Are: A Memoir.* HarperCollins.

Colvin, G. (2019). Mary Barra's leadership at GM: Lessons from the crisis. *Fortune,* 180(7), 48–54.

Conger, J. A. (1991). Inspiring others: The language of leadership. *Academy of Management Executive*, 5(1), 31–45.

De Dreu, C. K. W., & Weingart, L. R. (2020). Task versus relationship conflict, team performance, and team member satisfaction: A meta-analysis. *Journal of Applied Psychology*, 92(5), 741–749.

Denning, S. (2020). *The Leader's Guide to Storytelling: Mastering the Art and Discipline of Business Narrative*. Wiley.

Edmondson, A. (2019). *The Fearless Organization: Creating Psychological Safety in the Workplace for Learning, Innovation, and Growth*. Wiley.

Elsbach, K. D., & Stigliani, I. (2020). How leaders shape the organizational culture of innovation. *California Management Review*, 62(4), 25–47.

Gates, H. (2020). *Conversations with Ruth Simmons: Leadership and Inclusion*. Harvard University Press.

Goleman, D. (2006). *Social Intelligence: The New Science of Human Relationships*. Bantam Books.

Goleman, D., Boyatzis, R., & McKee, A. (2020). *Primal Leadership: Unleashing the Power of Emotional Intelligence*. Harvard Business Review Press.

Grant, A., & Sandberg, S. (2019). The balancing act of assertiveness and openness in leadership. *Journal of Leadership and Organizational Studies*, 26(2), 169–182.

Gross, J. J., & John, O. P. (2003). Individual differences in two emotion regulation processes: Implications for affect, relationships, and well-being. *Journal of Personality and Social Psychology*, 85(2), 348–362.

Hackman, J. R., & Wageman, R. (2016). When and how team leaders matter. *Research in Organizational Behavior*, 26(1), 37–74.

Helms, L. (2020). Christine Lagarde and European leadership during the financial crisis: Balancing conviction and diplomacy. *European Political Science Review*, 8(3), 525–540.

Hirshman, L. (2019). *Sisters in Law: How Sandra Day O'Connor and Ruth Bader Ginsburg Went to the Supreme Court and Changed the World*. Harper Perennial.

Hitt, M. A., Ireland, R. D., & Hoskisson, R. E. (2021). *Strategic Management: Competitiveness and Globalization*. Cengage Learning.

Holmes, K. (2011). *Max Perutz and the Secret of Life*. University of Chicago Press.

Hülsheger, U. R., Alberts, H. J., Feinholdt, A., & Lang, J. W. (2013). Benefits of mindfulness at work: The role of mindfulness in emotion regulation, emotional exhaustion, and job satisfaction. *Journal of Applied Psychology*, 98(2), 310–325.

Karelaia, N., & Van Knippenberg, D. (2020). Conviction and leadership: How firm beliefs shape team performance. *Leadership Quarterly*, 31(4), 401–417.

King, M. (2018). *The Good Neighbor: The Life and Work of Fred Rogers*. Abrams Press.

Kornelius, S. (2021). *Christine Lagarde: The Authorized Biography*. Penguin Random House.

Kraus, M. W. (2017). Voice-only communication enhances empathic accuracy. *American Psychologist*, 72(7), 644–654.

Luthans, F., Youssef-Morgan, C. M., & Avolio, B. J. (2015). *Psychological Capital and Beyond*. Oxford University Press.

Maddox, B. (2002). *Rosalind Franklin: The Dark Lady of DNA*. HarperCollins.

Mannix, E., & Neale, M. A. (2020). What differences make a difference? The promise and reality of diverse teams in organizations. *Psychological Science in the Public Interest*, 20(2), 62–89.

Mayer, R. C., Davis, J. H., & Schoorman, F. D. (1995). An integrative model of organizational trust. *Academy of Management Review*, 20(3), 709–734.

McGuinness, W. (2020). Ngozi Okonjo-Iweala: Leading through crisis with empathy and conviction. *New Zealand Journal of Leadership*, 8(1), 11–23.

Mehrabian, A. (1972). *Nonverbal Communication*. Aldine-Atherton.

Nadella, S. (2017). *Hit Refresh: The Quest to Rediscover Microsoft's Soul and Imagine a Better Future for Everyone*. HarperBusiness.

Nooyi, I. (2019). *My Life in Full: Work, Family, and Our Future*. Penguin Random House.

Pearce, C. L., & Conger, J. A. (2003). *Shared Leadership: Reframing the Hows and Whys of Leadership*. SAGE Publications.

Perlow, L. A., Williams, S., & Balachandra, L. (2017). The importance of intentional pauses: Leadership lessons from mindfulness practice. *Journal of Management*, 43(5), 1204–1224.

Powell, C. L. (2012). *It Worked for Me: In Life and Leadership*. HarperCollins.

Ray, K., & Eagly, A. (2020). The role of nonverbal communication in leadership: Effects of leaders' voice and body language. *Journal of Applied Psychology*, 105(5), 432–450.

Sampson, A. (2018). *Mandela: The Authorized Biography*. HarperCollins.

Schultz, H. (2011). *Onward: How Starbucks Fought for Its Life without Losing Its Soul*. Rodale.

Taylor, M. (2021). Arne Sorenson: A legacy of grace in leadership. *Harvard Business Review*, 99(4), 67–72.

Ting-Toomey, S. (1999). *Communicating Across Cultures*. Guilford Press.

Ury, W. (1993). *Getting Past No: Negotiating with Difficult People*. Bantam Books.

Weger, H., Bell, G., & Emmett, M. C. (2019). Active listening in the workplace: The effects on trust and team performance. *Journal of Business Communication*, 56(1), 77–95.

Yukl, G., & Mahsud, R. (2020). Leadership in organizations: The importance of decisiveness in tough times. *Leadership Quarterly*, 31(2), 257–273.

Zak, P. J. (2018). *The Moral Molecule: How Trust Works*. Penguin.

Chapter 8

Campbell, J. (2008). *The Hero with a Thousand Faces*. New World Library.

Cialdini, R. B. (2016). *Pre-Suasion: A Revolutionary Way to Influence and Persuade*. Simon & Schuster.

Crystal, B. (2013). *Still Foolin Em: Where I've Been, Where I'm Going, and Where the Hell Are My Keys?* Henry Holt and Co.

Denning, S. (2021). *The Leader's Guide to Storytelling: Mastering the Art and Discipline of Business Narrative*. Jossey-Bass.

Fischer, T., Dietz, J., & Antonakis, J. (2017). Leadership process models: A review and synthesis. *Journal of Management*, 43(6), 1726–1750.

Gill, R. (2015). Why the PR Strategy that Worked for Apple Won't Work for You. *Harvard Business Review*.

Gillett, J. (2014). *Acting on the Stage: Techniques for the Modern Actor*. Methuen Drama.

Green, M. C., & Brock, T. C. (2000). The role of transportation in the persuasiveness of public narratives. *Journal of Personality and Social Psychology*, 79(5), 701–721.

Greenleaf, R. K. (2002). *Servant Leadership: A Journey into the Nature of Legitimate Power and Greatness*. Paulist Press.

Guber, P. (2011). *Tell to Win: Connect, Persuade, and Triumph with the Hidden Power of Story*. Crown Business.

Hasson, U., Ghazanfar, A. A., Galantucci, B., Garrod, S., Keysers, C. (2012). Brain-to-brain coupling: A mechanism for creating and sharing a social world. *Trends in Cognitive Sciences*, 16(2), 114–121.

Heath, C., & Heath, D. (2007). *Made to Stick: Why Some Ideas Survive and Others Die*. Random House.

Khanna, T. (2018). *Trust: Creating the Foundation for Entrepreneurship in Developing Countries*. Berrett-Koehler Publishers.

Leach, R. (2010). *Meyerhold on Theatre*. Routledge.

McGuinness, D. (2020). Jacinda Ardern: The leader who wowed the world with compassion. BBC News.

Morgan, N. (2015). *Power Cues: The Subtle Science of Leading Groups, Persuading Others, and Maximizing Your Personal Impact*. Harvard Business Review Press.

Oreg, S., & Berson, Y. (2019). Leadership and employees' reactions to change: The role of leaders' personal attributes and organizational context. *Personnel Psychology*, 72(4), 695–726.

Olson, R. (2015). *Houston, We Have a Narrative: Why Science Needs Story*. University of Chicago Press.

Pitches, J. (2006). *Vsevolod Meyerhold*. Routledge.

Schultz, H., & Gordon, J. (2011). *Onward: How Starbucks Fought for Its Life without Losing Its Soul*. Rodale Books.

Sirleaf, E. J. (2014). *This Child Will Be Great: Memoir of a Remarkable Life by Africa's First Woman President*. Harper Perennial.

Vonnegut, K. (1999). *Bagombo Snuff Box: Uncollected Short Fiction*. G. P. Putnam's Sons.

Zak, P. J. (2013). *The Moral Molecule: The Source of Love and Prosperity*. Penguin Group.

Zak, P. J. (2014). Why your brain loves good storytelling. *Harvard Business Review.*

Zak, P. J. (2015). *Trust Factor: The Science of Creating High-Performance Companies.* American Management Association.

Chapter 9

Aronson, J., & Steele, C. (2005). Stereotypes and the fragility of academic competence, motivation, and self-concept. In A. J. Elliot & C. S. Dweck (Eds.), *Handbook of Competence and Motivation* (pp. 436–456). Guilford Press.

Bongwe, S. (2021). *Interview on creating platforms for youth dialogue.* News24.

Covey, S. R. (2013). *The 7 Habits of Highly Effective People.* Simon & Schuster.

Dalio, R. (2017). *Principles: Life and Work.* Simon & Schuster.

Earley, P. C., & Ang, S. (2003). *Cultural Intelligence: Individual Interactions Across Cultures.* Stanford University Press.

Edmondson, A. C. (2018). *The Fearless Organization: Creating Psychological Safety in the Workplace for Learning, Innovation, and Growth.* Wiley.

Goleman, D. (2013). *Emotional Intelligence: Why It Can Matter More Than IQ.* Bantam Books.

Groysberg, B., & Slind, M. (2012). Leadership Is a Conversation. *Harvard Business Review.*

Iacoboni, M. (2008). *Mirroring People: The New Science of How We Connect with Others.* Farrar, Straus and Giroux.

Kauffmann, S. (2018). Macron's Public Conversations: Building a Narrative for France. *Le Monde.*

Paul, R., & Elder, L. (2019). *The Thinker's Guide to Socratic Questioning.* Foundation for Critical Thinking.

Pentland, A. (2012). The New Science of Building Great Teams. *Harvard Business Review.*

Rogers, C. R., & Farson, R. E. (2015). *Active Listening.* University of Chicago Press.

Salas, E., et al. (2015). Team dynamics and effectiveness: Key insights for building stronger teams. *Journal of Organizational Behavior,* 36(4).

Schein, E. H. (2016). *Humble Inquiry: The Gentle Art of Asking Instead of Telling*. Berrett-Koehler Publishers.

Scott, S. (2002). *Fierce Conversations: Achieving Success at Work and in Life One Conversation at a Time*. Viking Penguin.

Stone, D., Patton, B., & Heen, S. (2010). *Difficult Conversations: How to Discuss What Matters Most*. Penguin Books.

Tschannen-Moran, B., & Tschannen-Moran, M. (2018). *Coaching Conversations: Transforming Your School One Conversation at a Time*. Corwin Press.

Woolley, A. W., Chabris, C. F., Pentland, A., Hashmi, N., and Malone, T. W. (2010). Evidence for a collective intelligence factor in the performance of human groups. *Science*, 330(6004), 686–688.

Yousafzai, M. (2018). *We Are Displaced: My Journey and Stories from Refugee Girls Around the World*. Little, Brown Books for Young Readers.

Zak, P. J. (2015). Why Inspiring Stories Make Us React: The Neuroscience of Narrative. *Harvard Business Review*.

Zenger, J., & Folkman, J. (2016). The Ideal Praise-to-Criticism Ratio. *Harvard Business Review*.

Chapter 10

Bakker, A. B., Breevaart, K., Scharp, Y. S., & de Vries, J. D. (2023). Daily self-leadership and playful work design: Proactive approaches of work in times of crisis. *Journal of Applied Behavioral Science*, 59(2), 314–336.

Bakker, A. B., Scharp, Y. S., Breevaart, K., & De Vries, J. D. (2020). Playful work design: Introduction of a new concept. *Spanish Journal of Psychology*, 23, e19, p. 1–6.

Brown, S., & Vaughan, C. (2009). *Play: How It Shapes the Brain, Opens the Imagination, and Invigorates the Soul*. Penguin.

Catmull, E., & Wallace, A. (2014). *Creativity, Inc: Overcoming the Unseen Forces that Stand in the Way of True Inspiration*. Bantam Books.

Clifford, J. (2013, May 31). Toyota production system: What it all means. *Toyota UK Magazine*.

Csikszentmihalyi, M. (1997). *Finding Flow: The Psychology of Engagement with Everyday Life*. Basic Books.

Csikszentmihalyi, M. (2008). *Flow: The Psychology of Optimal Experience*. Harper Perennial (Originally published 1990).

Edmondson, A. C. (2019). *The Fearless Organization: Creating Psychological Safety in the Workplace for Learning, Innovation, and Growth*. Wiley.

Edmondson, A.C. (2023). *Right Kind of Wrong: The Science of Failing Well*. Atria Books.

Harter, J. (2024). *U.S. Engagement Hits 11-year Low*. Gallup.

IKEA. (2017). (rep.). *Play Report 2017: A spark of play every day* (vol. 3, pp. 1–41). IKEA.

Johnson, S. (2016). *Wonderland: How Play Made the Modern World*. Riverhead Books.

Kestly, T. A. (2014). *The Interpersonal Neurobiology of Play: Brain-Building Interventions for Emotional Well-Being*. Norton.

LEGO. (2018). (rep.). *Play Well Report*. The LEGO® Foundation.

Li, J. (2013). Continuous improvement at Toyota manufacturing plant: applications of production systems engineering methods. *International Journal of Production Research*, 51(23–24), 7235–7249.

Liu, W., Bakker, A. B., Tse, B. T., & van der Linden, D. (2023). Does playful work design "lead to" more creativity? A diary study on the role of flow. *European Journal of Work and Organizational Psychology*, 32(1), 107–117.

Panksepp, J. (1998). *Affective Neuroscience: The Foundations of Human and Animal Emotions*. Oxford University Press.

Panksepp, J., & Biven, L. (2012). *The Archaeology of Mind: Neuroevolutionary Origins of Human Emotions*. Norton.

Panksepp, J., Siviy, S., & Normansell, L. (1984). The psychobiology of play: Theoretical and methodological perspectives. *Neuroscience & Biobehavioral Reviews*, 8(4), 465–492.

Petelczyc, C. A., Capezio, A., Wang, L., Restubog, S. L. D., & Aquino, K. (2018). Play at work: An integrative review and agenda for future research. *Journal of Management*, 44(1), 014920631773151

Rice, D. (Host). (2024, April 17). Managing the talent market challenge and the move to skills based orgs [Audio podcast]. People Managing People.

245

Bibliography

Roos, J., & Victor, B. (2018). How it all began: the origins of LEGO® Serious Play®. *International Journal of Management and Applied Research*, 5(4), 326–343.

Roos, J., Victor, B., & Statler, M. (2004). Playing seriously with strategy. *Long Range Planning*, 37(6), 549–568.

Seymour, B., Singer, T., & Dolan, R. (2007). The neurobiology of punishment. *Nature Reviews Neuroscience*, 8(4), 300–311.

Steel, A., Silson, E. H., Stagg, C. J., & Baker, C. I. (2019). Differential impact of reward and punishment on functional connectivity after skill learning. *Neuroimage*, 189, 95–105.

Suffren, S., La Buissonnière-Ariza, V., Tucholka, A., Nassim, M., Séguin, J. R., Boivin, M., Kaur Singh, M., Foland-Ross, L. C., Lepore, F., Gotlib, I. H., Tremblay, R. E., Maheu, F. S. (2022). Prefrontal cortex and amygdala anatomy in youth with persistent levels of harsh parenting practices and subclinical anxiety symptoms over time during childhood. *Development and Psychopathology*, 34(3), 957–968.

Trezza, V., Achterberg, E. J., & Vanderschuren, L. J. (2019). The neurochemistry of social play behaviour in rats. In P.K. Smith & J. L. Roopnarine (Eds.), *The Cambridge Handbook of Play: Developmental and Disciplinary Perspectives* (pp. 30–48). Cambridge University Press.

Van Vleet, M., & Feeney, B. C. (2015). Play behavior and playfulness in adulthood. *Social and Personality Psychology Compass*, 9(11), 630–643.

Vanderschuren, L. J., & Trezza, V. (2013). What the laboratory rat has taught us about social play behavior: role in behavioral development and neural mechanisms. In S. L. Andersen & D.S. Pine (Eds.), *The Neurobiology of Childhood* (pp. 189–212). Springer.

Vanderschuren, L. J., Achterberg, E. M., & Trezza, V. (2016). The neurobiology of social play and its rewarding value in rats. *Neuroscience & Biobehavioral Reviews*, 70, 86–105.

Wheeler, S., Passmore, J., & Gold, R. (2020). All to play for: LEGO® SERIOUS PLAY® and its impact on team cohesion, collaboration and psychological safety in organisational settings using a coaching approach. *Journal of Work-Applied Management*, 12(2), 141–157.

Acknowledgments

Writing a book is work mostly done in solitude; but not done alone. There are a great many people who helped make this book possible.

When I wrote my last book, our "nest" was not yet empty. My early morning writing would be interrupted by the need to wake up our then-teenage sons, Henry and Oliver, fix them breakfast, and then scurry them out the door for school. The house is much quieter now, with those boys now men making their own way in the world. My wife, Lisa, has been a trusted advisor for nearly 40 years, but now our boys are as well. I'm eternally grateful for their love and support.

I am also indebted to the students I teach at Purdue University and the participants in the professional development workshops I get to lead. Their curiosity and engagement have enriched this work.

The students in my Engineering Leadership graduate course have been keenly instrumental in helping me develop the content of this book, because much of it began as classroom lectures and discussions.

I also want to give a special acknowledgment to the many scientists, engineers, and administrators at Lawrence Livermore National Laboratory, where I've had the privilege of leading over a dozen Executive Presence and Leadership Biodynamics programs. Their enthusiasm, insights, and dedication have been instrumental in refining the ideas presented in this book.

And finally, I would like to thank the team at Wiley. This is the second time I've had the privilege of working with Jeanenne Ray. Sherri-Anne Forde and Michelle Hacker were so very supportive, as was the rest of the Wiley team

To all of you, thank you for helping me shape and share the insights on these pages.

—**Scott Hutcheson**

About the Author

Scott Hutcheson, PhD, is a biosocial scientist and senior lecturer at Purdue University. His teaching, research, and professional practice focus on leadership, team, and organizational performance from a biology-of-behavior perspective.

With his 30-plus years of experience, Scott has engaged with hundreds of organizations from industry, higher education, and the public and nonprofit sectors—from across the United States and internationally. These organizations include the White House, Department of Commerce, National Science Foundation, USDA, and other federal agencies in the design and execution of strategies and programs for managing complex challenges related to competitiveness, innovation, sustainability, and public health. Scott's impact is global, having worked with over 4,000 leaders from 147 different countries.

He writes for academic journals, magazines, and newspapers. *Strategic Doing: Ten Skills for Agile Leadership* was released in 2019 by Wiley. It became a #1 Amazon New Release in six different categories and appeared on multiple lists as one of the Best Business Books of that year. Scott is also a *Forbes* contributor, where his column is in the top 1% in readership.

Scott is an in-demand speaker, frequently giving keynotes and leading workshops at conferences and other events. His TED Talk "Prospection: Reminiscing Forward" on the science of prospection has been viewed more than 1.3 million times on YouTube.

Scott is married to Lisa Hutcheson, who works in mental health policy. Together, they co-founded Hutcheson Associates. Her work focuses on public policy and advocacy. Scott and Lisa have two adult sons, Henry and Oliver, and two dogs named Pippa and Cosette. Scott and Lisa reside near Indianapolis, Indiana, in the historic town of Ulen.

You can connect with Scott in the following ways:

Hutcheson Associates: www.scotthutcheson.com

Speaking: www.bookscotttospeak.com

LinkedIn: www.linkedin.com/in/scotthutcheson/

Instagram: www.instagram.com/bookscotttospeak/

Forbes: www.forbes.com/sites/scotthutcheson/

Index

4-7-8 breathing technique, 28, 31
"36 Questions That Lead to Love," 179

Abstract concepts, tangibility, 168
Accessibility, impact, 66
Action, clarification, 150–152
Active listening, 86, 128, 176
Adaptability, 11, 14
Adversity (overcoming), conversation tool
    (usage), 195
Affective systems, 201
Alignment, challenges (overcoming), 153
Align (verb), usage, 152
And, But, Therefore (ABT), 154, 157, 159
Angelou, Maya, 89
Appearance, importance, 59
Approachability, 89–92
Ardern, Jacinda, 135–136
Assertiveness, 59
Assessment/adaptation, usage, 17
Audience
    approach, adaptation, 129
    communication adaptation, 125
    reactions, attention, 169–170
Authenticity/openness, 185–186, 189–190
Authority, signaling, 138
Autonomic nervous system (ANS), 201

Backstage presence, 55
Bailey, George, 92
Balance, guardians, 8–12
Barra, Mary, 129
Beaver
    architect role, 8
    behavior, plasticity, 5
    foundation building, 3–8, 16
    leadership lessons, 6–7
Behavioral adaptability, 7, 9
Behavioral change, sustaining, 69
Behavioral clarity, 66
Behavioral plasticity, 13
    display, 4
Behavior patterns, 1–2

Biohacking
    leadership strategies, 3
    personal connection, 79–80
    usage, 82–84
Biological dynamics, impact, 22
Biological process, leadership (equivalence),
    21–23
Biology
    integration, steps, 32–33
    movement, connection, 33–34
Biomechanical mastery, coaching, 49–50
Biomechanics, 150
    application, 39–44
    concept (Meyerhold), 36
Body language
    shift, 35
    usage, 43
Bonds (strengthening), dialogue (usage),
    193–194
Boundaries
    maintenance, 106
    respect, 162
Boyatzis, Richard, 81
"Boy Meets Girl," 156
Brain development, play (importance), 202
Breath control, usage, 48
Breathing exercises, 32
Brown, Stuart, 202
Buffer time, visible prioritization, 112
Burns, James MacGregor, 57
Burns, Ursula, 132
Bush, George H.W., 79
Business schools, cultural influence, 57–58

"Call to Adventure," 154
Calm
    ripple effect, creation, 31
    science, 133–134
Campbell, joseph, 154
Capra, Frank, 92
Carter, Jimmy, 117
Challenge
    anticipation, 115
    skill, balance, 206

251

Change
  driving, 168, 195
  management, narrative, 158
Character development techniques, 47
Character journals, usage, 48
Charisma, 59
Check-ins, usage, 80
Checklists, usage, 115
Churchill, Winston, 57
Cialdini, Robert, 147
Clarity, 130–131
Cognitive complexity, ethology insights, 4
Cognitive flexibility, 6
Collaboration
  building, 70
  impact, 6
  usage, 64
Collaborative atmosphere, fostering, 178
Collaborative environment
  creation, 17
  performance, improvement (case study), 69–71
Collaborative success, gravitas (foundation), 142
Command-and-control leadership, 59–60
Communication
  enhancement, 70
  gaps, 69
  impact, 45
  nonverbal communication, 125
  prioritization, 104
  tailoring, 126
  transparency, 132, 135
Community dynamics, 5–6
Competence, 63–64, 121–122
  biohacking, 97
  confidence, contrast, 98–101
  core behaviors, embodiment, 100
  importance, 98
  play, expression, 206–208
  workshops, 68
Composure
  biohacking, 133–134
  maintenance, 132–136
  modeling, 134
  strengthening, 134
  usage, 140
Confidence
  competence, contrast, 98–101
  complementary role, 101
  instilling, poise (maintenance), 140
Conflict (resolution), patience/composure (usage), 140
Connection
  biodynamics, 74–75
  customization, 79–80
  personal level, 78–82
  power, 63
  signals, 205
  strengthening, 176
  warmth, usage, 95–96
Constructive conflict
  engagement, 129
  management, 128
Construct validity, 67
Context, story
  relationship, 164
  tailoring, 165
Continuous learning
  culture, fostering, 170–171, 197–198
  emphasis, 18
Controlled breath, power, 27–39
Conversation
  advice, 186–188
  approach, selection, 185
  avoidance, 187–188
  biohacker, becoming, 179–180, 196–198
  catalyst, role, 190
  challenges, 190–196
  constant conversation, 174
  culture, fostering, 197–198
  decision-making dynamics, equivalence, 177–179
  dominance, 186, 192, 193
  dynamics, 174
  emotional connector, equivalence, 176
  ethics, 187
  guiding, 182–183
  neurology, 175–176
  neuroscience, 173
  power, 196
  psychology, 175–176
  science, 175–180
  structures, 178, 180–183
  synchrony, 175
  usage, strategic dialogue (usage), 184–190
Conversations/concerns, follow-up, 93
Conviction, biohacking, 127–128
Corporate culture, influence, 57–58
Court, biomechanics, 37–38
Credibility, importance, 98
Cross-cultural adaptability, 67
Crystal, Billy, 160
Cultural influences, 57–58
Cultural insensitivity, 164
Cultural misunderstandings, 191–192
  navigation, 193

Dams, beaver building (instinct), 4
Data, usage, 102, 115
Decision-making dynamics, conversations (equivalence), 177–179
Decisions
  anchoring, 132
  informing, data (usage), 102
Decisiveness, 130–131
  empathy, balance, 132
Decorum/grace
  action, 139–142
  biohacking, 139–140
Deep breathing, 27
Delays, transparent handling, 112
Dialogues
  crafting, 180–183
  encouragement, 187
  usage, 193–195
Digital tools, utilization, 118
Dignified leadership, usage, 140
Diplomacy, biohacking, 127–128
Disruptions, inevitability, 132–133
Distractions, management, 77
Diverse perspective
  encouragement, 17
  navigation, 164
Diversity
  promotion, 14, 17, 19
  sea star champions, 12–16
Doubt, creation, 152–153
Dynamics, balancing, 16, 19

Ecosystems architects, 2
Edmondson, Amy, 209
Effort, acknowledgment, 83
Eisenhower Matrix, 102
Embodied cognition, 44–45
Embodied leadership, 46
Emotion
  leadership, equivalence, 28–29
  power, harnessing, 28
  unethical manipulation, 162
Emotional acknowledgment, 83
Emotional bonds, fostering, 179
Emotional connection, 177
Emotional connectors, conversations (equivalence), 176–177
Emotional contagion, addressing, 32
Emotional echoes, 28–29
Emotional intelligence, usage, 140
Emotional recall journaling, 48
Emotional regulation, 29, 133–135
Empathy, 131
  decisiveness, balance, 132
  demonstration, 80
  listening, 141

Engagement
  customization, 87
  depth, 137
  dialogues, crafting (impact), 180–183
  truth, balancing, 163–164
Environmental play cues, conveyance, 204–205
Environments, diversity, 9
Erlanger, Jeff, 81
Erving, Julius "Dr. J," 37
Ethical boundaries, navigation, 186–188
Ethics, navigation, 161–163
Evers, Medgar, 89
Evolutionary adaptation, 4–5
Evolutionary biology, impact, 3–4
Evolutionary drivers, 2–3
Executive presence, 55
  leadership scholars, criticism, 61–62
  redefining, 65
  rethinking, 56–58
  traditional model, 58–61
  understanding/limitations, 56–57
Exercise, usage, 27
Experiment, observe, adapt, 169–170, 196–197
Expert consultation, insights, 65
External expression, internal narrative (contrast), 149–150
External selves, internal selves (alignment), 152–153
Eye contact
  maintenance, 76
  usage, 43, 51, 83

Face validity, 66
Facial feedback, impact, 45
Fact, Story, Ask (FSA), 154, 157, 158, 159
Failures, reframing, 210
Feedback, 206
  assessments, 68
  basis, 170
  scores, improvement, 68
  seeking, 165
  times, regularity, 90–91
  tools, usage, 68
Feedback loops
  real-time feedback loops, 68
  usage, 50
Feelings, articulation, 28
Finch, Atticus, 85
Flow
  ingredients, 206–208
  recognition, 208
  systems, creation, 208
Foundations
  beaver builders, 3–8, 16
  building, 18–19
"From Bad to Worse," 156–157

Gestures, 45–46
Ghosn, Carlos, 168
Goals, achievement, 120
Gravitas, 64
    behaviors, 123
    biohacking, 123
    foundation, 142
    modernization, 65
    play, exploration, 208–210
    purpose, clarity, 128
    workshops, 68
Growth, opportunities (creation), 93
Gut feeling, 22

Hanks, Tom, 114
Heart rate variability (HRV), 24, 26
    monitoring, 31
    regulation, 30
    role, 26–27
    training, 33
Hero's Journey, application, 155–156
"Hero's Journey, The," 154
Hero with a Thousand Faces, The
    (Campbell), 154
Hesitation, creation, 152–153
Hierarchical barriers, reduction, 178
Hierarchical norms, 59–60
High-stress product launch, leading, 31–32
Homeostasis, 201–202
Humility
    demonstration, 91
    practice, 87
    prioritization, 141

Ibarra, Herminia, 60
Ideas, simplification, 126
Impact, measurement, 70
Impulses, control, 110
Impulsiveness
    avoidance, 108–110
    biohacking, 108–109
    challenges, 108
Inclusive language, usage, 90
Inclusivity
    environment, fostering, 141
    fostering, 14–16, 138
    invitation, silence (usage), 137
    stories, inclusivity, 162–163
Individual goals
    collective goals, balance, 11
    team goals, alignment, 18
Individual selection, focus, 2
Influence, storytelling (relationship), 147–149
Information overload, prevention, 137
Innovation, driving, 168
Inside-out leadership, 29–31

Insights, usage, 115
Intent (alignment), execution (usage), 170, 197
Intentional action, 153
Intentions, 187
    clarification, 150–152
    usage, 162
    verbal intention, 170
Interactions (guiding), emotional intelligence
    (usage), 140
Internal consistency, 67
Internal intentions
    external actions, misalignment, 39
    external expression, disconnect, 149
Internal narrative, external expression
    (contrast), 149–150
Internal selves, external selves (alignment),
    152–153
Intervention development, 67–69
Iterative refinement, testing/adjusting, 66
It's a Wonderful Life (Capra), 92

Jerath, Ravinder, 27

Keystone leaders, 1
Keystone species, 1–2
Kinsey Goman, Carol, 41
Kinship selection, collaboration emphasis, 2
Knapp, Mark, 43
Kondo, Marie, 121
Kuan Yew, Lee, 168–169

Language, mindfulness, 165
Leaders
    choice, 100–202
    coaching, 49
    embodied cognition applications, 46
    example, 99–100
    focus, 126
    gap (bridging), storytelling (usage),
        144–145
    internal commitment, external expression
        (misalignment), 152–153
    posture/movements/eye contacts, 41–42
Leadership
    approaches, 99–100
    biological basis, 23
    biological process, equivalence, 21–23
    biology, 21, 32–33
    biomechanics, 33–34, 35
        application, 39–44
        continuous practice, 53
        embodied cognition, impact, 44–45
    breathing, usage, 27–28
    composure, biohacking, 133–134
    consistency, importance, 43–44

constant conversation, 174
demonstration, behaviors (impact), 43
development, experience, 1
dichotomy, 36–37
dignified leadership, usage, 140
duration, 214
embodied experience, 39
embodiment, techniques, 43
emotion, equivalence, 28–29
exercises, 48
impact, enhancement, 40
influence, strengthening, 70
inside-out/outside-in approaches, 36
instinct, usage, 24
journey, 213
leading by example, 30–31
lesson, 14
outside-in leadership, 39–40
physiological response, 24
physiology, 23–28
presence, 69–70
resilience, HRV (role), 26–27
silence, biohacking, 136–137
storytelling, 160, 163–166, 168–169
techniques, 42–44
theater lessons, 47–48
truth, demonstration, 144
verbing, application, 150
Leadership Biodynamics Framework, 55,
62–64
building, 63–64
competence, 63–64
connection, power, 63
evidence-based foundations, 63
implementation, 69–70
influence, collaboration (usage), 64
methodological rigor, 64–66
rigor/relevance, commitment, 71
validation/refinement, construction,
63–65
warmth, 74
Leadership Biodynamics Profile, 213–214
Leadership BioPresence Profile, 213
Leading, stories (usage), 159–161
"Leaving a tip on the table" (concept),
160–161
Lincoln, Abraham, 77
Listening
biohacking, 76–77
quality, 75–78
Long-term success, 99

Macron, Emmanuel, 194
Mandela, Nelson, 138
"Man in Hole," 156
Manipulation, 161–163, 187

Masculine ideals, reliance, 61
McCraty, Rollin, 26
Media, influence, 57–58
Meditation, 33
Meetings, rehearsal, 115
Memory retention, storytelling (relationship),
147
Mentoring programs, implementation, 15
Merkel, Angela, 110
Message delivery, effectiveness,
124–127
biohacking, 124–125
challenges, 124
clarity/simplicity, 124–125
Meyerhold, Vsevolod, 35–36, 150, 152–153
Micro-behaviors
adjustments, 50–51
case study, 51–52
Mindfulness
practices, 32, 134
usage, 27, 51
Mindful presence, demonstration, 109
Mindset
results-driven mindset, 168
shift, 86
Mirror exercises, 48
Mirroring/rapport
connection, 46
impact, 45
Mirror neurons, impact, 204
Miscommunication, mitigation, 192–193
Misconnection, impact, 191
Mistakes, acknowledgment, 141
Motivation, boosting, 194
Motor cortex, activation, 145–146
Movement, usage, 46
Multifactor Leadership Questionnaire, 61
Mutual understanding, sense (fostering), 176

Nadella, Satya, 126
Narratives, 144
emotional power, 146–147
structures, 154–158
transportation, 148
Nature, lessons integration, 16–18
Needs, anticipation, 93
Neurological interplay, 176
Newport, Cal, 108
Nightingale, Florence, 95
Nonprofit organization, leader (situation),
160
Nonverbal communication, 125
Nonverbal cues
consistency, maintenance, 109
display, 43
validation, 83

Nonverbal engagement, 87
Nonverbal signals, alignment, 126

Objective-driven actions, usage, 47
Objective-driven interactions, 48
Objectives, defining, 210
Objects, leveraging, 206
Okonjo-Iweala, Ngozi, 167–168
Olson, Randy, 157
Ongoing learning, commitment, 171
Open body language
  maintenance, 76, 90
  usage, 83
Open dialogue, encouragement, 178
Openness, atmosphere (creation), 90
Organization, 117–121
  biohacking, 118–119
  challenges, 117–118
  digital tools, utilization, 118
  routine, maintenance, 119
  system, clarity/consistency
    (implementation), 118–119
Other-orientation, 85–89
Others, validation, 82–85
Outside-in approach, 41
Outside-in leadership, 40–41
Overembellishment, 163–164
Oxytocin triggers
  conversations, impact, 176–177
  usage, 31–32

Pankseep, Jaak, 201
Past actions, public reflection, 109
Patience, usage, 140
Pausing, importance, 76
Performance, perception (contrast), 98–99
Personal acknowledgments, recognition, 79
Personal cues, sending, 206
Personal flow, celebration, 208
Personal stories, sharing, 90
Persuasion science, 147–148
Philosophy in the Flesh (Lakoff/Johnson), 44
Physical posture/movements, impact, 40
Physical presence
  dynamic expression, 37–38
  power, 47
Physiological traits, 12
Planning tools, usage, 115
Plasticity, 5
Play
  definitions, 200
  exploration, 208–210
  expression, 206–208
  motivations, 203
  neurobiology, 201–203
  neuroscience, 199

Playful spaces, creation, 205
Playful work, 207
Poise, maintenance, 140
Postures
  adoption, 46
  micro-behavior, 51
Power posing, impact, 45
Praise, acknowledgment, 83
Preparation efforts, sharing, 115–116
Preparedness, 114–117
  biohacking, 114–116
  challenges, 114
Presence, 90
  demonstration, 80
Presentations
  leader preparation, 152
  rehearsal, 115
Priorities
  adjustment, 102–103
  communication, 102
Priorities, setting, 101–104
  biohacking, 102–103
  challenges, 101–102
Privacy, respect, 162
Proactive maintenance, usage, 6
Productive outcomes, conversations
    (guiding), 182–183
Progress, review/reflection, 119
Psychometric assessment, reliability/validity
    (ensuring), 66–67
Punctuality, 111–114
  biohacking, 111
  challenges, 111
Purpose, clarity, 128

Questions
  anticipation, 115
  leading, 180–181

Reaction, pause, 109
Reassure (verb), usage, 150–151
Reciprocal altruism
  cooperation, 2
  illustration, 13
Recovery, 14
Reflection
  encouragement, 137, 138
  usage, 18–20, 128
Reflective listening, 181–182
Reflective responses, 76
Relatability, 89–92
Relatedness, biohacking, 90–91
Relevance, 164
Reminders/alerts, visible use, 112
Resilience, 14, 99
  building, 167–168
  demonstration, 135

development, 18
  fostering, 195
  insight, 27
  modeling, 210
  setbacks, recovery, 134
Resource management, 14
Respect
  culture (fostering), dignified leadership
    (usage), 140
  environment, fostering, 141
Response
  care, usage, 141
  management, 87
Rest and recovery, public acknowledgment,
  106
Results-driven mindset, 168
Rice, Condoleezza, 104
Rizzolatti, Giacomo, 29
"Road of trials," highlighting, 155
Robinson, Ken (insights), 36
Rogers, Fred ("Mr. Rogers"), 29, 81–82, 141–142
Role-playing scenarios, 68
Role reversal simulations, 48
Rosenwald, Julius, 88–89
Round-robin discussions, usage, 192

Scenarios
  real-world scenarios, 66
  rehearsal, 49
Sea star
  buffer role, 15
  diversity, 12–17
  ecosystem buffering role, 13
  lesson leadership, 14
  regenerative abilities, 12–13
Self-assessments, 68
  leveraging, 68
Self-awareness, 153
Self-positioning, 155
Self-regulation, 31
Setbacks, recovery, 134
Shared recollections, 143–144
Shared vision, impact, 167
Short-term wins, long-term goals
  (balancing), 103
Silence
  authority/control, relationship, 136–137
  biohacking, 136–137
  usage, 136–138
Silent Language of Leaders, The
    (Kinsey Goman), 41
Siloed teams, impact, 69
Simplicity, embracing, 165
Situations, approach (selection), 188–189
Skilled storytelling, impact, 146
Small gestures, usage, 76
Smile, usage, 46

Social cues, meaning, 204
Social learning/development, 10
Socratic dialogue, 178
Socratic method, 180–181
Space, walking, 48
Stage, biomechanics, 37–38
Stakeholder engagement, improvement, 70
Standing one's ground, 127–129
Stanton, Edwin, 77–78
Steadiness, visibility, 128
Still Foolin' 'Em (Crystal), 160
Stories
  authenticity, 162
  context, 164–165
  crafting, 154–159
  cultural insensitivity, 164
  inclusivity, 162–163
  relevance, 164
  reliance, 162
  selection, intention (usage), 161
  sharing, 80
  usage, 159–161
Story shaping, 154, 156–157
Storyteller, alignment, 149–153
Storytelling
  advantage, real-world applications,
    148–149
  advice, 161–163
  biohacker, 169–171
  challenges, 163–166
  culture, fostering, 170–171
  frameworks, mastery, 159
  impact, 166–169
  influence, relationship, 147–148
  memory retention, relationship, 147
  neurological impact, 145–146
  neuroscience, 143
  refinement, 171
  science, 145–149
  strategic use, 160
Strategic competence, 65
Strategic conversations, power, 184–185
Strategic dialogue, usage, 184–190
Strategic Doing: Ten Skills for Agile
    Leadership (Hutcheson), 39
Strategic intervention, 10, 14
Strategic mindset, 98
Strategic questioning, 178, 182–183
Strategic resource management, 6
Strategy, dynamic expression, 37–38
Stress
  biological impact, 25
  management, controlled breath (power),
    27–28
  ripple effect, 25–26
  spread, documentation, 26
Structured turn-taking, usage, 192
Subtle adjustments, power, 50–51

257

Index

Subtext reading, 48
Sympathetic nervous systems, parasympathetic nervous systems (balance), 26

Targeted recognition, 93
Tasks
  batching, usage, 105–106
  breakdown, 118
Tata, Ratan, 167
Team
  anchoring, decisiveness/clarity, 130–131
  approachability/relatability, impact, 91–92
  balance, maintenance, 12
  cohesion, 11, 166–167, 193–194
  collaboration, strengthening, 70
  connection, impact, 81
  conversation, impact, 193
  decision-making processes, 178
  dynamics, 7–8, 176
  impulsiveness, avoidance (impact), 110
  leader management, 161
  motivation, shared vision (impact), 167
  organization, impact, 120
  other-oriented impact, 88
  performance, revitalization (case study), 11–12
  preparation efforts, sharing, 115–116
  preparedness, impact, 116–117
  priorities, impact, 104
  punctuality, impact, 113
  ripple effect, 134
  storytelling, impact, 166–169
  tension, leadership (impact), 25–26
  thoughtfulness, impact, 94–95
  validation, impact, 84–85
  workload management, impact, 107
Teamwork
  delegation, public commitment, 106
  impact, 6
Thatcher, Margaret, 57
Thayer, Julian, 26
Theater, focus, 38
Theatrical biomechanics, concept, 35–36
Thoughtful decision-making, communication, 109
Thoughtfulness, 92–95
  biohacking, 93–94
  tailoring, 93–94
Thoughtful questions, asking, 86
Thoughtful responses, usage, 76
Time blocking, usage, 105
Timeliness, public acknowledgment, 112
To Kill a Mockingbird, 85
Tone, mindfulness, 165
Top-down leadership, 59–60
Tough calls, making, 129–132

challenges, 130
Tough decision-making, biohacking, 130–131
Transparency, 131
  usage, 132
Trust
  building, 13, 31–32, 131, 167–168, 181–182, 195
  sense, fostering, 176
Truth
  adherence, 165
  engagement, balancing, 163–164
Two-day leadership biodynamics training, design, 67–68

Validation
  customization, 84
  impact, 181–182
  offering, 83
Values, anchoring, 129
Verbal affirmations, usage, 76
Verbal content, 197
Verbal intention, 170
Verbal signals, alignment, 126
Verbing, 150–153
Visible traits, 59
Vocal adjustments, importance, 51
Voice
  diversity, navigation, 191–192
  equity, ensuring, 192
  modulation, usage, 48
Vonnegut, Kurt, 154, 156
Vulnerability, 161

Warmth
  approachability, 89–92
  biohacking, 73
  expression, 92
  generation, tangible actions, 74–75
  highlighting, 65
  importance, 74
  play, connection, 203–206
  usage, 95–96
  workshops, 68
Washington, Booker T., 88–89
Wolves
  balance guardians, 8–12
  behavioral adaptability, 9
  leadership lessons, 10–11
  role, exploration, 11–12
  social structure, 9
Workload, management, 100, 104–108
  biohacking, 105–106
  challenges, 105

Yousafzai, Malala, 190